CAMBRIDGE STUDIES IN PHILOSOPHY

Knowledge and Evidence

CAMBRIDGE STUDIES IN PHILOSOPHY

General editor SYDNEY SHOEMAKER

Advisory editors J. E. J. ALTHAM, SIMON BLACKBURN,
GILBERT HARMAN, MARTIN HOLLIS, FRANK JACKSON,
JONATHAN LEAR, WILLIAM G. LYCAN, JOHN PERRY,
BARRY STROUD

Knowledge and Evidence

Paul K. Moser

Loyola University of Chicago

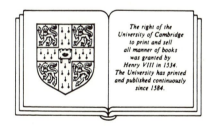

The right of the
University of Cambridge
to print and sell
all manner of books
was granted by
Henry VIII in 1534.
The University has printed
and published continuously
since 1584.

Cambridge University Press

Cambridge

New York   Port Chester   Melbourne   Sydney

Published by the Press Syndicate of the University of Cambridge
The Pitt Building, Trumpington Street, Cambridge CB2 1RP
32 East 57th Street, New York, NY 10022, USA
10 Stamford Road, Oakleigh, Melbourne 3166, Australia

© Cambridge University Press 1989

First published 1989

Printed in the United States of America

Library of Congress Cataloging-in-Publication Data
Moser, Paul K., 1957–
Knowledge and evidence / Paul K. Moser.
p.   cm. – (Cambridge studies in philosophy)
Bibliography: p.
Includes index.
ISBN 0 521 37028 0
1. Knowledge, Theory of.   I. Title.   II. Series.
BD161.M848   1989   88–31570
121 – dc19   CIP

British Library Cataloguing in Publication applied for

For Laura, Anna, and Denise
– three good reasons

Contents

Acknowledgments

Work on this book began in late 1985, shortly after the publication of my first book, *Empirical Justification*. Since that time my work has benefited from the support of various people and institutions. During the summer of 1986, Loyola University of Chicago funded a Summer Research Grant for my work on an early version of the book. And during the summer of 1987, the National Endowment for the Humanities funded a Summer Research Grant for completion of a second version of the book. My work on the book also benefited from an NEH Faculty Development Stipend for the summer of 1988. Without such financial assistance, this book surely would still be in progress.

Numerous philosophers have helped to improve the arguments of this book by means of discussions, written exchanges, anonymous referees' reports, and formal exchanges at professional meetings. I specifically thank Harry Gensler, Al Mele, and Arnold vander Nat for helpful comments on some of the chapters. And very special thanks go to Robert Audi, Richard Feldman, and an anonymous Cambridge University Press referee for extensive written comments on the penultimate version of the book. These philosophers prompted me to improve my proposals and arguments at various points. The book's style has benefited in various ways from the excellent copyediting of Jane Van Tassel, production editor for the Press.

For support of a different but equally important sort, I thank my wife, Denise, and daughters, Anna and Laura. Their daily friendship and encouragement are needed sources of intellectual energy and ambition.

A few sections of this book use revised parts of some of my articles: "Reliabilism and Relevant Worlds," *Philosophia* 19 (1989); "The Foundations of Epistemological Probability," *Erkenntnis* 29

(1988), 231–51; "Internalism and Coherentism: A Dilemma," *Analysis* 48 (1988), 161–3; "Propositional Knowledge," *Philosophical Studies* 52 (1987), 91–114; "Does Foundationalism Rest on a Mistake?" *Conceptus* 19 (1985), 9–22. I thank the editors of these journals for permission to draw on these articles.

P.K.M.

Chicago, Illinois

Introduction

Contemporary epistemology exhibits much disarray. These days epistemologists agree on little about the conditions for human propositional knowledge. Some hold that such knowledge requires justified true belief, while others claim that it does not. An innocent bystander will think that philosophy trades in disarray, and that its disagreements do not really matter anyway. But such innocence betrays naiveté. Human knowledge is a vital commodity whose conditions we can disregard only to our own detriment. Epistemologists recognize this, but philosophical agreement still escapes them.

Even among those holding that knowledge requires justified true belief, disagreements abound. Consider the justification condition. Foundationalism of any stripe is widely in disrepute in certain quarters, while in other quarters modest versions thrive and even multiply. Influential alternatives to foundationalism now include coherentism, contextualism, and certain versions of reliabilism. Consider next the truth condition. Truth as correspondence still has its proponents. But this conception of truth gets no serious hearing in certain philosophical circles. By way of alternatives to truth as correspondence, we now hear much about truth as coherence, truth as warranted assertibility, and truth as an instantiation of Tarski's famous schema. Consider finally the belief condition. Some epistemologists regard believing as a mere disposition to behave in a certain way, while others take it to require assent to a proposition. And still others appear to identify believing with assenting. Disagreement takes no holiday in epistemology.

In the eager rush away from foundationalism and truth as correspondence, many philosophers have neglected the moderate versions of post-Cartesian, even post–C. I. Lewis, foundationalism. And they have overlooked a simple, metaphysically inoffensive

1

variant of the correspondence theory of truth suggested long ago by Aristotle. In fact, some philosophers misrepresent foundationalism and the correspondence theory of truth in ways that betray serious confusions. For example, various philosophers claim, even these days, that foundationalism requires the certainty of some justified beliefs. And we often hear that a correspondence theory of truth requires a correspondence *criterion* of truth, if not a mysterious sort of metaphysical intuition. I need not pause to name names here, although I easily could. (Some of the names will surface in due course anyway.) Instead we now need to counteract such epistemologically harmful muddles with careful distinctions and arguments. This book pursues that cause.

Specifically this book provides an account of propositional knowledge that preserves what is indispensable in foundationalism and the correspondence theory of truth. At the same time, this account acknowledges the central role of explanation in epistemic justification, and thereby salvages what is crucially important in explanatory coherentism. But in requiring that all justified propositions have a basis in experience, my account escapes a fatal defect of epistemic coherentism: its allowing justified propositions to be improbable relative to experience. My account also contrasts with radical foundationalism according to which the foundations of knowledge are infallible, indubitable, or irrevisable. Its notion of foundations commits one only to *non*inferentially justified propositions, i.e., propositions justified independently of evidential relations to any propositions. On this modest foundationalism, the subjective nonconceptual contents of experience (e.g., what one seems to perceive) play a central role in the noninferential justification of foundational propositions. Thus on this view the foundations of knowledge are *not* self-justified; nor is anything else.

My account of knowledge is conceptually reductionistic in a desirable way. We might even say that it shows how to *naturalize* an important part of epistemology. It reduces the concepts of propositional knowledge and epistemic justification to familiar *non*epistemic, *non*-normative concepts such as those of explanation, entailment, causation, and experiential contents. In doing so, my account takes the apparent normative mystery out of epistemic concepts such as *justification* and *knowledge*. And my account leads to a straightforward meta-justification that allows us to see its ad-

2

vantages over competing accounts, including coherentism, reliabilism, and alternative versions of foundationalism. This meta-justification gives a dialectical edge to my theory, thus enabling it to be recommended over its competitors. Such an advantage is important. Much conceptual work in epistemology is seemingly done in an intellectual vacuum, with no serious regard for competing theories. But we cannot challenge theoretical opponents by ignoring them; nor will they thereby go away.

This book also faces skepticism head on, and argues that it can be effectively challenged, if not refuted. One important lesson is thus that nonskeptics need not ignore the skeptic, since they have the epistemological wherewithal to mount a serious challenge. Such a lesson should be comforting if only because we cannot ignore the skeptic with a clear epistemological conscience. This book gives us a forceful reply to both justification skepticism and knowledge skepticism. Part of my reply involves a new solution to the famous problem of the criterion that has vexed epistemologists since the time of Sextus Empiricus. This book also shuns the growing skepticism and despair about avoiding Gettier-style counterexamples, and provides a new analysis of knowledge that avoids such counterexamples in a highly intuitive manner.

This book focuses on the conditions for propositional empirical knowledge. Simply characterized, propositional knowledge is just knowledge *that* something is the case. It contrasts, for example, with knowledge *how to do* something. Empirical knowledge, also simply characterized, is just knowledge dependent on perceptual or sensory experience. It contrasts with *a priori* knowledge. My focus specifically is on propositional empirical knowledge that requires *justified true belief or assent*. Some philosophers deny that propositional knowledge requires belief or assent, and some philosophers deny that such knowledge requires justification. I shall not pursue the various examples used to support such denials, since we would soon find ourselves in what appears to be a verbal dispute. Even if there is a legitimate use of the term 'propositional knowledge' that does not involve the notions of belief, assent, and justification, one standard use does require those notions. In fact, since the time of Plato's *Theaetetus*, philosophers generally have acknowledged a notion of propositional knowledge that requires the notions of justification, truth, and belief. This standard notion occupies this

3

book. I shall offer some reasons for acknowledging this standard notion, but I shall not pretend to have shown that all alternative notions are incoherent or defective.

Chapter 1 provides general characterizations of the belief, truth, and justification conditions for propositional knowledge. It explains the belief condition via a *state–object* view according to which belief has two essential components: a dispositional state and a propositional object. On this view, we can easily contrast believing with assenting, coming to believe, and being merely disposed to believe. And we can deny that believing need be conscious in the sense that one somehow must be aware of one's believing. The latter point is important, because some philosophers have used examples involving unconscious belief to argue that knowledge does not require belief.

I claim that one sort of knowledge – dispositional propositional knowledge – requires belief. My reason for claiming this is that (a) one must be dispositionally as well as psychologically related to the propositions one dispositionally knows, and (b) belief is the only plausible candidate for what relates one dispositionally as well as psychologically to the propositions one dispositionally knows. Without one's belief relation to dispositionally known propositions, those propositions would not be dispositionally known *by oneself,* even if they are known by others. Yet I also propose that there can be a sort of knowledge – nondispositional propositional knowledge – that differs from dispositional knowledge only insofar as it includes an assent condition instead of a belief condition. In nondispositional knowledge, nondispositional assenting relates one psychologically to the propositions one knows.

The sort of truth required by propositional knowledge is, according to Chapter 1, truth as *minimal* correspondence, in the sense that Aristotle originally proposed and J. L. Mackie recently revived. Because of its truth condition, a known proposition must state *how things are*, at least with respect to a particular place and time. Thus according to the minimal correspondence definition, the claim that a proposition is true means simply that things are as they are stated to be by that proposition. Nothing more and nothing less should be involved in the definition of truth. The common inclination to think otherwise stems from a confusion of the *definition* of truth and the *criteria* for discerning truth. But of course we should avoid any such confusion.

4

Chapter 1 shows how the minimal correspondence definition entails Tarski's adequacy condition for a definition of truth: X is true if and only if P, where 'P' stands for a declarative sentence, and 'X' stands for the name of that sentence. And this of course is desirable. But Chapter 1 also explains why Tarski's adequacy condition does not entail the minimal correspondence definition. And this is desirable too, since Tarski's condition was not intended as a definition of truth. Chapter 1 defends the minimal correspondence definition against several likely objections, such as those suggested by Hilary Putnam, Nelson Goodman, and Richard Rorty. Thus this book relies on a notion of truth that is *non*doxastic and *non*epistemic in the sense that it allows for truth independent of belief, justification, and knowledge. Despite its being unpopular in certain quarters, this notion of truth withstands the objections in circulation. Popularity never was a good criterion of truth.

Chapter 1 also provides a general characterization of the justification condition for propositional knowledge. Unlike true belief, propositional knowledge excludes what is merely coincidental truth from the knower's perspective, such as lucky guesswork and correct wishful thinking. Propositional knowledge requires that one have *adequate indication* that a known proposition is true. But, it seems, a knower needs some sort of evidential justification to have adequate indication that a proposition is true. The belief/assent condition for propositional knowledge must be adequately related, from the knower's perspective, to the truth condition for knowledge. And an evidential justification condition is the only plausible candidate that provides for this relation. Thus I propose that propositional knowledge requires some sort of evidential justification. On my view, evidential justification is epistemic justification. But we should not infer that justified true belief is sufficient for propositional knowledge. Given Gettier-style counterexamples, such knowledge requires a fourth condition beyond the belief/assent, truth, and justification conditions. (Chapter 6 specifies what this elusive fourth condition is.)

Chapter 1 asks whether the concept of epistemic justification is a *normative* notion, either deontological or nondeontological. I contend that it is not. My main objection to normative notions of epistemic justification is that they are theoretically superfluous; that a non-normative notion of adequate evidence is all we need to characterize epistemic justification. Another problem is that the

5

normative notions of justification in circulation are intolerably vague. Chapter 1 gives an initial characterization of a non-normative notion of epistemic justification via the notions of adequate evidence and evidential probability.

CHAPTER 2 Chapter 2 continues with the topic of epistemic justification. It provides an account of *minimal* epistemic reasons, i.e., epistemic reasons that do not entail satisfaction of the justification condition for propositional knowledge. Such reasons make a proposition evidentially probable *to some extent*, but do not necessarily make a proposition evidentially more probable than its denial. Chapter 2 characterizes evidential probability in such a way that it contrasts with statistical, propensity, subjective, and recent epistemological interpretations of probability. One central feature of such probability is that it is relative to an evidence basis. But this raises the question of what constitutes the evidence basis of evidential probability. To answer this question, Chapter 2 begins with an examination of the following views stating that the evidence basis of such probability is purely propositional: Probability Coherentism, Probability Infinitism, the Thesis of Self-Probability, and the Thesis of Circular Probability. My general conclusion is twofold: (a) each of these views faces irremediable problems, and (b) it is implausible to suppose that evidential probability supervenes on an evidence basis that is purely propositional. I reach a similar conclusion for the view that propositional attitudes, such as mere belief states, provide the needed evidence basis.

Thus Chapter 2 asks whether evidential probability can have a *non*propositional evidence basis. This leads to distinctions among three general views on evidential probability: Radical Externalism, Moderate Externalism, and Internalism. According to *Radical Externalism*, the evidence basis in question consists at least in part of something external to one's psychological states, something of which one does not have any awareness. This view is represented mainly by certain causal-reliability theories of epistemic probability. According to *Moderate Externalism*, evidential probability supervenes on one's nonpropositional psychological states, such as sensory states, but one need not be aware of those states or of their contents. Such a view is suggested by various philosophers sympathetic to psychological behaviorism, including W. V. Quine. *Internalism*, in contrast, locates the relevant evidence basis either in

6

nonpropositional psychological states of which one is aware or simply in their contents of which one is aware.

Chapter 2 argues that a moderate version of Internalism is superior to the alternatives. According to *Moderate Internalism*, evidential probability derives ultimately from the subjective contents of one's nonpropositional psychological states, contents of which one is aware. Such states include one's nonconceptual states of seeming to sense and seeming to perceive (e.g., one's being appeared to by something). But Moderate Internalism does not require that one be aware of one's being in such states; it requires simply that one be aware of the contents of such states. Chapter 2 provides a taxonomy of experience that clarifies the notions of a psychological state and subjective contents relevant to Moderate Internalism. And it proposes a *non*epistemic notion of explanation that clarifies how propositions can derive evidential probability from the subjective contents of one's experiences. On my view, noninferential evidential probability derives from a proposition's explanatory power relative to the contents of one's nonconceptual experiences. Many philosophers assume that we should understand the notion of explanation via some notion of justification, but I contend that this assumption gets things backwards.

Not all evidential probability is occurrent. Some evidential probability-makers are nonoccurrent in the sense that they were present to awareness for a person, but are not now. Philosophers of an internalist persuasion have not given adequate attention to the conditions for nonoccurrent justification, or even to the general distinction between occurrent and nonoccurrent justification. Chapter 2 explains how probability-makers can be nonoccurrent when they are retrievable from memory in a certain way. The rejection of nonoccurrent probability-makers entails an implausible justification solipsism of the moment, and thereby raises serious problems for the possibility of justified belief in persisting physical objects.

Chapter 2 also explains how its commitment to Moderate Internalism entails a species of epistemic foundationalism. On this view some propositions can have evidential probability independently of evidential relations to any other propositions. Such a view involves a two-tier structure of evidential probability. Thus Chapter 2 explains how there can be not only unconditional, nonpropositional probability-makers, but also derivative, propositional

7

probability-makers. My account proposes that some propositional probability-makers are basic relative to all other probable propositions, insofar as their probability derives solely from nonpropositional experience. And it proposes that other propositional probability-makers are nonbasic insofar as their probability depends in part on other propositional items. Yet my account in Chapter 2 focuses only on minimal epistemic reasons, reasons that need only make a proposition evidentially probable, or justifiable, *to some extent*.

CHAPTER 3 Chapter 3 takes up the topic of *justifying* epistemic reasons. These are reasons sufficient for satisfaction of the justification condition for propositional knowledge. My first main conclusion is that a proposition's being evidentially more probable than its denial is *in*sufficient for that proposition's being epistemically justified. Justified propositions must be evidentially more probable than not only their relevant contraries but also their probabilistic competitors. When a proposition satisfies this requirement, it has what I call *maximal* evidential probability. Chapter 3 gives an account of maximal probability that relies solely on nonepistemic, nonnormative notions such as those of better explanation, entailment, causation, and subjective contents of experience. The account coincides with the Moderate Internalism of Chapter 2. And it allows for two special sorts of *contravening* of evidential probability relative to one's experience. In this respect, my account preserves the insight that epistemic justification is defeasible, at least for the most part.

Chapter 3 also offers a nonepistemic, non-normative account of what it is to *have* a justifying reason, and what it is for a belief to be *based on* a justifying reason. Such an account is crucial for a theory of knowledge, since propositional knowledge requires not only that one have a justifying reason, but also that one's believing or assenting be based on one's justifying reason. I characterize the evidential basing relation in part via the notion of a belief's being causally sustained by one's experience or by one's believing or assenting to a proposition for which one has a justifying reason.

Chapter 3 also explains that talk of justifying reason is crucially ambiguous between (a) the notion of a reason that makes a proposition *justifiable* and (b) the notion of a reason that makes a proposition actually *justified*. It clarifies this distinction via the concept of an evidential *association relation* that is essential to the notion of a justified proposition. The basic idea here is that a proposition is actually justified for one only if one has associated that proposition with its supporting evidence in a certain way. This idea isolates a basic distinction that current epistemology widely neglects. Such neglect, we shall see, does not indicate unimportance.

Finally Chapter 3 turns to justification skepticism. It argues that we can effectively challenge, if not refute, justification skepticism on explanatory grounds. Given my theory of justification, we can pose a dilemma for any skeptical view implying that no physical-object propositions are epistemically justifiable for us on the basis of our evidence. One horn of the dilemma demands that the skeptic provide a plausible notion of justification whose requirements are not satisfied by my account in Chapters 2 and 3. The other horn demands that the skeptic provide an explanation of our perceptual experiences that is at least as good as the explanation due to certain physical-object propositions. We shall see that the justification skeptic apparently cannot escape this dilemma.

Chapter 4 focuses on my theory's commitment to foundation- *CHAPTER 4* alism. It answers some likely objections to my foundationalism, such as the anti-foundationalist arguments of Richard Rorty and Wilfrid Sellars. And it challenges some prominent alternative accounts of justification, viz., certain versions of coherentism, contextualism, and reliabilism. Chapter 4 explains that there is sound motivation for my foundationalism in light of the famous epistemic regress problem introduced in Aristotle's *Posterior Analytics*. Thus I argue that modest foundationalism is a significant benefit, and in no way a disadvantage, from an epistemological point of view. I also argue that prominent versions of coherentism, contextualism, and reliabilism face serious problems that my foundationalism avoids. If these arguments are sound, we have grounds for recommending this book's foundationalism over its prominent competitors.

Chapter 5 introduces the topic of *procedural* epistemic rationality. *CHAPTER 5* An account of such rationality characterizes the epistemically rational way to be a truth-seeker. This account differs from an explanation of when one's evidence epistemically justifies one's beliefs. An account of procedural epistemic rationality, unlike an account of epistemic justification, involves guidelines for one's regulating the acquisition and the revision of beliefs. A belief has procedural epistemic rationality for one only if it is epistemically justifiable for one, but the converse does not hold. Chapter 5 thus

9

distinguishes conditions for procedural epistemic rationality from conditions for epistemic justification. Chapters 2–4 concern only conditions for justification. But Chapter 5 shows how we easily can extend the theory of those chapters to answer some basic questions about procedural rationality. Chapter 5 clarifies several notions of truth-seeking relevant to procedural rationality, and then argues for a notion that contains a distinctive evidence requirement. The needed evidence requirement stems from the Moderate Internalism of Chapters 2 and 3. It thus preserves the central role of explanation of experiential contents in epistemically rational belief.

Chapter 5 challenges a Cartesian approach to procedural rationality according to which one must refuse to believe, and even reject as false, uncertain propositions. Chapter 5 also identifies several prominent non-Cartesian approaches, such as those of Bernard Williams, Roderick Chisholm, Karl Popper, and Isaac Levi. But I find these approaches defective, largely for a single reason: they neglect the crucial role of maximal probability-makers in procedural epistemic rationality.

Chapter 6 completes my account of propositional knowledge by treating two major topics. The first topic is the fourth condition for propositional knowledge demanded by Gettier-style counterexamples. The second is the needed meta-justification that enables us to recommend this book's account of knowledge over its available competitors.

Regarding the fourth condition for knowledge, Chapter 6 assesses Robert Shope's initially promising use of the notion of epistemic explanation to diagnose Gettier-style counterexamples. I argue that Shope's diagnosis ultimately fails, but this does not mean that the notion of epistemic explanation is useless. Chapter 6 defends a straightforward fourth condition that we could formulate via a notion of epistemic explanation. But a more straightforward formulation uses the notion of *truth-resistant evidence* instead. Characterized roughly, truth-resistant justifying evidence is justifying evidence that is resistant to, or sustained by, the collective totality of truths. My characterization in Chapter 6 shows how we can dispense with the questionable notion of the totality of truths. Chapter 6 also explains how its fourth condition avoids the troublesome conditional fallacy in epistemology, and allows for more than one concept of propositional knowledge. The latter result is desirable, for philosophers have conflicting epistemic intuitions about certain Gettier-style counterexamples. My account of knowledge explains how we can account for such conflicting intuitions.

Regarding the needed meta-justification, one motivating factor is the problem of the criterion introduced in the skeptical writings of Sextus Empiricus. This problem suggests that we cannot know anything about the external world, on the grounds that (a) we cannot know physical-object propositions without first knowing epistemic principles about *how* we know such propositions, and (b) we cannot know epistemic principles about how we know physical-object propositions without first knowing some physical-object propositions. Chapter 6 denies that justification simply for physical-object propositions requires meta-justification, such as justification for believing that a physical-object proposition is justified via certain epistemic principles. Yet I also reject the particularist reply to the problem of the criterion, due to Chisholm and others, according to which we simply assume from the start that we know certain physical-object propositions. Such a particularist reply is patently question-begging against knowledge skepticism.

Thus Chapter 6 proposes a different strategy for solving the problem of the criterion. Called 'explanatory particularism', my strategy resembles the method of meta-justification in ethics relying on "reflective equilibrium." The basic idea is that the epistemologist does, and indeed must, begin with considered epistemic judgments, but that such judgments should be revised when doing so increases explanatory power relative to other considered epistemic judgments. Chapter 6 explains how the strategy of explanatory particularism improves on ordinary particularism, and gives skepticism a fair hearing in the competition among epistemological theories. Explanatory particularism, in contrast to traditional particularism, does not rule out skepticism from the start.

Chapter 6 also explains how explanatory particularism leads to a justification of this book's epistemological theory. Such a meta-justification requires that my account of knowledge exceed its available competitors in explanatory power relative to our considered epistemic judgments. Chapter 6 indicates how my account meets this requirement. It also emphasizes that the proposed meta-justification fits nicely with the sort of justification for physical-object propositions identified in Chapter 3. This point deserves emphasis, since meta-justification is itself a species of epistemic justification.

11

Overall, then, this book offers a new account of propositional knowledge that aims to improve on its predecessors. This account provides a challenger to the prominent epistemological theories in circulation, such as coherentism, contextualism, reliabilism, and competing versions of foundationalism. It aims specifically to surpass such competitors on explanatory grounds. Thus it strives to avoid the problem questions that hamper such competitors. And this of course is an important desideratum for a new account of knowledge. So even if this book fails to remove the disarray from contemporary epistemology, it at least provides a theory that adds to the field of competition.

1

Conditions for propositional knowledge

Human propositional knowledge is knowledge *that* something is the case. Such knowledge is necessarily knowledge *for* some human or other. It is thus perspectival, or person-relative. The relativity of propositional knowledge is illustrated by the fact that *my* knowing that something is the case does not require *your* knowing this too. We need to determine what exactly accounts for this relativity in order to understand what human propositional knowledge is. Thus we need to examine the various likely prerequisites for such knowledge to see how they provide for the relativity in question.

Since Plato's time, the main likely prerequisites for propositional knowledge have been the belief condition, the truth condition, and the justification condition. Examination of these conditions will reveal that propositional knowledge is doubly perspectival, owing to the person-relativity of the belief condition and the justification condition. But it will reveal also that such knowledge is not altogether perspectival, since the truth condition is not essentially person-relative.

1.1 Belief

One's believing is always one's believing *something*, and whatever one believes is of course an *object* of believing. An object of one's believing is a propositional truth-bearer: it is something that is true or false. For example, if I believe that the fawn is on the lawn, the object of my believing is either true or false: it is either true or false that the fawn is on the lawn.[1] Thus my talk of truth-bearers is

---

1 I shall not digress to Aristotle's well-known problem concerning statements about the future. For a useful discussion of this problem that supports my view that an object of believing is a truth-bearer, see Kneale and Kneale (1962, pp. 45–54).

really talk of truth-*value* bearers, since a truth-bearer is not necessarily true.

We may call a truth-bearer a *proposition*, so long as we understand a proposition to be anything that is either true or false. Familiar examples of propositions thus construed come from what is asserted or expressed in the making of a statement. My talk of propositions does not aim to commit us to abstract objects of the sort countenanced by Frege and Russell, for example. For this book's epistemological purposes, we can sidestep the vexing ontological question whether we need to posit propositions as abstract entities. Thus readers offended by talk of propositions can substitute talk of *statements*, so long as we do not confuse the expressed content of a statement and the making of a statement.[2]

One's simply believing a proposition contrasts with one's believing a proposition *with regard to an object*. The former believing is *de dicto*, since its object is *just* a proposition; whereas the latter believing is *de re*, since its object is not merely propositional or conceptual. *De re* believing is illustrated by my believing *about a fawn* that it is on the lawn. Such believing involves an "aboutness relation" to an object – in this case a fawn – that is not found in *de dicto* believing. But such believing is related also to a propositional object – in the present case the proposition that it is on the lawn, where 'it' is denotatively defined via a referential aboutness relation to a fawn. The nature of the aboutness relation in *de re* believing is a topic of considerable philosophical controversy.[3] I suspect that we can illuminate this topic via the notion of attention attraction introduced in §2.3.2. But the main point here is just that *de re* and *de dicto* believing both have propositional objects that are either true or false.

Even though all believing, being propositional, has a truth-bearer as an object, not all believing is *believing-true*.[4] For any proposition, P, believing-true is either believing it is true that P or believing

2 I shall not pursue, then, the ontological issue whether we must construe propositions as abstract entities. For some discussion of this issue, see Moser (1984) or, more generally, Church (1956), Quine (1970, Chap. 1), Armstrong (1973, Chap. 4), and Schiffer (1987, Chaps. 2–5).
3 For some indication of the controversy, see Chisholm (1976, pp. 159–75), Burge (1977), Pollock (1982, pp. 60–80), and Bach (1987, Chap. 1).
4 This point has been overlooked by various philosophers, including Lycan (1988, p. 137), Foley (1986, p. 352), Cohen (1984, p. 279), and Bernard Williams (1970, p. 137).

that P is true. One's believing-true that P is not entailed by one's believing that P. For the former believing, unlike the latter, requires something like one's having ascribed either the operator 'it is true that' or the predicate 'is true' to a proposition. One can believe that P even though one has not ascribed either that operator or that predicate to the proposition that P. For instance, I can believe that a fawn is on the lawn, even though I do not believe that it is true that a fawn is on the lawn, or that the proposition that a fawn is on the lawn is true. This will become clear in light of the subsequent account of believing. Believing-true, then, is conceptually more complex than simple believing. So let us not confuse believing with believing-true.

My believing that there is a fawn on the lawn requires my having assented, perhaps unconsciously, to the proposition that there is a fawn on the lawn. We need this requirement of assenting to preserve the distinction, to be drawn below, between one's actually believing and one's being merely disposed to believe.[5] In particular, this requirement is essential to a straightforward notion of nonoccurrent dispositional belief. One's genuinely assenting to a proposition is simply one's sincerely and understandingly affirming it.[6] Such affirming need not be a verbal utterance or inscription. (We believe many things that have been neither uttered nor inscribed.) Instead, assenting requires subjective, psychological affirmation of a proposition. One's assenting is conscious when one is aware of it; otherwise it is unconscious. Clearly the assenting required by believing need not be conscious. We are unaware of much of the assenting that underlies our believing.

One can stand in any of three logically possible relations to a proposition one considers: the relation of believing it, the relation of disbelieving it (i.e., believing its denial), and the relation of withholding it (i.e., refraining from believing it and its denial). These relations are not *actions*, but rather are *states* of a person, since

---

5 For some compelling evidence for this claim, see Lycan (1988, Chap. 3). Lycan, however, apparently does not appreciate the importance of the requirement of assenting, since he does not endorse it.

6 This approach to assenting is compatible with various accounts of conditions for sincerity and understanding. For instance, we might say that assenting is sincere when and only when it is not accompanied by one's wanting to deceive; and we might say that one understands a proposition only when one is capable of representing its truth conditions. My own views on the conditions for understanding and for one's having a concept are sketched in Moser (1988a).

they have the dispositional character of existing while not always being manifested, or occurrent. My believing that $2 + 2 = 4$, for instance, is not extinguished when I am thinking solely about matters nonarithmetical. But my *assenting* to $2 + 2 = 4$ is, where assenting to a proposition is one's sincerely and understandingly affirming that proposition, consciously or unconsciously. Thus assenting, like acting, must be manifested in the sense of being occurrent; but believing, being dispositional, need not. In fact, assenting is often just the *manifestation* of a dispositional belief state. A state of believing is dispositional in the sense that if one is in a belief state with respect to a proposition, P, then one will assent to P in any circumstance where one sincerely and understandingly answers the question whether it is the case that P.

Coming to believe, however, is not dispositional, since it is just a matter of belief *formation.* One comes to believe a proposition, P, if and only if a state of believing is formed with respect to P for one. And a state of believing is formed with respect to P for one only if one assents to P. (Once again, we need this requirement to distinguish between actual believing and a mere disposition to believe.) Specifically, one's assenting to P marks the beginning of a belief state when such a state is formed. Thus one comes to believe that P only if one assents to P. And since one's genuinely assenting to P requires one's understandingly affirming that P, the same is true of one's coming to believe that P. (But of course one might assent to P even though one does not come to believe that P; assenting to P need not result in a dispositional belief state regarding P.) And since one is in a state of believing that P only if one has come to believe that P, every state of believing with respect to a proposition requires that that proposition has been understandingly affirmed by the person in that belief state. But none of this requires that one be conscious of one's assenting or one's belief formation.

One's coming to believe a proposition contrasts conceptually with the *maintaining,* or the *sustaining,* of one's believing a proposition. The latter presupposes that a belief has been formed, and involves the conditions for the preservation of the already formed belief. The maintaining of a belief can depend on various factors. One's believing a proposition might be maintained simply because something caused one to come to believe that proposition while nothing ever interfered with the continuation of the state. In such a case, the cause of one's maintaining a belief is identical with the

16

cause of one's coming to believe. Yet there can be cases where such an identity does not hold. It might be that one causal factor is responsible for one's coming to believe a proposition, and a second causal factor is responsible for one's maintaining the belief, because without the second factor, a third causal factor would extinguish the state of believing.

I have anticipated the important but widely neglected distinction between one's believing a proposition and one's *being merely disposed to believe* a proposition. Clearly if one believes a proposition, one is disposed to *assent* to it under certain circumstances. But one's being merely disposed to believe a proposition is not logically sufficient for one's believing a proposition. One can be merely disposed to believe a proposition that one has not yet affirmed or even entertained. For example, ten minutes ago, before I had even thought about the proposition that $128 + 23 = 151$, I was merely disposed to believe that proposition. But ten minutes ago, I had not yet come to believe that proposition, since I had not yet affirmed it. Thus I did not believe that proposition ten minutes ago. My being merely disposed to believe that proposition ten minutes ago involved my being disposed to come to believe it upon my sincerely and understandingly answering the question whether that proposition is true. Clearly there are many propositions that we are thus disposed to believe, even though we do not actually believe them.[7]

Believing, then, is a dispositional *state* of a person that is related to a propositional *object*. This in short is *the state–object view of belief.* On this view a belief has two essential components: a dispositional state and a propositional object. These two components exist not only in *de dicto* belief, where a belief state is related only to a propositional object, but also in *de re* belief, where a belief state is related to a nonpropositional object as well as a propositional object. We need to distinguish these two components of belief, since what is relevant to the assessment of one of the components can be irrelevant to the assessment of the other. For example, assessments of truth and falsity apply directly to a propositional *object* of belief, but do not apply directly to a belief *state*. Our ordinary use of

7 Neglecting the distinction between believing and being merely disposed to believe, many philosophers have assumed implausibly that every person believes an infinite number of propositions. See, for example, Harman (1986, p. 12). A needed corrective to this assumption has been suggested by Audi (1982). Some critical discussion of Harman's view of believing can be found in Moser (1987).

'belief' is often ambiguous between these two components. We can avoid such ambiguity, whenever it threatens, by using 'believing' or 'belief state' to refer to the psychological state of belief and 'proposition believed' to refer to the propositional object of such a state.

My talk of the possibilities of believing, disbelieving, and withholding might seem to imply that believing is voluntary. Yet it really does not imply this at all. The claim that believing, disbelieving, and withholding are *logical possibilities* is quite compatible with the claim that believing is not actually voluntary. The issue whether human believing is voluntary is of course an empirical matter that we cannot settle apart from psychological investigation. Yet it seems that believing is voluntary in one respect but not in another. Since I am psychologically unable to change every belief state of mine just by an act of will, not all believing is *directly* voluntary, even if all believing is *indirectly* voluntary. Even if I have the power to *employ means* to bring about believing, disbelieving, or withholding, I do not have the power to control all my believing just by an act of the will.

Indirect control over believing seems to be a live option. For instance, I evidently can bring myself to believe a proposition by focusing on compelling evidence for that proposition, and by ignoring all evidence to the contrary. Or more extremely, I evidently can bring myself to believe, disbelieve, or withhold a proposition by subjecting myself to hypnosis or to some other means of (indirect) control over belief formation. Since these latter possibilities are evidently psychological as well as logical, we may plausibly assume that at least some believing is indirectly voluntary. But again this is an empirical point that we cannot recommend solely on conceptual grounds. Justified belief, as characterized in Chapters 2–4, does not require voluntary belief of either a direct or an indirect sort.

Drawing together the main points thus far, we now can set forth this definition of one's *believing a proposition*:

A person, S, believes a proposition, P, at a time, $t = df$. (i) S has assented to P (consciously or unconsciously) either before t or at t, and (ii) as a nondeviant result of his assenting to P, S is in a dispositional state at t whereby he will assent to P in any circumstance where he sincerely and understandingly answers the question whether it is the case that P.

Clause (ii) raises familiar questions about the possibility of deviant causal chains.[8] But let us not digress; these questions are not peculiar to my account, and my account is compatible with a wide range of plausible answers. Instead, let us proceed with the intuitive notion of a well-behaved, nondeviant causal chain, thereby construing (ii) so as to exclude causal deviance.

Contrast my definition of believing with the suggested definition of one's *being merely disposed to believe a proposition*:

> A person, *S*, is merely disposed to believe that *P* at a time, *t* = *df.* (i) *S* does not believe that *P* at *t*, but (ii) *S* is in a dispositional state at *t* whereby he will come to believe that *P* upon his sincerely and understandingly answering the question whether it is the case that *P*.

One's believing a proposition requires one's having assented to that proposition, whereas one's being merely disposed to believe a proposition does not require this. One's believing a proposition at a time does not require one's assenting to that proposition *at that time*. Thus the assent required by believing need not exist now. But it must have existed at some time, and it must mark the beginning of the belief state.

The account of justified believing in this book will presuppose the notion of believing just characterized. Yet nothing in the debate between my theory of justification and its rivals will depend on my notion of believing. Thus proponents of an alternative notion of believing are not epistemologically doomed from the start, at least not because of my notion of believing.

The logical relation between knowledge and believing is straightforward. Dispositional propositional knowledge requires believing, but believing does not require propositional knowledge of any sort. Believing does not require propositional knowledge, for (a) such knowledge requires truth, but believing does not, and (b) such knowledge requires justification, but believing does not. Dispositional propositional knowledge requires believing, because believing is what relates the believer dispositionally as well as psychologically to a dispositionally known proposition. Apart from my believing that *P*, dispositional knowledge that *P* will not actually be *mine*. It might then be someone else's or it might be something

---

8 On such questions, see, for example, Peacocke (1979, Chap. 2) and Searle (1983, pp. 136–40).

I am merely *disposed* to acquire; but it will not actually be mine. This point does not necessarily conflict with the familiar talk of one's knowing something but not actually believing it. Apparently such talk typically indicates one's not *consciously* believing something one knows. (Characterizations of self-deception sometimes involve such talk.) Dispositional knowledge does not require one's being conscious of one's believing. Instead it requires that one simply believe.

One might propose that something other than believing relates a knower psychologically to dispositionally known propositions. For example, one might appeal to a special sort of representational capacity that does not entail believing. It is of course impossible to assess such a view apart from a clear account of the capacity in question. And I am unaware of any such account in circulation. Yet I do not pretend to have shown that no such account is possible. I find rather that believing is now the only plausible candidate for relating a knower psychologically to dispositionally known propositions, and on this basis I propose that dispositional knowledge requires believing.[9]

But I doubt that all propositional knowledge requires believing. *Non*dispositional knowledge is just like dispositional knowledge except that it involves mere genuine assent rather than belief toward a known proposition. Nondispositional knowledge does not require that a knower be dispositionally related via belief to a known proposition, but it does require the satisfaction of all the other conditions for knowledge. Thus suppose that P is true, that P is justified for me on the basis of my (Gettier-proof) justifying evidence, and that I assent to P, but do not believe that P, on the basis of that evidence. I do not believe that P in this case because my assenting to P has not generated the required sort of disposition; perhaps I even have a physiological or psychological defect that precludes my having the sort of disposition required by belief. The problem is *not* that there is insufficient time for the formation of a dispositional belief state. I grant that there can be a *momentary* dispositional belief state. The problem is that my assenting to P has not generated a dispo-

---

9 For some support for this proposal by way of answering several objections, see Armstrong (1973, Chap. 10), Lehrer (1974, Chap. 3), and Swain (1981, pp. 28–36). For dissenting views, see the survey in Shope (1983, pp. 171–92). (Lehrer has since rejected the view that knowledge requires belief; see his [1983, 1986] and the discussion in Davis [1988].)

sitional belief state. But this does not preclude knowledge. There seems to be a clear sense in which I have knowledge that P in the case in question, even though I do not believe that P. Let us call this *nondispositional knowledge*. In such knowledge, mere genuine assent rather than belief relates a knower psychologically to a known proposition.

I should expand briefly on my controversial point about the belief condition. Believing requires one's having a tendency to affirm a proposition under certain circumstances. Call this the *tendency requirement* of believing. Given this requirement, one believes that P only if one will affirm that P, with lawlike regularity, under certain circumstances. The very notion of a tendency or a disposition involves the idea of lawlike regularity.

Consider now my imaginary friend, Mr. Lawless. He is relevantly similar to us from the standpoint of psychological makeup, except for one notable difference. Lawless has a central nervous system that, owing to a very rare congenital defect, fails to sustain the sort of law-conforming tendency to affirm that is demanded by the tendency requirement of believing. Lawless has no problem whatsoever affirming propositions. He can understand propositions, and he can endorse propositions with as much sincerity as we ourselves can muster. The problem is that Lawless endorses propositions quite independently of the sort of law-conforming tendency that we believers represent. Thus the fact that Lawless sincerely affirms that P at one moment does not guarantee, in any lawlike manner, that he will reaffirm that P at a later time under certain circumstances. Lawless represents lawless behavior regarding the affirmation of propositions. But he nonetheless affirms some propositions.

We can imagine a plausible physiological account of the irregular condition of Lawless. Suppose that one's satisfying the tendency requirement of believing requires one's being able to remember certain propositions (and perhaps one's psychological relations to them), but that Lawless has sufficient brain damage to cause memory failure. This failure could be due of course either to lack of storage or to inability of retrieval. If the tendency requirement depends on memory, we can make sense of Lawless by appeal to certain impaired functions of his brain. Thus the case of Lawless appears not to be inordinately far-fetched.

It seems then that one's affirming that P need not be coupled with one's being disposed to affirm that P, with lawlike regularity, under certain circumstances. One's affirming that P might be coupled with one's being unable to sustain (physiologically or otherwise) the sort of lawlike affirmation behavior demanded by the tendency requirement of believing. In such a case, we have affirming without believing. Whenever Lawless affirms that P, he is in such a case; and thus he always fails to believe that P.

Suppose now that Lawless shares our common awareness of justifying (Gettier-proof) evidence for the true proposition that there is a white piece of paper before us. Lawless *seems* to see a white piece of paper – he has the requisite images; and he is unaware of any defeaters of his supporting evidence. Lawless also sincerely affirms that there is a white piece of paper before us; but of course, in contrast to the rest of us, he fails to believe this proposition. Lawless does not satisfy the tendency requirement of believing. But he does have (Gettier-proof) justified true affirmation with regard to the proposition that there is a white piece of paper before us. (And we could suppose also that the relevant justifying evidence causally sustains Lawless's affirmation; this would satisfy the evidential-basing relation for propositional knowledge.)

The *only* relevant difference between Lawless and us is that we alone satisfy the tendency requirement of believing. But how is this difference relevant to whether Lawless *knows*? I find that it is irrelevant, at least for one sort of propositional knowledge. Lawless does not have *ongoing* propositional knowledge, since his psychological relation to the affirmed proposition is not ongoing, at least not in the dispositional sense in which believing is ongoing. But Lawless does have transitory propositional knowledge. After all, he does have (Gettier-proof) justified true affirmation regarding the proposition in question. And the mere fact that his affirmation is nondispositional does not affect the *epistemic* status of this affirmation. Thus the case of Lawless illustrates the possibility of knowing without believing.

The standard belief condition for knowledge serves to guarantee that a knower is psychologically related, via a propositional attitude, to the propositions he knows. But why should we think that believing, with its essential tendency requirement, must provide the needed psychological relation? My answer: we should not think this.

Instead, we should distinguish two relevantly different sorts of propositional knowledge: dispositional (or ongoing) knowledge and nondispositional (or transitory) knowledge. Dispositional knowledge requires a belief condition, but nondispositional knowledge does not. The mere fact that nondispositional knowledge is transitory, owing to the knower's nondispositional propositional attitude, does not undermine its genuine epistemic status. People like Lawless can have knowledge, however transitory; they simply cannot have *dispositional* knowledge. The opposing view, stating that Lawless cannot be a knower, risks confusion between the nondispositional doxastic status and the epistemic status of a psychological state. We should shun that confusion. Similarly we now should shun any analysis of knowledge, such as the standard analysis, that requires a belief condition for every sort of propositional knowledge.

Since knowledge requires believing or at least assenting, and believing and assenting are perspectival in the sense that they are relative to a person, knowledge is similarly perspectival. My knowing that P does not entail your knowing that P, since my knowing that P does not require your believing or assenting to P. Thus we should reject as invalid the inference from one person's knowing something to another person's knowing it too. We should recognize that knowledge is perspectival because it requires belief or assent.

As I noted, one's believing that P does not require one's believing either that P is true or that it is true that P. Believing that P does not require the ascribing of the predicate 'is true' or the operator 'it is true that' to a proposition. Similarly knowledge that P does not require such ascribing either. Thus knowledge that P does not require knowledge *that P is true*, if the latter knowledge entails believing or affirming that P is true. Let us allow, then, that one can know that P even if one does not believe or affirm either that P is true or that it is true that P. (Yet ordinarily if one believes that P, one is disposed to believe that P is true.) Knowledge that P requires belief or assent only in the sense that it requires that one believe or assent to P, perhaps unconsciously.

Let us turn now to the truth condition for propositional knowledge.

1.2 Truth as minimal correspondence

One's believing a false proposition, P, is incompatible with one's knowing that P. A false proposition cannot be an object of knowledge. Knowledge requires true belief or assent in the sense that its belief/assent condition must be related to a true proposition. That is, knowledge that *P* requires that one believe or assent to *P* *and* that *P* be true.

We need to specify what sense of 'true' applies to the truth condition for propositional knowledge. I assume (a) that one knows that *P* only if it is true that *P*, and (b) that it is true that *P* only if *it is the case that P*. Thus I assume that one's knowing that *P* entails its being the case that *P*. It is conceptually confusing to say that one knows that *P* but it is not the case that *P*. (The student's claim that the Ptolemaic astronomers *knew* that the geocentric hypothesis is true ordinarily means nothing more than that these astronomers *believed* that they knew this hypothesis.) The notion of its being the case that *P* seems to be *non*epistemic: it seems not to involve the notion of evidence, justification, or knowledge. Instead this notion seems to involve the notion of *how reality is*. Let us try to relate this point to the truth condition for propositional knowledge.

1.2.1 Truth as correspondence

The familiar correspondence definition of truth is a likely means of relating the notion of truth to a nonepistemic notion of how reality is. According to the simplest version, the claim that a proposition is true means that the proposition *corresponds* to an actual state of affairs or an existing situation. Variations on this view occur in the writings of Aristotle, Russell, and the early Wittgenstein, among many others. The basic idea of the theory in its post-Aristotelian garb is that the truth of a proposition consists in its picturing, in terms of isomorphic representation, the way things actually are. Some proponents require a correspondence relation only of true *atomic* propositions, i.e., true logically simple propositions. According to these philosophers, the truth of nonatomic propositions is a function of their atomic constituents.

But the most pressing question is: what *kind* of correspondence is definitive of truth? How exactly does the true proposition that I am reading a book, for example, *correspond* to the way things actually are? The answers to these questions are far from obvious. So it is no surprise that proponents of the theory have not agreed on a precise account of correspondence.[10] Yet proponents do agree that truth concerning the nonpropositional world is defined via a specific representational relation, often called 'isomorphic representation', between propositions (or their constituents) on the one hand and nonpropositional reality on the other. Such truth is supposedly a distinctive representational connection between the two sides of a proposition/world duality.

Even if we had a detailed account of isomorphic representation, a serious problem would remain: there are propositions whose truth does not consist in any straightforward way of correspondence as pictorial isomorphic representation. Consider for example: (a) true propositions about unrealized situations (e.g., 'I shall pay my taxes next year' and 'If I were a physical education instructor, I would be in better physical shape than I am as a philosophy professor'); (b) true propositions about normative considerations (e.g., 'I *ought* to devote more time to assisting people in poverty'); and (c) true propositions that are mathematical or logical (e.g., '5 + 5 = 10' and 'It is not the case that both P and $\sim P$'). It is quite unclear how correspondence between the two sides of a proposition/world duality defines the truth of such propositions. In fact, it is not even clear that such propositions are *solely* about isomorphically representable features of the actual world. Thus it is not clear that their truth is a function only of their relation of correspondence, construed as isomorphic representation, to the actual world. Perhaps there is a straightforward notion of isomorphic representation that accommodates the truth of such propositions. But until we find it, we should look elsewhere for a definition of truth.

There is an additional, equally serious problem facing the view that correspondence as isomorphic representation is definitive of truth. On this view, if we assume that correspondence is precisely defined in some elaborate way in terms of isomorphic representation, there is the threat of preventing most people from believing that a proposition is true. Evidently we do need some rather elaborate definition to accommodate true propositions of the troublesome sorts just noted. But of course most people lack the relevant elaborate notion of correspondence; I, for one, lack this notion.

10 For overviews of various approaches to correspondence, see Prior (1967), O'Connor (1975, pp. 70–86, 112–36), and Hallett (1988, Chap. 1).

Thus such people will be unable to believe that a proposition is true, since correspondence, construed as isomorphic representation, is definitive of truth. But apparently many of us can believe that a proposition is true even though we lack the relevant elaborate notion of correspondence. As long as correspondence is defined via a complicated notion of isomorphic representation, this problem will persist.[11]

Thus we need to avoid an elaborate notion of correspondence in our definition of truth. We need a *minimal* notion of correspondence.

1.2.2 The minimal correspondence definition

A minimal version of the correspondence definition promises to succeed where the traditional version failed. This version surfaces in Book IV of Aristotle's *Metaphysics*: "To say of what is that it is not, or of what is not that it is, is false, while to say of what is that it is, or of what is not that it is not, is true." This minimal correspondence notion of truth emerges more recently from John Mackie's view that to say that a statement is true is to say that things are as they are stated to be by that statement.[12] The only possible relevant difference between Aristotle's and Mackie's representations of the minimal correspondence definition is that Aristotle's view makes truth a feature of a *saying* whereas Mackie's view makes truth a feature of a *statement*. It is not obvious that every statement is a saying, especially if a saying requires an utterance in contrast to an inscription. In any case, Mackie does stress that by 'statement' he means the *content* of a statement rather than the *act* or performance of stating.

If we continue to use 'proposition' to designate the content of a statement, we can put the minimal correspondence definition simply as follows:

> The claim that a proposition, *P*, is true means that things are as they are stated to be by *P*.

This qualifies as a correspondence definition because it makes truth a function of a representational relation between the two sides of

---

11 On some additional problems for traditional correspondence approaches, see Putnam (1981, pp. 56–74), Hallett (1988, Chap. 2), and Vision (1988, Chap. 3).
12 See Mackie (1970; 1973, pp. 48–58).

a proposition/world duality.[13] Specifically it makes truth a function of the statement relation between a proposition and how things actually are. If things are as they are stated to be by a proposition, then the proposition is true; otherwise it is false. But we have here a *minimal* correspondence notion, since it does not use any notion of one-to-one correspondence relations, or of isomorphic representation, between true propositions and features of the world.

Let us ask how the minimal correspondence definition relates logically to Tarski's familiar schema for truth, which may be called 'schema T':

X is true if and only if P,

where 'P' stands for a declarative sentence, and 'X' stands for the name of that sentence.[14] For example, given schema T, 'All philosophers are contentious' is true if and only if all philosophers are contentious. Tarski proposed that any acceptable definition of truth must accommodate all the instances of schema T. Specifically Tarski put forth schema T not as a definition of truth, but as an *adequacy condition* for a definition of truth, i.e., a condition that must be met by any adequate definition of truth. Thus by design, schema T specifies not the meaning of the predicate 'is true', but only an adequacy condition on its definition.

The minimal correspondence notion entails schema T, so long as we count (unambiguous) declarative sentences as propositions, but the converse entailment does not hold. The following argument shows that the proposed entailment holds:

1. 'P' stands for a declarative sentence, and 'X' stands for the name of that sentence. (Assumption)
2. 'X is true' means that things are as they are stated to be by X. (From the minimal correspondence definition, and the assumption that declarative sentences are propositions)
3. Things are as they are stated to be by X if and only if P. (From 1 and the notion of 'X states how things are')
4. If X is true, then things are as they are stated to be by X. (From 2)
5. So if X is true, then P. (From 3 and 4)

---

13 When a true proposition is solely about itself, we need to distinguish between the proposition *as what represents* and the proposition *as what is represented* in order to accommodate the notion of a proposition/world duality.
14 On schema T, see Tarski (1936, 1944, 1967). For relevant recent discussion, see Putnam (1960; 1983a, Chap. 4; 1983b), Davidson (1969, 1973), Field (1972; 1986, pp. 64–7), and Soames (1984).

6. If things are as they are stated to be by X, then X is true. (From 2)
7. So if P, then X is true. (From 3 and 6)
8. Hence X is true if and only if P. (From 5 and 7)

Given this argument, the minimal correspondence notion clearly does not conflict with Tarski's adequacy condition for a definition of truth; on the contrary, it requires it. This should be no surprise, since Tarski's adequacy condition was explicitly motivated by Aristotle's aforementioned statement of the minimal correspondence definition.

But the minimal correspondence definition is not equivalent to Tarski's schema T. Schema T does not entail the minimal correspondence definition, since schema T involves only sentences as truth-bearers and the minimal correspondence definition does not. And to the extent that it is implausible to restrict truth-bearers to sentences, the minimal correspondence notion is preferable to schema T, at least as a definition of truth.[15] Schema T states only an adequacy condition for a definition of truth, whereas the minimal correspondence notion, being a definition, states *the meaning* of the predicate 'is true'.

Let us ask whether the minimal correspondence notion faces the objection I raised against the traditional correspondence definition. The relevant objection is that the traditional definition, by implication, places an excessive demand on one's believing that a proposition is true. According to the minimal correspondence notion, one believes that a proposition is true if and only if one believes that the proposition states how things are. This claim seems not to be excessive; it seems quite plausible to suppose that one has the concept of truth only if one has the concept of how things are. The latter concept is basically the concept of what items (e.g., objects, features of objects, relations between objects and/or features), if any, exist (perhaps only at a particular place and time). Whereas the concept of how things are is essential to the concept of truth, I doubt that the same is true of the concepts of coherence, pragmatic value, warranted assertibility, and correspondence as isomorphic representation. Thus I prefer the minimal correspondence notion to definitions of truth that employ the latter concepts.

Let us turn now to some likely objections to the minimal correspondence definition.

15 On the need for truth-bearers beyond sentences, see the works cited in note 2.

1.2.3 Criticisms and replies

The first objection sounds Kantian: it is simply that the very notion of how things are independently of conceivers is unintelligible.[16] We must ask what sort of argument can make this objection even initially compelling. Perhaps one candidate argument runs as follows: (1) Every intelligible concept is conceiver-relative. (2) The concept of how things are independently of conceivers is not conceiver-relative. (3) Thus the concept of how things are independently of conceivers is unintelligible.

The main problem with such an argument is that it equivocates on the term 'conceiver-relative'. A concept might be conceiver-relative in the sense that it is *possessed* by a conceiver; or it might be conceiver-relative in the sense that it *makes essential reference* to a conceiver. The concept of a stone, for example, is possessed by various conceivers, but it does not make essential reference to a conceiver. One can have the concept of a stone without having the concept of a conceiver. The concept of how things are is similar to the concept of a stone in that regard. This point is compatible of course with the fact that how things are may comprise *mind-dependent facts*; so we have not excluded mental reality automatically.

Given the two senses of 'conceiver-relative', premise (1) is evidently false if construed as the claim that every intelligible concept makes essential reference to a conceiver. There is no reason to think that for every concept, *C*, one's possessing *C* requires one's having the concept of a conceiver. On the other hand, premise (1) is arguably true if construed as the claim that every intelligible concept is possessed by some conceiver or other. Given a non-Platonist view of concepts, a concept exists only as the psychological feature of some conceiver or other. But on the latter construal premise (2) is false, or at least question-begging. Premise (2) is true only on the construal where to be conceiver-relative is to make essential reference to a conceiver. Thus barring equivocation, if premise (2) is true, then premise (1) is false, and if premise (1) is true, premise (2) is false. We do not have here, then, an argument showing that the notion of how things are is unintelligible.

---

16 Various philosophers have suggested this objection. See, for example, Goodman (1960; 1978, pp. 3–4), Putnam (1981, pp. 49–54, 60–4), and Rorty (1982, pp. xxvi, 14–15, 192). Cf. Post (1987, pp. 293–8) for expansion on Goodman (1960).

A more familiar argument derives from the verificationist assumption that the intelligibility of a concept requires the verifiability of the conditions for its being instantiated or its not being instantiated. The argument, put simply, is: (1) A concept is intelligible only if its instantiation conditions are verifiable. (2) The instantiation conditions for the concept of how things are are not verifiable. (3) Thus the concept of how things are is not intelligible.

Premises (1) and (2) are uncompelling mainly because of the vagueness of the term 'verifiable'. Regarding premise (1), let us grant, if only for the sake of argument, that a concept is intelligible only if one could *in principle* be justified in believing that it is instantiated or that it is not instantiated. (See Moser [1988a] for some discussion of this view.) Such a concession does not threaten the minimal correspondence definition, since we have no reason to think that it is logically impossible for one to be justified in believing a proposition about how things are. Thus premise (2) needs support, and it is unclear what this support might be. If verifiability requires only defeasible justifiability, premise (2) will be initially uncompelling, or at least question-begging; and if a stronger notion of verifiability is introduced, premise (1) will be implausible. Thus the overall argument seems more troublesome than the notion it aims to discredit.

A serious problem also threatens the conclusion that the concept of how things are is unintelligible. Given that conclusion, we can ask whether it itself is a claim about how things are. If it is, we can ask whether it itself is intelligible *given its own claim*. And if it is not a claim about how things are, we need to ask what sort of claim it is. One reply is that it is a claim not about how things are, but only about what we are *justified in affirming*. Thus the relevant conclusion would be that we are justified in affirming that the concept of how things are is unintelligible. But we can ask of that conclusion also whether it itself is a claim about how things are. If it is, we can ask again whether it itself is intelligible given its own claim. And if it is not a claim about how things are, we need again to ask what sort of claim it is. If it is a claim solely about what we are justified in affirming, we have the iterative conclusion that *we are justified in affirming that we are justified in affirming* that the concept of how things are is unintelligible. But if we take this approach, then because of the foregoing line of questioning, we face a regress of increasing levels of epistemic iteration. Such a regress is unacceptable, since it is doubtful that we have the sort of iterative evidence it requires.

Thus it is not clear how to make sense of the claim that the concept of how things are is unintelligible. Barring an unpalatable regress, that claim evidently presupposes the very concept it finds unintelligible.

Another argument against the minimal correspondence definition resembles a familiar criticism of John Locke's representational theory of perception. It runs in outline as follows: (1) A correspondence definition of truth requires that we be able to compare propositions with unconceptualized reality. (2) We have no access to unconceptualized reality. (3) So a correspondence definition of truth is unacceptable.[17]

The premises of this argument fail to convince. Regarding premise (1), there is no reason to think that a correspondence definition of truth demands our being able to compare propositions and unconceptualized reality. The minimal correspondence definition does not require unconceptualized reality; it is perfectly compatible with thoroughgoing idealism. One might endorse premise (1) if one acknowledged a nonconceptual world and confused a correspondence definition of truth with a set of conditions for *finding out* whether a proposition is true. But the minimal correspondence definition is not designed as a criterion for finding out whether a proposition is true; it is simply a definition of truth. And as a definition, the minimal correspondence approach has no bearing whatsoever on the issue whether we can compare propositions with unconceptualized reality.

Premise (2) is equally troublesome given the vagueness of 'access'. There is perhaps a trivial sense in which we have no *conceptual* access to unconceptualized reality, given that actualized conceptual access to reality makes it conceptualized. But that truism hardly lends any support to the conclusion (3). Nor should that truism lead one to think, as some philosophers apparently do, that mind-independent unconceptualized reality is ineffable or unconceptualizable. My main point, however, is that, owing to its first premise, the foregoing argument is unsound, and thus does not threaten the minimal correspondence definition.

17 This sort of argument is suggested in various recent writings of Hilary Putnam. See, for instance, Putnam (1981, pp. 49, 130, 134; 1983a, pp. viii, 162, 166).

Another variation on the foregoing sort of argument has been offered recently by Hilary Putnam. It is:

The trouble [with a correspondence theory of truth] is not that correspondences between words or concepts and other entities don't exist, but that *too many* correspondences exist. To pick out just *one* correspondence between words or mental signs and mind-independent things we would have already to have referential access to the mind-independent things. You can't single out a correspondence. . .between our concepts and the supposed noumenal objects without access to the noumenal objects.[18]

Putnam's basic argument seems to be this:

(1) There are a great many similarities (= correspondences) between a proposition and the world.
(2) Not just any similarity between a proposition and the world is definitive of truth.
(3) So the correspondence theorist must identify the sort of similarity between a proposition and the world that is definitive of truth.
(4) The only way to identify a truth-definitive similarity between a proposition and the world is by means of referential access to the mind-independent world.
(5) We cannot have referential access to the mind-independent world.
(6) So a correspondence definition of truth is unacceptable.

Premises (1)–(3) seem unobjectionable. Premise (1) receives support from Putnam's well-known model-theoretic argument against metaphysical realism, which concludes that "no matter what operational and theoretical constraints our practice may impose on our use of a language, there are always *infinitely many different reference relations* (different 'satisfaction relations', . . . or different *correspondences*) which satisfy all of the constraints" (1983a, p. ix; cf. pp. 1–25, 85).[19] I shall not quarrel over premises (1)–(3).

Premises (4) and (5) raise serious problems. Putnam does not give any arguments that make these premises compelling, and it is unclear what such arguments might be.

In fact, premise (4) is arguably false. The task of identifying the sort of correspondence definitive of truth *can* be accomplished without referential access to the mind-independent world. For the definition of truth via the minimal correspondence definition does not at all require the existence of a mind-independent world. That

18 Putnam (1981, pp. 72–3; cf. pp. 45–7, 51, 64–6). See also Putnam (1983a, pp. 277–8).
19 For replies to Putnam's model-theoretic argument against correspondence truth and realism, see Devitt (1984, Chap. 11), Forbes (1986, pp. 38–41), and Lewis (1984).

definition is a *semantic* thesis that does not by itself state any meta-physical thesis such as that there is a mind-independent world. Thus as I suggested, the minimal correspondence definition is logically compatible with a form of idealism stating that there are only minds. So premise (4) is gratuitous at best.

Premise (5) is similarly ungrounded, but let us not pursue that point. For (a) we have found Putnam's argument to be uncompelling apart from (5), and (b) the minimal correspondence definition does not depend on the denial of (5). Perhaps Putnam endorses the false premise (4) because of a confusion between the conditions definitive of truth and the conditions for finding out whether a proposition is true. In any case, the minimal correspondence definition has escaped unscathed.

A final noteworthy objection to the minimal correspondence definition is that it is trivial. Such an objection is frequently raised against Tarski's schema T, but it is quite unclear what its concern actually is. Ordinarily the objection that a position is trivial means that the position is obviously correct and undeniable by any sensible person. But the minimal correspondence definition is far from trivial in that sense. Many sensible philosophers have defended alternatives to it. Yet if the objection is simply that the minimal correspondence definition is obviously correct, I do not take the objection as threatening. This section maintains that the minimal correspondence definition is actually correct, even if not obviously correct.

Perhaps the real concern of the objection is that the minimal correspondence definition is insufficiently *informative* about the nature of truth. But it is not obvious that a definition of truth needs to be more informative; nor is it clear that it can be in general. Surely the objector needs to show that a definition of truth can be more informative. Perhaps the basic worry here is simply that the minimal correspondence definition does not enable us to find out whether individual propositions are true. Apparently this is a common worry among critics of a correspondence theory of truth. But such a worry only betrays confusion: a confusion between the conditions for a proposition's *being* true and the conditions for our *finding out* whether a proposition is true.

Given the basic distinction between such conditions, we cannot fault a *definition* of truth for failing to specify means for finding out whether a proposition is true. A definition of truth need not specify such means; nor does the minimal correspondence definition intend to do so. For generally a definition of a general concept is one thing, and a criterion for finding out whether something instantiates that concept is something else. The failure of the minimal correspondence definition to provide the latter sort of criterion does *not* distinguish it from most definitions of general concepts. (Consider, for instance, the concepts of animal, conscious being, and sentient being.) Thus there seems to be no harmful sense in which the minimal correspondence definition is trivial or uninformative.

We can illustrate an important advantage of the minimal correspondence definition over traditional correspondence theories via propositions whose truth does not consist, in any straightforward sense, in correspondence construed as isomorphic representation. Earlier I mentioned three sorts of propositions: (a) true propositions about unrealized situations, (b) true propositions about normative considerations, and (c) true mathematical or logical propositions.

Regarding (a), consider again the true proposition that if I were a physical education instructor, I would be in better shape than I am as a philosophy professor. It is very difficult to specify a clear sense of 'correspondence' involving isomorphic representation according to which that proposition corresponds to the world. But on the minimal correspondence definition, we need have only the notion of things being such that if I were a physical education instructor, I would be in better shape than I am as a philosophy professor. Similarly regarding (b) and the true proposition that I ought to spend more time helping poor people, the minimal correspondence definition requires only the notion of things being such that I ought to spend more time helping poor people. And regarding (c), if a true logical or mathematical proposition, *P*, is necessarily true, the minimal correspondence definition requires only the notion of things being such that necessarily *P*. The example 'There are no martians' follows suit: the minimal correspondence definition requires only the notion of things being such that there are no martians.

The minimal correspondence definition does not require that the definition of truth involve an elaborate notion of isomorphic representation between the constituents of the relevant true proposition and the features of the world. Instead this notion of a true proposition requires only the notion of a proposition's stating *how things actually are*. Such simplicity is clearly an advantage of the minimal correspondence definition, given the widely divergent means of representation among various natural languages. This definition enables us to free the definition of truth from the peculiarities of natural languages. One resulting benefit is that the notion of truth is not necessarily enslaved to the notion of a natural language. This is indeed a benefit, because it is conceivable that some propositions are true while there are no natural languages.

Overall then we plausibly can endorse the minimal correspondence definition of truth. Specifically we plausibly can take this definition to characterize the sort of truth required by propositional knowledge. I am unaware of a better notion of truth. This book will assume, then, that the truth condition for propositional knowledge comes from the minimal correspondence definition of truth. Thus necessarily if one knows that P, then P is true in the sense that P states how things actually are.

1.3 Epistemic justification

Having defined truth via the minimal correspondence definition, we now may say that if one knows that P, then P states how things actually are. But the same is not true of justified belief that P; justified belief is not necessarily related to a proposition that states how things actually are. Justified belief can be false, and in that respect it contrasts with knowledge.

This section gives a preliminary account of the justification condition for propositional knowledge. It argues that propositional knowledge does require justification, and that the notion of epistemic justification is not a normative concept in either a deontological or a nondeontological sense. Chapters 2–4 complete this chapter's preliminary account of epistemic justification.

Clearly one's believing a true proposition, P, is inadequate for one's knowing that P. True belief does not exclude coincidental truth, such as lucky guesswork; but propositional knowledge does, since it requires that the knower have *adequate indication* that a known proposition is true. Such adequate indication is on any viable construal a sort of *evidence* indicating that a proposition is true. Since such evidence just is epistemic justification, we may infer that epistemic justification is needed to provide adequate indication that a known proposition is true. Thus propositional knowledge evidently requires a justification condition.[20] (Readers who reject the latter claim should simply recognize that this book focuses on the sort of propositional knowledge that does require justification.)

Plato

Since the time of Plato's *Theaetetus*, many philosophers have held that a justification condition is needed for a plausible distinction between knowledge and mere true belief. A common understanding of the justification condition is that it is what makes a proposition *highly likely to be true* for a person. But philosophers disagree over precisely what sort of likelihood is relevant. Philosophers commonly think of epistemic justification as *evidence* or *warrant* for a proposition,[21] although there is again disagreement over what exactly qualifies as justifying evidence. Chapters 2–4 aim to resolve such disagreements by developing a new account of evidential probability.

My argument in support of a justification condition for propositional knowledge has a general form. The belief/assent condition for propositional knowledge must be *adequately related*, from the knower's perspective, to the truth condition for knowledge. If they are not thus related, there is room for coincidentally true belief such as lucky guesswork, in which case there is not knowledge. Coincidentally true belief that P will be excluded only if there is adequate indication that one's belief that P is true. But this requirement of adequate indication, on any plausible construal, is a requirement of evidence, which entails a justification condition. Thus propositional knowledge requires justification.

Epistemic justification, then, is needed to exclude coincidentally true belief such as lucky guesswork, and to provide for the adequate relation between the belief (or assent) and truth conditions for propositional knowledge. In Chapters 2 and 3 I shall clarify the relevant notion of adequate relation in detail.

Chs 2–3

Since our concern is *epistemic* justification, our focus is on the concept of justification required by the concept of propositional knowledge. Epistemic justification, I have suggested, is needed for a plausible contrast between coincidentally true belief and knowledge. But given Gettier-style counterexamples, we cannot say that propositional knowledge is simply justified true belief. Such knowl-

20 For additional support for this claim, see, for example, Butchvarov (1970, pp. 32–8) and Swain (1981, pp. 40–3). For dissenting views, see Hamlyn (1970, pp. 80–2, 99–100) and the survey in Shope (1983, pp. 192–6).
21 One recent defense of this view can be found in Feldman and Conee (1985).

edge requires a fourth condition, beyond the justification, truth, and belief (or assent) conditions.

Chapter 6 will explain how Gettier-style counterexamples arise in circumstances where there is a certain sort of knowledge preventive, i.e., (roughly speaking) a true proposition that, when conjoined with one's actual justification for a true belief, ultimately contravenes that justification. In such circumstances one has a justified true belief that is coincidentally true (in a sense to be clarified later) and thus does not qualify as knowledge. So in such circumstances a fourth condition is needed to explain the lack of knowledge.

Chapter 6 will introduce the notion of _truth-resistant_ justification to provide the needed fourth condition. Given this notion, we shall see that the fourth condition for knowledge is just a restriction on the justification condition. Thus although Gettier-style counterexamples show that epistemic justification is not sufficient to rule out coincidentally true belief of all sorts, such justification is still _necessary_ for that purpose. But let us not digress now to complications from Gettier-style counterexamples. Instead, let us recognize that epistemic justification is needed to distinguish knowledge from coincidentally true belief, such as lucky guesswork, but that later, in §6.2, we shall need to qualify the justification condition to handle Gettier-style cases.

The foregoing argument for a justification condition seems unexceptionable. But difficult questions emerge when we try to say anything more specific about the nature of epistemic justification. Some of these questions concern the sort of noncoincidental connection to truth provided by justification. Others concern the sort of psychological relation, if any, a knower must have to justifying evidence. And still others concern the structure of inferential justification, i.e., the sort of justification where one belief is justified by another. Such questions lead to debates over the nature of epistemic probability, over internalism versus externalism, and over foundationalism versus coherentism. And there are still other pressing questions, such as questions about the very concept of justification: is it a normative, or evaluative, concept, and if so, is it a deontological concept concerning how one _ought_ to believe? A theory of justification must answer all such basic questions. Chapters 2–4 will offer definite answers, but some preliminary comments on the _concept_ of epistemic justification are appropriate now.

A controversial issue is whether the concept of epistemic justification is normative. It might be normative in either of two ways: it might be a deontological notion involving the notions of obligation and permissibility; or it might be a nondeontological notion involving, not the former notions, but an evaluative notion such as that of goodness, preferability, or desirability. Philosophers who take the concept of justification to be normative have disagreed about which of these options is correct.

On the deontological side Roderick Chisholm has proposed that the claim that a proposition is epistemically justified for one *means* that it is false that one *ought* to refrain from accepting the proposition.[22] A more common statement of this view is that to say that a proposition is epistemically justified is to say that believing it is *epistemically permissible*. Proponents of a deontological notion of justification typically rely on a notion of *epistemic obligation* that contrasts with notions of moral obligation. But there is no uniform view on just what our epistemic obligations are, as Chapter 5 will make clear.

William Alston (1985) has proposed an alternative to a deontological concept of justification. The basic idea of his nondeontological normative concept of justification is this: '*S* is justified in believing that *P*' means that *S*'s believing that *P*, as *S* does, is a good thing from the epistemic viewpoint of maximizing truth and minimizing falsity. This concept aims to specify a sort of epistemic evaluation that is logically independent of the notion of epistemic obligation. On Alston's view the relevant good-making characteristic, from the epistemic point of view, is a belief's being based on adequate grounds in the absence of overriding reasons to the contrary. This latter addition to the view is implausible, however, if it is taken to specify the only good-making characteristic. For a proposition can be justified for one even if one fails to believe it. The denial of this point makes the belief condition for knowledge redundant. Since there is no reason to think that a proposition's justification for one requires one's actually believing it, let us construe the relevant good-making characteristic as a *proposition's* being

22 See Chisholm (1956a, 1956b). (It is not clear that Chisholm still holds this view.) A deontological construal of the concept of epistemic justification has been proposed also by BonJour (1985, p. 8), Alvin Goldman (1986, pp. 25, 59), Pollock (1986, pp. 124–5), Lycan (1988, p. 128), and Alan Goldman (1988, p. 40).

supported by adequate grounds in the absence of overriding reasons to the contrary.

The notion of adequate grounds needs explanation of course, but let us postpone that task. Chapters 2 and 3 will give it full attention. For current purposes we can work with a rough notion of adequate grounds according to which the truth of a proposition is neither necessary nor sufficient for its being supported by adequate grounds. One's adequate grounds for a proposition are, roughly speaking, considerations that make that proposition evidentially more probable than its denial and its other, probabilistic competitors from one's own overall evidential perspective. Chapters 2 and 3 will clarify in detail the key notions of evidential probability and probabilistic competition.

What, if anything, can resolve the disagreement over a deontological and a nondeontological concept of epistemic justification? Alston holds that a case of cultural isolation should lead us to decide in favor of his nondeontological concept. Suppose I have grown up in an isolated community where everybody accepts as authoritative the community's traditions. And suppose also that I have not confronted anything that calls into question the authority of these traditions. In such a situation, according to Alston, there is nothing I could reasonably be expected to do that would change my believing in accord with the community's traditions; but nonetheless the fact that a proposition, P, is supported by those traditions could be a bad reason for my believing that P. More generally, Alston faults the deontological concept of justification on the ground that, given that concept, "we may have done the best we can, or at least the best that could reasonably be expected of us, and still be in a very poor epistemic position in believing that P; we could, blamelessly, be believing P for outrageously bad reasons" (1985, p. 34). On this ground Alston denies that the deontological concept is the notion of justification essential to the notion of propositional knowledge.

But the objection from cultural isolation and the general criticism at hand are inconclusive. They confuse conditions of epistemic *permissibility*, or *rightness*, with conditions of epistemic *blamelessness*.[23] The example of cultural isolation does not obviously satisfy

---

23 Alston also conflates a deontological concept and a blame concept in his (1986a, p. 4; 1986b, pp. 196–8).

the conditions for epistemic permissibility, or rightness, even if it clearly satisfies the conditions for epistemic blamelessness. And regarding the general criticism, one's believing that P blamelessly, or in such a way that one has done the best one can, does not entail that one's believing that P is epistemically permissible, or right.

Ethical theorists commonly distinguish the conditions for moral permissibility, or rightness, from the conditions for moral blamelessness in such a way that one's being blameless in performing an action does not entail the rightness of that action. The mere fact that one cannot be faulted for performing an action, perhaps because of one's morally deprived upbringing, does not entail that this action is right in the sense that it is permitted by the correct, or appropriate, right-making moral rules. Analogously epistemic blamelessness does not entail epistemic permissibility. The mere fact that one cannot be blamed for holding a particular belief does not entail that that belief is permitted by the correct right-making epistemic rules. The notion of epistemic permissibility is, in a sense, more objective than the notion of epistemic blamelessness. The former notion is defined solely in terms of what (potential) beliefs are permitted by the correct right-making epistemic rules, whereas the latter notion is defined in terms of what reasonably can be expected relative to an individual's special circumstances. Thus Alston has not given us a decisive reason to reject the deontological concept of justification.[24] And it appears that Goldman (1986) and Pollock (1986), for example, understand their deontological notions via the concept of epistemic (right-making) permissibility, and not via the concept of epistemic blame.

Of course the failure of Alston's objection does nothing to recommend the deontological concept of justification. Nor do I want to recommend either that concept or its nondeontological counterpart. Both of these normative concepts involve superfluous components. That is, they involve notions that are not essential to the concept of epistemic justification. A simple dilemma illustrates this

---

24 Alston (1985, 1986b) also criticizes the deontological notion on the ground that it requires a sort of doxastic voluntarism. But once we free the deontological notion from the notion of epistemic blame, it is doubtful that this notion requires doxastic voluntarism. Epistemic rightness of one's belief, construed as permissibility relative to right-making epistemic rules, seems not to require one's direct or indirect control over belief.

point. Either the normative concepts of justification include an adequate evidence requirement or they do not. If they do not, they can be rejected in light of cultural-isolation cases of the aforementioned sort; for then they will allow for epistemic justification in cases where one lacks adequate evidence. On the other hand, if the normative concepts do include an adequate-evidence requirement, they will be impervious to cultural-isolation cases, but then it will be unclear what essential role their normative components serve. That is, it will be doubtful that their notions of epistemic goodness and epistemic permissibility play an essential conceptual role. In fact, these normative notions will then be superfluous. This argument does not presuppose or intend to show that normative notions cannot have non-normative criteria of application. Its main point rather is simply that the concept of propositional knowledge does not require a normative notion for its justification condition. Chapters 2 and 3 will show that we can explicate the notion of adequate evidence without normative notions.

The notion of epistemic obligation presupposed by the deontological concept of justification is a philosopher's technical notion that is inessential to the concept of propositional knowledge. One difficulty with this notion of obligation, as a proposed component of the concept of knowledge, is that it is very unclear what our epistemic obligations actually are. Thus this has been a topic of debate among philosophers at least since the famous James–Clifford exchange. Given the serious unclarity in the notion of epistemic obligation, which will be emphasized in Chapter 5, we would do well to free the notion of epistemic justification from it. Similar points apply straightforwardly, I believe, to the notion of epistemic blamelessness.

One might propose that our epistemic obligation is simply to believe propositions that have epistemic goodness, which requires, at least on Alston's view, that a proposition be supported by adequate evidence. Surely we need some such appeal to adequate evidence to avoid the aforementioned problem from cultural isolation. And on this proposal the difference between the deontological and nondeontological concepts is virtually negligible.[25] Of

25 Alston might claim that one significant difference between the two concepts is that the deontological concept requires at least indirect voluntary control over be-

41

course we still might recommend the nondeontological concept on grounds of simplicity: it makes do without the unclear notion of epistemic obligation.

But the nondeontological concept of epistemic goodness is also a philosopher's technical notion that is inessential to the concept of propositional knowledge. What is extraneous to the concept of knowledge is the notion of *goodness from the epistemic point of view*. It seems that one can have the concept of epistemic justification and even the concept of propositional knowledge without one's having the technical philosophical concept of goodness from the epistemic viewpoint of maximizing truth and minimizing falsehood. And the latter concept involves complications extraneous to the concept of knowledge: complications concerning how maximizing truth and minimizing falsehood are to be related in terms of relative epistemic importance. In fact, that concept is seriously unclear because of this. Chapter 5 will illustrate this point in some detail. Thus we should free the concept of epistemic justification from the nondeontological normative concept as well as from its deontological counterpart.

An improved alternative to the normative concepts of justification is the notion of justification as *an adequate indication, relative to one's total evidence, that a proposition is true*. Such an adequate indication is provided for one by something that makes a proposition, *P*, evidentially more probable for one, on one's total evidence, than not only ~*P* but also *P*'s probabilistic competitors. This notion enables us to avoid unnecessary complications from the proposed analogies to ethical concepts, and to say that the normative concepts of justification are dispensable without loss. This non-normative notion does all the real work in the concept of epistemic goodness and in any concept of epistemic obligation able to avoid the problem from cultural isolation. The notion of an adequate indication that a proposition is true is quite familiar, since it is equivalent to the familiar notion of evidence that makes a proposition evidentially more probable than its denial and its probabilistic competitors.

There are of course some notions that need clarification here,

<hr>

lieving, whereas his nondeontological concept does not. Yet I have suggested that if we free the deontological concept from the notion of epistemic blame, and understand it as connoting permissibility relative to right-making epistemic rules, it is doubtful that that concept requires even indirect voluntary control over believing. At least, we then need considerable argument for such a requirement.

such as the notion of evidential probability, the notion of an indication that a proposition is true, and the notion of a probabilistic competitor. Chapters 2 and 3 will clarify these notions in such a way that neither the deontological nor the nondeontological normative concept of justification is presupposed. The resulting notion of epistemic justification will thus be semantically independent of those normative concepts. In fact, it will be semantically independent of any normative concept. Yet the resulting notion of justification will still be useful in clarifying certain normative concepts of procedural epistemic rationality. Chapter 5 will illustrate the latter point.

We now have a rough sketch of a notion of epistemic justification that does not require the concept of epistemic obligation or the concept of epistemic goodness. On this notion, an epistemic justifier of a proposition is simply a certain sort of truth indicator, or evidential probability-maker, for that proposition. (Truth indicators, according to the theory developed in Chapters 2 and 3, are identical to evidential probability-makers.) A justifying truth indicator for P, on this view, is neither necessary nor sufficient for P's actually being true. And what is a justifier of P for one can cease to be a justifier of P for one upon one's coming to possess additional truth indicators. In that sense, as Chapters 2 and 3 explain, epistemic justification is *defeasible*. Thus we should not confuse the notion of epistemic justification with any notion of certainty that requires irrevisability or logical conclusiveness.

Further, a truth indicator for P need not itself be true. For, as Chapter 2 explains, the subjective contents of *non*propositional experiences can be truth indicators, and such contents, being nonpropositional, are neither true nor false. And believed propositions can be truth indicators for a person even when they are false. Such propositions need only be supported by a certain sort of truth indicator. The threat of an endless regress of required propositional truth indicators is undercut, as Chapters 3 and 4 explain, by the role of the subjective contents of nonpropositional experiences as truth indicators.

Given my general characterization of epistemic justification in terms of truth indicators, we can see that justification, unlike truth, is perspectival. Since truth indicators are necessarily truth indicators *for a person*, justification is also necessarily justification *for a person*. Given the person-relativity of truth indicators, a proposition that

43

is justified for one person can be unjustified for another. This relativity is not due to the person-relativity of believing or assenting, since neither one's possessing a truth indicator nor a proposition's being justified for one requires one's believing or assenting to a proposition. The person-relativity of justification is thus independent of the person-relativity of believing and assenting. (We could make the same point by talking about evidential probability-makers.) So since propositional knowledge requires justification as well as believing or assenting, such knowledge is doubly perspectival.

Contemporary philosophers disagree considerably about what counts as a justifying reason appropriate to knowledge, i.e., an epistemic justifier. Given my proposed general notion of justification, this is basically a disagreement about what are justifying truth indicators. For epistemic reasons are necessarily indicators that a proposition is true. (In contrast, *non*epistemic reasons for belief, such as prudential and moral reasons, are not essentially truth indicators; they are indicators that a belief *state* has certain nonalethic features, such as prudential well-being and moral goodness.) Two main issues motivate this disagreement. First, can there be justifying truth indicators for a person that are not conceptual states of that person, i.e., that are not states essentially involving conceptualization or predication, whether *de re* or *de dicto*? Second, if there can be such justifying truth indicators for a person, can they be independent of what the person has been aware of? The first issue can be called the question of *conceptualism* regarding justification; the second, the question of *externalism* regarding justification.

In Chapters 2–4, this book opposes both conceptualism and externalism regarding epistemic empirical justification. In doing so, it defends a broadly foundationalist account of epistemic justification, according to which the justification of any empirical proposition derives ultimately from truth indicators, or evidential probability-makers, provided by the subjective contents of nonconceptual experiences. Given the central epistemic role I shall attribute to a certain sort of explanation, we can call this account *experiential explanationism*, for lack of a better term. The development of this view in Chapters 2–6 will lead to a straightforward resolution of debates over foundationalism vs. coherentism, inter-

44

nalism vs. externalism, skepticism vs. nonskepticism, the Gettier problem, and the problem of the criterion.

I have provided some general reasons for the traditional view that propositional knowledge requires justified true belief or assent. However, a belief's being true and justified is not sufficient for knowledge, even if the belief enjoys the sort of Gettier-proof truth-resistant justification mentioned earlier. One might have a justified true belief that P while believing that P solely on grounds other than those that actually justify P. That is, one might believe that P solely for the "wrong reasons," even though P is justified and true. In such a case, one does not know that P. Thus propositional knowledge requires that one's believing that P be "adequately related" to the justifying evidence for P. In other words, such knowledge requires that one's believing that P be *based on* the justifying evidence. This is called the *basing-relation requirement* for propositional knowledge.

A paradigm case where the basing relation is satisfied comes from one's believing an argument's conclusion as a direct result of an *inference* from its premises. But, as we shall see in §3.4, there are other equally important cases, including those where a belief is based on a nonpropositional evidence basis. Let us keep the general basing-relation requirement in mind for now, but postpone its clarification until §3.4, when more details about evidence are available.

1.4   Conclusion

We now have a preliminary sketch of what human propositional knowledge essentially involves: true belief or assent supported by epistemic justification of a certain sort. The remainder of this book fills out this sketch by explaining the nature of epistemic justification, including truth-resistant justification that is impervious to Gettier-style counterexamples. The resulting explanation aims to take the apparent normative mystery out of the notion of epistemic justification.

This book's analysis of knowledge is exclusively an account of *propositional* knowledge, i.e., knowledge *that P*. Thus it does not aim to capture the notion of knowing *how* or the notion of knowing *who*, for example. For the most part, this book's account of epistemic justification is an account of *empirical* justification, the sort of justification depending on perceptual or sensory experience. Yet I shall make some general suggestions concerning *a priori* justification and knowledge, the sort of justification and knowledge that does not depend on perceptual or sensory experience.

Given the minimal correspondence definition of §1.2.2, we can say that the truth condition for propositional knowledge is not essentially perspectival in the way that the belief/assent condition and the justification condition are. That is, the truth condition is not essentially dependent upon a person, since how things are is not thus dependent. Perhaps truth-bearers would not *exist* if there were no persons, but this does not mean that their *being true* (or, that in virtue of which they are true) depends on persons. The truth-maker of a proposition, on the minimal correspondence definition, is how things are, and how things are can be quite person-independent, even though it need not be. Thus this chapter allows us to conclude that propositional knowledge is essentially perspectival on two counts, owing to its belief/assent condition and its justification condition, but is not thus perspectival on a third count, owing to its truth condition.

Another important lesson thus far is that the belief/assent and truth conditions for propositional knowledge are *non*epistemic since they themselves do not require knowledge or justification. Any adequate epistemology must accommodate this basic lesson. Otherwise conceptual confusion will reign.

Let us turn now to the topic of epistemic reasons, specifically *minimal* epistemic reasons.

2

Minimal epistemic reasons

Epistemically justified belief, generally conceived, is belief supported by epistemic reasons. Thus an account of epistemically justified belief requires an account of epistemic reasons. This chapter begins the needed account. It focuses on *epistemic* reasons, the sorts of reasons appropriate to propositional *knowledge*, in contrast to moral, prudential, and economic reasons, for example. In §2.1 I briefly explain the distinction between epistemic and nonepistemic reasons.

This chapter focuses on *minimal* epistemic reasons, i.e., epistemic reasons that do not entail satisfaction of the justification condition for propositional knowledge. Such reasons make a proposition evidentially probable *to some extent*, but do not necessarily make a proposition more probable than its denial. Thus minimal epistemic reasons make a proposition justifiable to some extent, but do not necessarily make a proposition sufficiently justifiable to satisfy the justification condition for propositional knowledge. As Chapter 3 will explain, such minimal reasons make a proposition justifi*able* to some extent, but do not make a proposition actually justifi*ed* to some extent. The topic of *justifying* epistemic reasons, i.e., reasons entailing satisfaction of the justification condition for propositional knowledge, must await Chapter 3.

2.1 Minimal epistemic reasons for belief

An epistemic reason is simply an indicator for a person that a proposition is true. But of course one's having an indicator that a proposition, *P*, is true does not entail that *P* is actually true. Epistemic reasons *for a belief* are indicators that a believed proposition is true. Our talk of epistemic reasons for believing, i.e., for a belief state, is often just elliptical for talk of epistemic reasons for a believed proposition. Belief *states*, being neither true nor false, do not have indicators that they themselves are true or false, although their propositional objects can of course be supported by truth indicators. In §3.4 I shall introduce a straightforward notion of reason-based believing.

As I suggested in §1.3, some philosophers hold that epistemic reasons are indicators that a belief state is *epistemically good*. On this view a belief state's epistemic goodness is basically its conformity to the twofold epistemic objective of acquiring true belief and avoiding, or at least minimizing, false belief. But this approach to epistemic reasons does not lend real clarification, since it simply presupposes the key notion of epistemic reasons as indicators that a proposition is true. The relevant notion of the epistemic goodness of a belief state, *B*, requires the notion of an indicator that the propositional object of *B* is true. Clearly the epistemic goodness of *B* does not require that *B* be related to an *actually true* proposition. Instead it requires that *B* be accompanied by an *indication* that it is related to a true proposition. Thus let us focus on epistemic reasons as indicators that a proposition is true.

Epistemic reasons contrast with nonepistemic reasons for belief. Epistemic reasons are indicators that a proposition is true, whereas nonepistemic reasons are indicators that a belief *state* has a certain nonalethic feature. For example, moral reasons for belief are indicators that a belief state has a certain moral value; prudential reasons for belief are indicators that a belief state has a certain prudential value; and aesthetic reasons for belief are indicators that a belief state has a certain aesthetic value. Directly analogous points hold for the other kinds of nonepistemic reasons, e.g., psychological, political, and economic reasons. Such nonepistemic reasons for a belief are *not* necessarily indicators that a believed proposition is true; so they should not be confused with epistemic reasons.

Prudential reasons for one's belief, for instance, indicate that one's belief state is prudentially valuable for one, but do not thereby indicate that the relevant believed proposition is true. In fact, it is quite unclear what it would mean to claim that a *proposition* by itself is prudentially valuable for one. Clearly an indication of the prudential value of a belief state is not logically sufficient for an indication that the proposition thereby believed is true. It might be prudent for me to believe, for example, that I shall recover from an illness even though there is no indication whatsoever that I shall

48

recover. Thus we can distinguish between epistemic and nonepistemic reasons on the ground that epistemic reasons, unlike nonepistemic reasons, are necessarily indicators that a proposition is true.[1]

The notion of an epistemic reason also contrasts with the notion of an *explanatory reason* for one's holding a belief. An explanatory reason for a belief is a special kind of nonepistemic reason: it is a reason that *explains why a belief state has been formed or maintained.* The familiar notion of a reason as a cause suggests a notion of an explanatory reason, i.e., a notion of a *causal explanation* of a belief state's being formed or maintained. Clearly an explanatory reason for a belief state is not necessarily an indicator that the proposition thereby believed is true. And an epistemic reason for a believed proposition is not necessarily an explanatory reason for the relevant belief state. Conceivably what explains why a belief state has been formed or maintained is one thing, and what indicates that the proposition thereby believed is true is quite another. So let us not confuse the notion of an explanatory reason for a belief state with the notion of an epistemic reason.

We can clarify the key notion of *an indication that P is true* in two steps. The first step clarifies the notion of *P's being true.* I have taken this step already in §1.2. Thus we may introduce this partial definition: X is an indication that P is true = $df.$ X is an indication that P states how things actually are. Given §1.2, the relevant notion of *how things are* is sufficiently familiar to lend some elucidation. As I suggested earlier, it is basically the notion of what items (e.g., objects, features of objects, relations between objects and/or features), if any, exist (perhaps only at a particular place and time.) Given this minimal correspondence notion of truth, we should avoid any confusion of the conditions for *P's* being true and the conditions for *our determining* whether P is true. The latter conditions concern justification or warranted assertibility, and are not definitive of truth itself. This point needs recognition if we are to maintain the commonplace notion of a justified false proposition or an unjustified true proposition.

The second step is less straightforward, as the notion of *an in-*

1 For further discussion of some species of nonepistemic reasons, and of their relation to epistemic reasons, see Moser (1985, Chap. 6). A somewhat different approach to nonepistemic reasons comes from Foley (1987, Chap. 6).

dication that a proposition is true resists easy clarification. Let us use the term *truth indicator* to designate anything that provides an indication for one that a proposition is true in the sense that it makes the proposition *probably true to some extent* for one. I noted earlier that a truth indicator need not make a proposition sufficiently probable to satisfy the justification condition for propositional knowledge. Since the relevant kind of probability is evidential, let us say that truth indicators are *evidential probability-makers*. In fact, I take the notion of a truth indicator to be conceptually identical to the notion of an evidential probability-maker. Thus we now need an account of evidential probability-makers.

The kind of probability essential to knowledge and justification is evidential in the sense that it is relative to a body of *evidence*. To clarify the notion of such probability, let us begin with the general characterization of *epistemological probability* by Henry Kyburg:

Not empirical: Probabilities are not frequencies, measures on events or sets of events or sequences; they are not propensities or chances.

Not subjective: Probabilities are not opinions, or beliefs, or degrees of belief, or dispositions to bet or act. Probabilities are not even rational degrees of belief.

But logical: Probabilities reflect an objective inferential relation between a body of evidence and propositions.[2]

Consider the proposition that the probability of getting a two with a throw of a die is one in six. Kyburg's epistemological interpretation implies that this proposition is true relative to one's evidence if and only if one's evidence supports the proposition that one-sixth of the tosses of a die result in a two. Kyburg takes the sense of this proposition to be simply: one's rational corpus makes acceptable the measure statement that about one-sixth of the tosses yield a two.

The characterization in the quotation above does not imply that all epistemological probability values are measurable by real numbers. It allows that some such values may be only comparatively or qualitatively specifiable. In addition, that characterization does *not* endorse Kyburg's independent assumption that all epistemological probabilities reflect an objective logical relation between an

2 Kyburg gives this characterization in his (1983a, p. 153). For further elaboration on this view, see Kyburg (1970a, Chap. 7; 1971).

evidential body of *statements*, or propositions, and other statements. A central conclusion of this chapter will be that evidential probabilities must be relative ultimately to *non*propositional evidence, i.e., evidence not constituted by the possible conceptual, or predicational, contents of a doxastic state. After reaching that conclusion, I shall explain the nature of the relevant nonpropositional evidence and of the objective inferential relation between such evidence and evidentially probable propositions.

The structure of my argument for a nonpropositional basis of evidential probability is straightforward. My strategy is to identify the available alternatives for the view that the basis of evidential probability is propositional, and then to argue that each alternative is ultimately inadequate. The notion of *the basis* of evidential probability is just the notion of that by means of which a proposition has evidential probability to some extent. I suggested earlier that one's evidential probability basis for a proposition need not be the same as the causal process by means of which one believes the proposition. One's believing a proposition can be caused by one source, while the probability of that proposition for one is due to a different source. Thus let us not confuse the notion of a belief's *causal origin* with the notion of a believed proposition's *evidential probability basis*.

We can characterize the notion of an evidential probability basis via the notion of what evidential probability *supervenes* on. Let us say that the evidential probability of a proposition supervenes on a property (or set of properties), R, if and only if R is necessarily such that whatever has it has that evidential probability.[3] Kyburg's characterization of epistemological probability suggests that R is an inferential relation between a proposition and a body of evidence. We can thus distinguish between the *inference basis* and the *evidence basis* for evidential probability. Questions about the inference basis concern the sorts of inferential relation that hold, or can hold, between an evidentially probable proposition and relevant evidence. For now I construe 'inference' broadly, to allow for such propositional relations as coherence and explanation. Questions about the evidence basis concern the sorts of evidence that underlie, or can underlie, (an inference to) an evidentially probable proposition. We

3 For discussion of this notion of supervenience in connection with the notion of epistemic justification, see Sosa (1980a, 1980b) and Van Cleve (1985).

thus need to specify what sorts of evidence and what sorts of inference are essential to evidentially probable propositions.

Our characterization of the evidence basis must accommodate the distinctions between: (a) what an evidence basis comprises, (b) that in virtue of which an evidence basis provides evidential probability for a proposition for one (e.g., an inferential relation), (c) one's awareness of the adequacy of an evidence basis for the evidential probability of a proposition, and (d) the necessary and sufficient conditions for evidential probability. Initially we shall focus on what an evidence basis comprises. We shall see eventually that one's having a particular evidence basis does not entail one's being aware of its adequacy for the evidential probability of a proposition. We turn now to the view that an evidence basis can consist solely of propositions.

2.2 Propositional probability-makers

Let us continue with the assumption of Chapter 1 that propositions are possible objects of an act of judgment *that* something is the case, where such objects necessarily have a truth value. The view that the evidence basis of evidential probability is exclusively propositional has these two general options:

I. The evidential probability of a proposition, P, for a person, S, supervenes on P's inferential relation to an evidence basis consisting of a proposition or a set of propositions that itself is not evidentially probable at all for S.

II. The evidential probability of P for S supervenes on P's inferential relation to an evidence basis consisting of a proposition or a set of propositions that itself is evidentially probable to some extent for S.

Option I implies that the evidential probability of a proposition has its evidence basis in a proposition or a set of propositions that is not itself evidentially probable at all. In contrast, option II implies that the propositional evidence basis is evidentially probable to some extent.

Option I apparently has no explicit proponents.[4] And its lack of

4 Yet this view is suggested by Wittgenstein (1969, §§253, 166, 136). I do not pretend to know, however, what Wittgenstein's overall account of evidence actually is; nor do I find much help in the cryptic remarks in his (1953, §§482–6; 1969, §§110, 204). See Shiner (1977), Morawetz (1978), and Wright (1985) for attempts at a reconstruction. Cf. Moser (1985, Chap. 2).

popularity is not surprising. If we suppose that a proposition, Q, is not probable at all for Jones, we shall be hard put to explain how another proposition, P, can be probable for Jones just in virtue of Q. Clearly Q's simply entailing P will not confer probability on P for Jones, since Q itself is not probable at all for Jones. If we allow that one nonprobable proposition confers evidential probability on another proposition for one, then we apparently risk allowing that *every* nonprobable proposition confers such probability. From the standpoint of conferring evidential probability, there seem to be no relevant differences among nonprobable propositions. But of course it is implausible to suppose that *every* nonprobable proposition confers evidential probability for a person. For example, it is implausible to hold that the nonprobable propositions Jones does not understand confer evidential probability for him.

In reply, we might restrict the set of relevant nonprobable propositions to the propositions one believes. But this move only shifts the mystery enshrouding option I; it does nothing to remove this mystery. We still need an explanation of how a believed nonprobable proposition can confer evidential probability on another proposition for one. If we allow that one believed nonprobable proposition confers evidential probability on another proposition for a person, we apparently risk allowing that *every* believed nonprobable proposition confers such probability. From the standpoint of conferring evidential probability, there seem to be no relevant differences among believed nonprobable propositions. But it is implausible to suppose that *every* believed nonprobable proposition confers evidential probability for a person. It is implausible to hold, for example, that believed contradictory propositions and believed *obviously* fictional propositions confer evidential probability for one.

We still face the basic question of what evidential probability supervenes on. To make progress on this question, we must turn to the variations on option II, since option I leaves us in mystery. Let us keep in mind the basic distinction between (a) a proposition's *being probable*, and *making probable, to some extent,* and (b) a proposition's *being more probable than not*, and *making more probable than not*. Being more probable than not entails being probable to some extent, but the converse does not hold. This chapter mainly concerns evidential probability to some extent, or *minimal* evidential probability. Chapter 3 will explain the conditions for a proposition's being evidentially more probable than its denial, and the conditions for a proposition's being sufficiently probable to satisfy the justification condition for propositional knowledge.

The main variations on option II are these:

Thesis of Self-Probability: The evidential probability of a proposition supervenes on its inferential relation to an evidence basis consisting of a proposition or a set of propositions that is evidentially self-probable, i.e., that has its evidential probability just in virtue of itself.

Probability Infinitism: The evidential probability of a proposition supervenes on its inferential relation to an evidence basis consisting of a proposition or a set of propositions that has its evidential probability just in virtue of its being at the head of an infinite inferential regress of propositions.

Thesis of Circular Probability: The evidential probability of a proposition supervenes on its inferential relation to an evidence basis consisting of a proposition or a set of propositions that has its evidential probability just in virtue of its being a member of an inferential circle of propositions.

Probability Coherentism: The evidential probability of a proposition supervenes on its inferential relation to an evidence basis consisting of a proposition or a set of propositions that has its evidential probability just in virtue of its membership in a comprehensive system of interconnected propositions.

Conceivably one might try to combine some of these views, but this will not avoid the main problems that face the combined views individually. If each of these views is inadequate to provide the basis of evidential probability, we cannot remove such inadequacy simply by combination. Subsequent arguments will clarify this.

Thus we have four main variations on the thesis that evidential probability supervenes on a propositional evidence basis that is probable to some extent: probability via (a) self-probable propositions, (b) infinite regresses of propositions, (c) inferential circles of propositions, and (d) comprehensive systems of interconnected propositions. These variations exhaust the basic ways to develop the thesis in question. If each of these variations fails, we shall need to look to a *non*propositional evidence basis for evidential probability. I shall argue that each does fail.

2.2.1 Against the Thesis of Self-Probability

The Thesis of Self-Probability locates the evidence basis for evidential probability in propositions that are *self*-probable, i.e., evidentially probable just in virtue of themselves.[5] On this view inferential chains of probability-providing propositions end in an evidence basis of propositions that acquire their evidential probability *from themselves*. Thus on this view evidential probability supervenes on an evidence basis of probable propositions, but there is no need for inferential circles or endless regresses of probability-providing propositions. For there are basic starter propositions that provide evidential probability without their being in need of it from further propositions. The Thesis of Self-Probability thus commits one to a two-tier structure of evidentially probable propositions. The basic tier consists of self-probable propositions, and the secondary tier consists of probable propositions that owe their evidential probability to the basic tier.

The Thesis of Self-Probability faces problems from its commitment to self-probable propositions. The very notion of an evidentially self-probable proposition is conceptually ill formed. We can illustrate this by asking why, or in virtue of what, *only some propositions and not others* are evidentially self-probable. Let us grant that every proposition, *given itself*, is evidentially probable to some extent. On the assumption that this is all self-probability requires, if any proposition is evidentially probable just in virtue of itself, then *every* proposition is. For propositions do not differ on the evidential probability they provide for themselves. Every proposition, given itself, is evidentially probable. But of course it is false that every proposition is evidentially self-probable for one and provides evidential probability for other propositions for one. For example, the propositions one does not understand are not evidentially self-probable for one. Thus we need a stronger notion of self-probability.

Evidentially self-probable propositions have their self-probability

5 Such a view is suggested, but not explicitly endorsed, by Chisholm (1977). He claims (p. 118) that "probability is a relation between propositions." Apparently on his view evidential probability is a relation between propositions that are justified to some extent. Chisholm also apparently holds (p. 21) that some justified propositions have a basis in self-justified propositions. If self-justification entails self-probability, Chisholm apparently is committed to some variant of the Thesis of Self-Probability. See Chisholm (1964; 1966, pp. 8–9, 27–9) for earlier suggestions of this variant.

for one either in virtue of their constituent ontological features, i.e., what they consist of, or in virtue of their semantic features, i.e., what they are about. But it is doubtful that a proposition can have self-probability just in virtue of its ontological features, for there is no relevant difference among propositions with respect to their ontological features. On one plausible view, they all consist of concepts related by some form of predication. Perhaps some propositions are *true* solely in virtue of the meaning of their constituent terms. But we should not confuse conditions for evidential probability with conditions for truth. The former conditions are necessarily relative to an evidence basis, whereas the latter are not, as Chapter 1 suggested.

It is also doubtful that evidential self-probability can derive from what a proposition is about. So long as a proposition, *P*, is not self-referential, what *P* is about will be different from *P* itself; and so *P* will not be *self*-probable in any literal sense. The probability of *P* will then derive from something other than *P* itself. We cannot salvage the view at hand by the stipulation that all self-probable propositions are solely about one's own subjective psychological states. For there are *obviously* false, highly improbable propositions about one's subjective psychological states. Consider, for example, the proposition that I now seem to see a square circle. Perhaps one's psychological states can make a proposition evidentially probable for one. But even if Jones's seeming to perceive something makes probable a proposition for Jones, the proposition in question would not have evidential *self*-probability for Jones. One's psychological states are *not* identical to the propositions they might make probable. Jones's *seeming to perceive* something is one thing; *the proposition* that he seems to perceive something is something else.

Thus the notion of an evidentially self-probable proposition faces serious problems. The main problem is that the notion itself is highly mysterious; it seems on its likely construals to allow for self-probable propositions that obviously are not self-probable. A theory of evidential probability would do better without this notion. So we should look elsewhere for the evidence basis of evidential probability.

2.2.2 *Against Probability Infinitism*

Probability Infinitism finds the evidence basis of evidential probability in propositions that are probable in virtue of their being at the head of an infinite regress of propositions. This view assumes that inferential chains of probability-providing propositions extend endlessly, that they do not terminate. Thus unlike the Thesis of Self-Probability, this view does not endorse a two-tier structure of evidentially probable propositions. Given Infinitism, all evidentially probable propositions have the same sort of evidence basis: propositions at the head of an endless regress of propositions.

Infinitism faces a problem from its commitment to endless regresses of probability-providing propositions. The most troublesome question is, How can evidential probability supervene on such regresses? This question raises problems once we distinguish between *actual* probability-providing infinite regresses and *merely potential* probability-providing infinite regresses.[6] An actual probability-providing infinite regress contains only evidentially probable propositions as members, whereas a merely potential probability-providing infinite regress does not. Yet both kinds of infinite regress contain only members with successors that *would* jointly make those members evidentially probable *if* the successors themselves were evidentially probable.

Consider the proposition that there are perfect numbers greater than 100, and assume that S is a person whose mind is sufficiently powerful to believe every member of this endless regress:

(1) There is at least one perfect number greater than 100.
   There are at least two perfect numbers greater than 100.
   "   three   "

Suppose S's only information about perfect numbers is that a perfect number is a whole number equal to the sum of its whole factors less than itself. In that case the proposition that there are perfect numbers greater than 100 is not evidentially probable for S. For none of the members of (1) is then evidentially probable for S. Thus (1) is a *merely potential* probability-providing regress for S. If any member of (1) were evidentially probable for S, its predecessors would be also (at least in ordinary cases). But this subjunctive conditional does not make any member actually probable for S.

6 An analogue of this distinction is discussed in Sosa (1980a, pp. 12–13) and in Moser (1985, pp. 107–15). The following examples used to illustrate the distinction are suggested by Sosa.

An *actual* probability-providing regress has only members that are actually evidentially probable. Suppose that S believes the following infinite series of propositions:

(2) There is at least one even number.
   There are at least two even numbers.
       "   three   "

           .
           .
           .
           .

For (2) to be an actual probability-providing regress, S needs a proof, or some kind of evidence, making it evidentially probable that there is a denumerable infinity of even numbers. How else could *every* member of (2) be made evidentially probable for S? The need for such evidence does not undermine the infinite regress of probability-providers, each of which is actually probable. On the contrary, such evidence enables each member of the regress to be an actual, rather than a merely potential, probability-provider.

But why are the members of regress (1) merely potential probability-providers, whereas the members of (2) are actual probability-providers? The answer is that the members of (1), unlike the members of (2), are not made evidentially probable by any information external to, or probabilistically independent of, the regress. Thus a probability-providing infinite regress is actual if and only if there is information external to the regress that makes every member of the regress evidentially probable. Lacking such external information, a probability-providing regress is merely potential. We can defend this proposal via an examination of regress (1).

Let us assume that S believes each member M_n of (1), and knows that M_n entails M_{n-1} and is entailed by M_{n+1}. And again let us suppose that S has no other belief about perfect numbers, aside from the belief involving the standard definition of a perfect number. Given just these assumptions, is any member of (1) evidentially probable for S, such as the proposition – call it M_0 – at the head of (1)? Apparently a member M_n is evidentially probable for S *if* its successor M_{n+1} is. But is any successor M_{n+1} evidentially probable for S? For instance, is the proposition that there are at least a thousand perfect numbers greater than 100 evidentially probable for S? It seems not, since nothing we have assumed thus far makes this proposition evidentially probable for S.

Our example does allow us validly to infer this conditional: *if* the successor of a proposition M_n is evidentially probable for S, then M_n is also probable for S. But given only the assumptions of our example, S is not epistemically justified to any extent in affirming the antecedent of this conditional, since it is not actually evidentially probable for him. And a similar point applies to every member of regress (1). At most S is justified to some extent in affirming *the conditional itself.*

Here is the correct way to portray the sort of regress suggested by Probability Infinitism:

(3) ... *if* probable, M_n makes probable M_{n-1}, ..., if probable, M_1 makes probable M_0.

A question-begging way to depict the regress suggested by Probability Infinitism is:

(4) ... M_n makes probable M_{n-1}, ..., M_1 makes probable M_0.

(4) begs the key question whether the member at the head of an infinite regress such as (1) is actually evidentially probable. Thus (3), being non–question-begging, is preferable to (4) as a portrayal of the sort of infinite regress suggested by Probability Infinitism.

The member M_0 at the head of a regress such as (3) is merely *conditionally* probable. That is, barring considerations external to the regress, M_0 will be evidentially *non*probable for S unless the antecedent of the relevant conditional is true, i.e., unless M_1 is evidentially probable for S. But M_1 is also merely conditionally probable for S, for its probability depends on the probability of M_2, which is similarly conditionally probable. And a directly analogous point holds for M_3 and for every other member of a regress represented by (3). Thus once we portray the regress of Infinitism via (3), i.e., as a merely potential probability-provider, we see that such a regress is inadequate to make the member at its head evidentially probable. So we can challenge Infinitism with this question: why should we grant that, apart from external information, any member of a regress represented by (3) is actually made evidentially probable by its successor? The foregoing considerations indicate that we should not grant this, and thus that Probability Infinitism is unconvincing.

We have not yet specified the exact nature of the external information required for an actual probability-providing regress. But a few points are now clear. First, because of the considerations opposing option 1 and the Thesis of Self-Probability, we should not suppose that the external information has an evidence basis in nonprobable propositions or in self-probable propositions. Second, because of the considerations opposing Probability Infinitism, we cannot plausibly assume that the external information has an evidence basis in a merely potential probability-providing infinite regress. Third, it is unhelpful to assume that the external information has an evidence basis in an actual probability-providing infinite regress. For such an assumption will only raise the question at hand once again at a single remove.

So let us assume that the required external information has its evidence basis in a *finite* regress of probability-providing propositions. And let us call this finite regress '*R*'. The first member M_n of *R* is either (i) made probable by some information external to *R*, (ii) nonprobable, (iii) self-probable, (iv) made probable by some set of members between M_n and the head of *R*, (v) made probable by virtue of membership in a system of interconnected propositions, or (vi) made probable by a nonpropositional evidence basis. Clearly option (i) either evades the issue at hand or begins an unacceptable merely potential probability-providing regress; and options (ii) and (iii) face serious problems from considerations already noted. Barring a nonpropositional evidence basis for the moment, we are thus left with options (iv) and (v), which correspond to the aforementioned options of the Thesis of Circular Probability and Probability Coherentism. So let us turn now to those options.

2.2.3 Circular probability and probability coherentism

The Thesis of Circular Probability locates the evidence basis of evidential probability in propositions that are probable in virtue of their membership in an inferential circle. Specifically, this view finds the evidence basis in this sort of regress:

M_n makes probable M_{n-1}, ..., M_1 makes probable M_0,

where M_0 makes probable M_n. If we could assume the transitivity of the making-probable relation, we could (a) infer that M_0 makes M_0 probable, (b) charge this kind of regress with literal circularity and a dubious sort of self-probability, and (c) conclude that so far as this kind of regress goes, it is undecided whether M_0 is actually evidentially probable.

But even if we bracket for now the question of the transitivity of the making-probable relation, a serious problem faces the view that evidential probability supervenes on an inferentially circular evidence basis. The most troublesome question is this: how can a proposition, P, that depends for its evidential probability on another proposition, Q, make Q evidentially probable? In other words, if P lacks probability apart from Q, how can Q derive its probability from P? After all, P itself is *non*probable apart from Q. We have already seen the implausibility of the view that the evidence basis of evidential probability consists of nonprobable propositions or self-probable propositions. How then can a closed inferential circle of propositions provide the basis for evidential probability?

From the standpoint of providing evidential probability for a person, one closed inferential circle is as effective as any other. At least, the Thesis of Circular Probability does not identify any relevant differences. But obviously not *every* closed inferential circle of propositions provides evidential probability for a person. Consider such a circle involving only obviously fictional propositions, such as propositions that are obviously science fiction. It is doubtful then that a closed inferential circle is sufficient to provide evidential probability. Thus we have good reason to reject the Thesis of Circular Probability, which commits us to circular evidence.[7]

We are left now with Probability Coherentism, the view that the evidence basis of evidential probability consists of propositions belonging to a comprehensive system of interconnected propositions. This view denies that the making-probable relation consists of linear relations between individual propositions, and endorses instead a network conception of the evidence basis. On this view evidential probability derives ultimately from a system of propositions that are sufficiently interconnected to be "coherent" in some sense. Proponents typically take coherence relations among propositions to be entailment or explanatory relations of some sort. Specifically, various philosophers hold that a proposition, P, coheres with a certain set of propositions if P entails or is entailed by some mem-

7 So we should resist Harman's claim (1986, p. 33) that "there is nothing wrong with circular justification in the coherence theory, especially if the circle is a large one." Harman does not identify relevant evidential differences between small and large inferential circles; nor does he anticipate the criticisms just raised.

bers of that set, or if P explains the truth of, or has its truth explained by, some members of that set. Probability Coherentism avoids the charge of literal circularity, given its claim that probability supervenes on a coherent *system* of propositions.

But however coherence relations among propositions are understood, Probability Coherentism faces a serious problem. Mere coherence of a system of propositions, however comprehensive, fails to provide evidential probability concerning how things actually are. There are comprehensive coherent systems of *obviously* false, evidentially gratuitous propositions, such as propositions in science fiction. And for virtually any coherent system of propositions, we can imagine an alternative system consisting mainly of the denials of the propositions in the first system. But of course two such coherent systems cannot both be probability-providing for a person concerning how things actually are. This is especially clear if we construe 'probable' as 'more probable than not'. For if a proposition, P, is evidentially more probable than its denial, $\sim P$, then $\sim P$ is not evidentially more probable than P. These considerations indicate that the mere coherence of a system of propositions does not make its members evidentially probable for a person. At most such coherence makes the members *possibly* true. But if coherence by itself is not probability-providing, a coherent system of propositions is not automatically probability-providing. Thus Probability Coherentism does not provide an adequate evidence basis for evidential probability.

One might reply that the kind of coherence relevant to Probability Coherentism is coherence among the members of the set of propositions that one *believes*, and not coherence among just any set of propositions. Given this reply, the proponent of Coherentism evidently can escape one part of the objection above. For apparently no one will believe *both* of the opposing sets of propositions I suggested.

But an equally serious problem remains. As the reference to science fiction propositions suggests, one could believe a set of coherent propositions that has nothing to do with, or simply denies the existence of, what one experiences. For example, I might have a throbbing toothache of which I am painfully aware, while the coherent sector of my belief system has nothing to do with toothaches, or, more radically, denies that there are throbbing toothaches. In such a case, given Coherentism, it would not be probable for me that I have a throbbing toothache (and it could even be probable for me that I do *not* have a throbbing toothache), even though I am acutely aware of my toothache. For in that case the coherent set of propositions that I believe would not make it probable for me that I have a throbbing toothache.

Even if in the imagined case I actually believed that I have a throbbing toothache, it would still not thereby be probable for me that I do, given Coherentism. For once again the coherent set of propositions that I believe would fail to make it probable for me that I have a throbbing toothache. But it is implausible to suppose that in the imagined case it would therefore not be evidentially probable for me that I have a throbbing toothache. Thus it seems that the coherent set of propositions one believes does not by itself have evidential probability-making effectiveness for one, with respect to what those beliefs are about. This point receives support from the fact that the coherent sector of one's belief system might be supported only by groundless conjecture, wishful thinking, or unbridled speculation. Such considerations indicate that coherence alone does not provide evidential probability, and thus that Probability Coherentism is an inadequate account of such probability. (See §4.1.1 for further criticism of epistemic coherentism as an account of epistemic justification.)

2.2.4 Summary and generalized argument

In sum, we have seen the inadequacy of each of the views implying that the evidence basis of evidential probability is only propositional: probability via nonprobable propositions, self-probable propositions, infinite regresses of propositions, inferential circles of propositions, and coherent systems of propositions. It seems clear that my objections to these views are equally troublesome for the possible combinations thereof. But let us not digress.

To simplify my various criticisms, we can formulate a general argument showing the inadequacy of the view that the evidence basis of evidential probability is only propositional. The key issue is, How can a proposition *by itself*, being the possible conceptual or predicational content of a doxastic state, confer evidential probability on some proposition for a person? If *any* proposition by itself confers such probability for a person, then *every* proposition does; for propositions by themselves do not differ in their evidential-probability–conferring effectiveness for a person. But of course it is false that every proposition confers evidential probability on some proposition for a person. For instance, a proposition one has never entertained or does not understand does not confer such probability for one. Thus we need an explanation why only some, and not all, propositions provide evidential probability for a person.

Apparently every proposition *given itself* is evidentially probable, but this does not explain the conferring of evidential probability for a person. An unanswered question concerns the conditions under which one is *given* a proposition in the sense that it is evidentially probable *for one*. Part of the needed answer is that the evidential probability of a proposition for a person is determined relative to the person's *evidence basis*. But mere propositions by themselves do not constitute an evidence basis for a person. A proposition is part of one's evidence basis only if one is somehow psychologically related to that proposition. The denial of this point risks the evidential relevance of *all* propositions; but of course not all propositions are determinants of evidential probability for one.

In reply, we might propose that the propositions one *believes* are probability-conferring for one, with regard to what they are about (so long as no conflicts arise among one's beliefs).[8] But this view falters on the fact that merely believed propositions might be evidentially supported only by groundless conjecture, wishful thinking, or unbridled speculation. A similar consideration counts against the view that propositions agreed upon by one's peers are probability-conferring for one.[9] Merely believed propositions are not necessarily constrained, in what they affirm, by what one has experienced, either perceptually or otherwise; nor are they necessarily constrained by anything else that is evidentially relevant. But this means that the reply at hand fails to provide an adequate distinction between evidentially probable propositions and propositions that obviously are not probable at all.[10] (I do not want to deny now, however, that one's *believing* a proposition might make it

---

8 Such a view has been suggested by Pollock (1979, pp. 105–11) and by Harman (1986, pp. 32, 46). (Apparently Pollock no longer holds this view; see his [1986, pp. 19–25].) Ducasse (1944, pp. 337–40) too has proposed that some propositions are made "evident" for one just in virtue of one's believing them.

9 Such an approach to epistemic justification has been suggested by Rorty (1979, Chaps. 4–7). I shall assess this approach in more detail in §4.1.2.

10 For additional criticisms of such a view, see Moser (1985, Chaps. 2, 3) and Foley (1987, Chap. 7).

evidentially probable for one that one believes it; I shall deny this later by implication.) Nor can we make any mileage here by appealing to *probable* belief instead of mere belief, since the evidence basis of probable belief is the very matter under dispute.

Perhaps one's believing a proposition can make some, but not all, propositions evidentially probable for one. Such a view has been suggested by Richard Foley (1987), and this view merits our attention here. We need to ask how one's believing some *but not all* propositions can give one an epistemic reason to think they are true. Foley holds that one's own reflective epistemic standards can provide the answer. According to Foley (1987, pp. 52–3), if a person, S, on careful reflection would think that his believing that P makes P sufficiently likely to be true, then on S's own epistemic standards, his believing that P itself tends to make the proposition that P epistemically rational for him. So let us ask whether our believing some propositions, given our epistemic standards, tends to make those propositions epistemically rational for us.

Foley suggests, by way of example, that on careful reflection many people would think that most relevant possible situations in which they believe they are in pain are situations in which they actually are in pain. And he holds that many people would think this also of many of their other conscious psychological states. Thus he infers that "the proposition that they believe they are in such a state tends to make epistemically rational for them the proposition that they are in this state" (p. 53). Foley's view implies also that if one of these people, S, believes that he is in such a state (call the relevant proposition 'R'), and S does not believe the premises of an argument (that on careful reflection S would regard as sufficiently truth-preserving) either for ~R or for the proposition that (it is false that if S believes that R, then R), then S's believing that R actually makes R epistemically rational for S (pp. 64–5). Foley takes such subjective self-justification to be the basis of all epistemic rationality.

Foley's appeal to what a person would believe *on careful reflection* might seem to introduce an objective component into his conditions for self-justification. But this is not really so. Foley defines 'careful reflection' simply as a person's "reflecting [on his beliefs without manipulation] until his view stabilizes, until further reflection would not alter his opinion of the argument in question" (p. 35). Careful reflection, on Foley's view, is not constrained by anything beyond one's beliefs and epistemic standards. The results of such reflection do manifest one's reflective epistemic standards. But on Foley's view these standards themselves are just one's reflective beliefs concerning what is sufficiently likely to be truth-preserving relative to the goal of obtaining truth and avoiding error (p. 55). Thus Foley's self-justified foundations of epistemic rationality are indeed subjective.

I doubt that Foley's subjective self-justification is sufficient either for a proposition's satisfying the justification condition for knowledge or for a proposition's being evidentially probable to some extent. An example will confirm this doubt.

Suppose Jones is a highly impressionable beginning university student who has heard his new roommate, an eloquent philosophy major, endorse eliminative materialism concerning the existence of pains. Jones believes, as a result of his roommate's endorsement, that eliminative materialism regarding pains is correct and thus that there are no throbbing headaches (since there are no throbbing pains). Because Jones believes that there are no throbbing headaches, he also believes that N [= he, in particular, does not have a throbbing headache]. And Jones is one of those many people, mentioned by Foley, who on careful reflection think that most relevant possible situations in which they believe they are in a certain conscious psychological state, such as the state of being headache-free, are situations in which they are actually in that state. In addition, Jones does not believe the premises of an argument (that on careful reflection he would regard as sufficiently truth-preserving) either for ~N or for the proposition that (it is false that if Jones believes that N, then N). Jones is consistently committed to eliminative materialism, and he is very confident, especially on reflection, that his current beliefs about his conscious psychological states are highly reliable.

As a result of reading too much philosophy in one sitting, Jones is acutely aware of an apparent throbbing headache. This awareness consists, at least in part, of Jones's attention's being distracted by his apparent throbbing headache. His apparent headache even prevents him from doing any further reading, and so interrupts the completion of his term paper in defense of eliminative materialism concerning pains. Adding quandary to injury, Jones, being a beginner at philosophy, is also unable to explain the occurrence of his apparent throbbing headache in a way agreeable to his newfound eliminativism. He has not yet acquired sufficient familiarity with the details of eliminativism and neurophysiology to provide a materialist account of his apparent throbbing headache. But as a result of his roommate's influence, he sticks to his eliminativist guns, refrains from believing that he has a throbbing headache, and maintains his belief that N. (None of this assumes, incidentally, that Jones has direct control over his believing.)

What should we say about the epistemic status of Jones's belief that N? Foley's account implies that this belief is self-justified for Jones. On this account, Jones's believing that N tends to make N epistemically rational for Jones; and Jones does not believe the premises of a relevant argument for $\sim N$ or for the proposition that (it is false that if Jones believes that N, then N). Yet something has gone wrong. Jones's apparent throbbing headache is negatively relevant to the justification of his belief that N. Specifically, it is a *potential underminer* of that justification, since if Jones cannot account for it via an acceptable explanation that can incorporate N, his belief that N will be unjustified. Apart from such a neutralizing explanation, Jones's belief that N will be epistemically defective in the sense that it will be accompanied by a potential underminer that is not neutralized for Jones by an acceptable explanation. Since epistemically justified belief is incompatible with such epistemic defectiveness, Foley's view is incorrect in its implication that Jones's belief that N is self-justified. And since such epistemically defective belief is an inadequate basis for inferential justification, Foley's view is also incorrect in its implication that Jones's belief that N is an adequate basis for the justification of other beliefs.

Jones's belief that N in the imagined situation is not only epistemically unjustified, but also evidentially nonprobable for Jones. Jones's belief that N is a *mere* belief, since nothing in the imagined situation makes it evidentially probable to some extent. This belief is not made evidentially probable for Jones by his new roommate's endorsement of eliminative materialism concerning pains. Nothing in the imagined situation gives Jones evidence making it probable that his roommate's endorsement is correct. We consistently can suppose that relative to Jones's total evidence, his roommate's endorsement is *at best* coincidentally correct. Similarly, Jones's belief that N is not made probable by his reflective belief that his beliefs about his conscious psychological states are highly reliable. For nothing in the imagined situation gives Jones evidence making it probable that this reflective belief is correct. We consistently can suppose that relative to Jones's total evidence, this reflective belief also is at best coincidentally correct. Thus we have no reason to think that Jones's belief that N is evidentially probable for him.

Foley's account assumes that epistemic justification is a function only of "our nature as believers and [of] our willingness on reflection to trust what that nature recommends to us" (p. 111). This assumption is actually just a variation on the familiar coherentist thesis that epistemic justification is a function only of one's *beliefs*, actual and reflective (p. 94).[11] But Foley's assumption, like the familiar coherentist thesis, runs afoul of the apparent fact that one's beliefs, actual or reflective, can be completely unsupported by considerations indicating that they are true.

My example of Jones suggests that the subjective contents of one's sensory and perceptual experiences (e.g., what one seems to perceive) are part of one's total empirical evidence, at least as potential underminers, and thereby place constraints on what one is justified in believing. Yet such contents need not be uniformly represented in one's beliefs, even if they often are. My example of Jones illustrates just such points. Thus a theory such as Foley's that makes justification a function only of actual and reflective beliefs neglects an important constraint on justification. Such a theory allows that one can be justified in believing an empirical proposition that is insufficiently probable relative to one's total empirical evidence. For it allows that one can be justified in believing an empirical proposition that is made improbable by a potential underminer in one's experiential contents. More to the point, a theory such as Foley's allows for justified beliefs that are not supported *at all* by considerations indicating that they are true. Thus Foley's theory does not lend credibility to the view that evidential probability for some propositions can derive just from one's beliefs, including one's reflective beliefs.[12]

In sum, I have argued that evidential probability does not supervene on an evidence basis consisting solely of propositions or

---

11 This coherentist thesis is very popular among contemporary philosophers; its proponents include Lehrer (1974, Chap. 8), Rorty (1979, Chap. 4), Davidson (1983), BonJour (1985, Chap. 4), Harman (1986, Chap. 4), and apparently Lycan (1988, Chap. 8). I shall say more about this thesis in §4.1.1.

12 For additional critical discussion of Foley's subjective foundationalism, see Moser (1989a, 1989b).

of belief states. Extending this lesson, we now can conclude that it will not help to appeal to any other sort of intentional state with a propositional object. For any such state, being propositional, will require something in virtue of which its object is evidentially probable. A propositional state can be an evidential probability-maker for one only if its object itself has evidential probability for one. The notion of a *self*-probable propositional object is also unhelpful here. We have already found this notion to be troublesome, in part because every proposition is probable given itself, but not every proposition is evidentially probable for a person. And owing to the considerations just raised about mere belief, the mere fact that one has an intentional attitude toward a proposition does not make that proposition evidentially probable for one (the *possible* exception being a proposition that simply affirms the existence of that intentional state). Thus we should look to a *non*propositional basis of evidential probability.

Before turning to nonpropositional evidence, we should note that the foregoing considerations bear directly on what kind of thing can be a truth indicator *in and of itself*, i.e., without depending for its being a truth indicator on some other truth indicator. Since truth indicators are evidential probability-makers, the arguments above concerning evidential probability-makers apply directly to truth indicators. We need to ask now what sort of nonpropositional item can serve as an *unconditional* truth indicator, i.e., a truth indicator in and of itself. Let us approach this question via the topic of nonpropositional probability-makers.

2.3   Nonpropositional probability-makers

There are three main variations on the view that evidential probability has a nonpropositional basis:

> *Radical Externalism*: For some proposition, P, the nonpropositional evidential probability of P for a person, S, supervenes on P's inferential relation to an evidence basis consisting at least in part of facts or items that exist independently of, and are not represented in, S's psychological states and their contents.

> *Moderate Externalism*: For every proposition, P, if P has nonpropositional evidential probability for S, that probability supervenes on P's inferential relation to an evidence basis consisting only of S's nondoxastic psychological states (e.g., sensory states), but S need

not be aware of his being in those states or of the contents of those states.

Internalism: For every proposition, *P*, if *P* has nonpropositional evidential probability for *S*, that probability supervenes on *P*'s inferential relation to an evidence basis consisting only of either *S*'s nondoxastic psychological states of which he is aware or simply their contents of which he is aware.

These views concern only *non*propositional evidential probability. They do not aim to characterize or to preclude an evidence basis including propositional items. In §2.4 I shall explain how a version of internalism about nonpropositional evidence fits with an account of derivative, propositional probability-makers.

Radical Externalism implies that one's nonpropositional evidence basis for some propositions consists at least in part of something ontologically independent of one's psychological states and their contents, something of which one may not be aware. (In §2.3.2 I shall clarify the notion of the *contents* of a nondoxastic psychological state.) Moderate Externalism implies that one's nonpropositional evidence basis consists only of one's nondoxastic psychological states, but it does not require that one be aware of one's being in those states or of their contents. In contrast, Internalism takes one's nonpropositional evidence basis to consist only of either one's nondoxastic psychological states of which one is aware or their contents of which one is aware.[13]

I now intend the foregoing three views to concern only *minimal* evidential probability-makers, which make a proposition evidentially probable to some extent, but not necessarily evidentially more probable than its denial. And I now intend those views to concern only *occurrent* evidential probability, i.e., the sort of evidential probability where the relevant probability-maker is in some sense present to one. (In §2.5 I shall consider the topic of *non*occurrent evidential probability.) Philosophers rarely give attention to the distinction between occurrent and nonoccurrent evidence. This is surprising, since this distinction is crucial to the important distinction between occurrent and nonoccurrent justification and knowl-

---

13 It would be pointless to pursue here the issue whether awareness is itself an event or a state. Certainly awareness can be statelike in the sense that no change need occur during it. But I do not want to suggest that awareness is a dispositional state in the way that believing is. (See §1.1 on believing as a dispositional state.)

edge. I shall clarify these distinctions in the remainder of this chapter.

2.3.1 Against Externalism

Radical Externalism and Moderate Externalism fail to accommodate the distinction between occurrent and nonoccurrent evidence. I shall explain this problem for each of these views in turn.

a. Against Radical Externalism

The most prominent versions of Radical Externalism are causal-reliability theories that make epistemic justification a function of the reliability of belief-forming causal processes.[14] Such reliability theories typically provide conditions for justified *belief*, and say little, if anything, about the conditions for a *proposition's* being justified for one, apart from one's believing it. This is not surprising, given these theories' appeal to *belief*-forming processes. So I shall present their suggested approach to evidential probability in terms of probable belief.

The reliability theories in question assume that a belief is evidentially probable to some extent so long as it has been causally produced and sustained, in the absence of underminers, by a belief-forming process (e.g., memory, perception, introspection) that is reliable to some extent. These theories assume that the reliability of a belief-forming process is a function of either the ratio or the arithmetical difference between the true beliefs and the false beliefs it produces. But these theories divide over the difficult question of the exact situations, actual or counterfactual, in which reliability confers evidential probability. (See §4.3 on this question.) On such reliability theories, it is the *objective* truth-conduciveness of a belief-forming process that determines evidential probability. And on such theories, a probability-conferring process often consists of facts or items that are external to the believer in the sense that they

14 Versions of such causal-reliability theories have been presented by Alston (1976, pp. 268–9), Goldman (1976; 1979; 1986, Chap. 4; 1988), and Meyers (1988, Chaps. 4, 6). (Alston apparently no longer holds such a view.) My discussion will not focus on the requirement of no underminers that causal-reliability theorists often invoke, since this requirement cannot save Radical Externalism or epistemic reliabilism from the sorts of objection I raise. See §4.3 for more on this point.

exist independently of, and are not represented in, the believer's psychological states and their contents.

Two serious problems face any version of Radical Externalism. We can illustrate the first problem via a causal-reliability variation on Radical Externalism, while overlooking the familiar difficult question of relevant identity conditions for belief-forming processes.[15] Suppose that my empirical belief that P has been causally produced and sustained by a belief-forming process, F, that is highly truth-conducive. Suppose also that all my empirical evidence present to me (e.g., current perceptual experiences and occurrent beliefs describing and adequately explaining those experiences) fails to provide any indication that F exists, and so also fails to provide any indication that my belief that P has been produced and sustained by F. Clearly in that case my belief that P would not be occurrently evidentially probable for me *because of its being due to F*. Of course that belief might still be probable due to other considerations, but this possibility is irrelevant now.

Nothing in the empirical evidence present to me indicates, or makes it probable, that F exists and is causally responsible for my belief that P. Thus F is an inadequate basis for the occurrent evidential probability of my belief that P, even if F is in fact a truth-conducive cause of this belief. So long as the empirical evidence present to me fails to indicate that F exists, my empirical beliefs due to F are, barring support other than F, at best coincidentally true relative to that empirical evidence. But of course no empirical belief that is occurrently evidentially probable for me is at best coincidentally true relative to the empirical evidence present to me. Since any version of Radical Externalism is open to this sort of objection, such externalism is an unacceptable view about occurrent evidential probability. (In §4.3 we shall see that a generalization on this objection challenges various reliabilist theories of epistemic justification.)

My objection assumes that an empirical proposition, P, is occurrently evidentially probable for one only if P is not at best

15 This question concerns the degree of generality with which belief-forming processes can plausibly be characterized on the view that they confer probability or justifiability. The difficulty of this question has been emphasized by Pollock (1984, pp. 108–11; 1986, pp. 118–19) and by Feldman (1985). Suggested answers can be found in Goldman (1986, pp. 49–51) and Sosa (1988, pp. 179–82).

coincidentally true relative to the empirical evidence present to one. The Radical Externalist might reply that in the suggested case the fact that my belief that *P* has been causally produced and sustained by a truth-conducive process *is* part of the empirical evidence present to me. Yet this reply is unconvincing. There is no clear sense of 'evidence present to one' via which it is plausible to say that the fact in question is, in the suggested case, part of the evidence present to me. Clearly not all facts involving causal relations to one are part of the evidence present to one. Mere facts involving causal relations to one do not automatically generate occurrent evidence for one. We obviously are not quite so fortunate in our acquisition of evidence.

Thus the Radical Externalist owes us a straightforward notion of occurrent evidence enabling us plausibly to say that something is part of one's occurrent empirical evidence even though it exists independently of, and is not represented in, one's psychological states and their contents. This notion must preserve the conceptual distinction between mere facts involving causal relations to one and one's occurrent evidence. Since Radical Externalists have not provided such a notion, Radical Externalism is uncompelling as a view about occurrent evidential probability.

The second problem bears on Radical Externalism as an account of nonoccurrent or occurrent probability. The problem is that Radical Externalism seriously limits our opportunity to challenge Humean probability skepticism. Such skepticism claims that no beliefs affirming the existence of mind-independent items are evidentially probable for us. Given Radical Externalism, for some propositions the claim that these propositions are evidentially probable *presupposes* a claim that affirms the existence of certain mind-independent items, such as the existence of a reliable belief-forming process that involves a physical object. But the Humean skeptic will demand independent argument for such a claim.

If the demanded independent argument itself presupposes physical-object claims, then to challenge the skeptic, this argument will require still another argument that does not presuppose such claims. To provide a challenge, the latter required argument must either be nonprobabilistic or involve only probabilities that do not presuppose physical-object claims. So far as Radical Externalism goes, it is quite unclear what the details of either option might be. In either case, then, Radical Externalism leaves a lot to be desired. Or less charitably, it appears to limit our opportunity to challenge Humean probability skepticism.

b. Against Moderate Externalism

Moderate Externalism might seem to improve on Radical Externalism. One familiar variation on Moderate Externalism stems from the familiar empiricist view that all nonpropositional evidence comes from one's sensory stimulations, i.e., one's sensory receptors' being stimulated in certain ways.[16] Such sensory stimulations are purely physical reactions to input from a physical environment. They do not essentially involve any awareness of psychological states or of the contents of such states. For example, when one is simply looking at, i.e., in the direction of, a blue book under suitable conditions of illumination and perspective, one's visual receptors are stimulated in a determinate way – a way determined in part by the rectangular blue images projected on one's retinas. But of course one need not be *aware* of an image of a rectangular blue book to have one's visual receptors stimulated by such a book. One might have such a stimulation while being aware only of something else, e.g., one's throbbing toothache. More generally, merely looking at *X*, even under suitable conditions of illumination and perspective, does not entail an awareness of *X*.

Thus the empiricist view at hand illustrates that Moderate Externalism is not equivalent to Internalism. It illustrates that Moderate Externalism does not require that nonpropositional evidence derive from one's awareness of a psychological state or of its contents.

Another variation on Moderate Externalism comes from some contemporary "reliable-indication" accounts of epistemic justification.[17] These accounts suggest that nonpropositional evidence

16 This view is suggested in some of Quine's epistemological writings. See, for example, his (1955, pp. 215–18; 1960, Chaps. 1–2; 1969, pp. 218, 223; 1974, Chap. 1).
17 Such accounts have been provided, for example, by Swain (1979; 1981, Chap. 4; 1985) and Alston (1985, pp. 43–5; 1986a, pp. 3–5; 1986b, pp. 215–17; 1988, pp. 270–6, 281). The accounts of Swain and Alston represent Moderate Externalism rather than Radical Externalism, since they restrict one's evidential grounds to one's internal psychological states. Alston's account explicitly provides for nonbelief ev-

consists solely of one's internal psychological states, such as sensory and perceptual states, that provide a reliable indication of the truth of the beliefs based on those states. Such a reliable indication is a truth-conducive indication in either the ratio sense or the arithmetical-difference sense noted in connection with the aforementioned reliable-process view. But reliable-indication theories do not share a uniform account of the exact situations, actual or counterfactual, in which reliability confers evidential probability. Nor do they share a single account of the conditions under which a belief is *based* on certain evidential grounds. Their relevant similarity is just that they make one's evidential grounds internal to one without requiring one's awareness of those grounds. Thus the reliable-indication theories in question exemplify Moderate Externalism rather than Internalism or Radical Externalism.

Moderate Externalism invites the sort of objection I raised against Radical Externalism. I shall illustrate this objection first via the aforementioned empiricist view, and then via reliable-indication theories.

Suppose that under suitable conditions of illumination and perspective the visual receptors in my retinas are stimulated by a blue book, but that I have no awareness either of an apparent blue book or of my being stimulated by such a book. Nor am I aware of any other indication of there being a blue book. In accord with Moderate Externalism, the empiricist view in question allows that in such a case, where there are no undermining considerations, some proposition such as (a) that there is a blue book, (b) that I see a blue book, or (c) that I seem to see a blue book, is occurrently evidentially probable for me to some extent.[18] But this allowance seems implausible. In the imagined case I have no awareness whatsoever of something that makes it probable that there is, that I see, or even that I seem to see, a blue book. Relative to all I am aware of, it is at best coincidentally true that there is, that I see, or even that I

idential grounds, but the same is not true of Swain's account. Moderate Externalism seems also to be represented by the reliability-oriented "virtue perspectivism" of Sosa (1985, p. 241; 1988, pp. 182–4).

18 In accord with standard usage, I use 'see', but not 'seems to see', as a success verb. Thus if one sees X, then X exists; but one can seem to see X even if X does not exist. While daydreaming, for instance, I might seem to see a huge yacht in my backyard, even though this yacht does not actually exist.

seem to see, a blue book. But no proposition that is occurrently evidentially probable for me is at best coincidentally true relative to all I am aware of.

The same problem faces the aforementioned reliable-indication variations on Moderate Externalism. Suppose that my belief that *P* has been formed, perhaps via inference of some sort, on the basis of my internal psychological state, *I*, that is a sensory state and is a reliable indication that *P* is true. Suppose also that I am now completely unaware of *I* and of its sensory contents. Reliable-indication theories, in accord with Moderate Externalism, allow that in this sort of case, where there are no undermining considerations, the proposition that *P* is now occurrently evidentially probable for me to some extent. But this seems wrong. For the proposition that *P* is at best coincidentally true relative to all I am now aware of. And no proposition that is now occurrently evidentially probable for one is at best coincidentally true relative to all one is now aware of.

My objection assumes that a proposition, *P*, is occurrently evidentially probable for one only if *P* is not at best coincidentally true relative to all one is aware of. The positive counterpart to this assumption is that occurrent evidence is evidence "present to one" in the sense that one is aware of it. Yet one might seek an alternative to this view in a thesis suggested by various proponents of Moderate Externalism. The thesis is that one's occurrent evidence for a belief need not be something of which one is actually aware, but need only be "the sort of thing whose instances are fairly directly accessible to their subject on reflection."[19] The notion of fairly direct accessibility is of course vague, but this is not my main criticism.

The crucial problem facing the accessibility thesis is that it conflates the distinct categories of occurrent evidence and nonoccurrent evidence. If one's *occurrent* evidence need only be fairly directly accessible to one, how does it differ from one's *non*occurrent evidence? The notion of accessibility is of course modal, and thus differs from the nonmodal notion of actualized access, or actual

19 Alston (1988, p. 275). For similar suggestions, see also Alston (1986b, pp. 211–13), Ginet (1975, p. 34), Chisholm (1977, p. 17; 1988; 1989, pp. 76–7), Swain (1981, pp. 79–81), and Pollock (1986, pp. 22, 133–5). None of these philosophers actually endorses the accessibility thesis as a view about occurrent evidence; instead, their suggestions about accessibility *overlook* the basic distinction between occurrent and nonoccurrent evidence.

awareness. One's evidence can be fairly directly access*ible* to one even if one does not have actualized access to it, i.e., even if one is not actually aware of it. So there is a genuine difference between evidence of which one is aware and evidence that merely is fairly directly accessible to one. Evidence of which one is aware is occurrent for one if any evidence is. But the same seems not to be true of evidence that merely is fairly directly accessible to one. If we take the latter sort of evidence to be occurrent, what then shall we take to be nonoccurrent evidence? There seems not to be a ready answer. And since it seems plausible to think that all one's evidence, including one's nonoccurrent evidence, is fairly directly accessible to one, it seems plausible to think that the accessibility thesis in question conflates the categories of occurrent evidence and nonoccurrent evidence.

Thus Moderate Externalism shares the main defect of Radical Externalism. It fails to provide the basis for a straightforward distinction between occurrent evidence and nonoccurrent evidence.

c. A positive lesson

The positive lesson here is that a nondoxastic psychological state is part of one's occurrent evidence only if one is aware of it or at least its contents. Neglecting this lesson, we shall be hard put to maintain a clear distinction between occurrent and nonoccurrent nondoxastic evidence. We shall be faced, for instance, with the view that *all* one's nondoxastic psychological states that are fairly directly accessible to one are part of one's occurrent evidence. But this view is implausible, as was illustrated by the examples supporting my criticisms of Radical and Moderate Externalism. We thus have motivation for turning to Internalism.

2.3.2 Internalism and unconditional probability-makers

We need to distinguish two main variations on Internalism:

Moderate Internalism: For every proposition, *P*, if *P* has nonpropositional evidential probability for *S*, that probability supervenes on *P*'s inferential relation to an evidence basis consisting only of *S*'s nondoxastic psychological states whose contents he is aware of, but he need not be aware of his being in those states.

Radical Internalism: For every proposition, *P*, if *P* has nonpropositional evidential probability for *S*, that probability supervenes on *P*'s inferential relation to an evidence basis consisting only of *S*'s nondoxastic psychological states that he is aware of his being in.

Radical Internalism requires that one have an awareness of one's being in the nondoxastic psychological states that constitute one's occurrent nonpropositional evidence, whereas Moderate Internalism does not. I shall characterize the sort of awareness relevant to Internalism in the following two sections. Let us remember that our quarry is still *occurrent* probability.

One might object that Moderate Internalism faces an analogue of my objection to Moderate Externalism. Consider a case where I am perceptually aware of an apparent blue book, but where I am completely *un*aware of my being perceptually aware of an apparent blue book, because my attention is wholly attracted by the apparent blue book itself. (Compare the parallel situation where one is so absorbed in what is happening on the movie screen that one is completely unaware of *one's watching* a film.) My talk of an *apparent* blue book does not imply that there is a blue book existing independently of perceivers.[20] So an apparent blue book can be presented to one even if it does not exist independently of oneself, and even if one is unaware of its appearing to oneself. Thus one's awareness of an apparent blue book does not entail one's being aware of an apparent blue book *as* something that appears to oneself. In the case at hand I am aware of *an apparent blue book*, but I am unaware of *my being aware of the apparent blue book*. Such second-order awareness in this case is foreclosed by the consuming first-order awareness I have of the apparent book itself. So this case falsifies any self-

20 Thus my use of 'apparent' emphasizes that 'is aware of', like 'seems to see', is *not* a success predicate. This emphasis is crucial, since we need to leave room for a non–question-begging challenge to probability skepticism concerning beliefs about the external world, such as the challenge provided in §3.5. For current purposes we can bracket worries about the *ontological* status of apparent perceptual "objects." My subsequent epistemological account fits with any plausible view on the ontological status of such "objects" that preserves appearing-language in some way. So my talk of apparent perceptual *objects* does not endorse a sense-datum theory; it is, rather, only a familiar way of talking about the *contents* of a perceptual experience that may or may not be veridical. Although my epistemological concerns do not require a special ontological account of such contents, I actually prefer the sort of adverbial account presented in Ducasse (1951, Chap. 13), Cornman (1975a; 1975b, Chap. 2), and Moser (1985, Chap. 5). For recent refinements on such an account, see Clark (1979, 1987) and Tye (1984).

intimation thesis according to which necessarily if one experiences X, then one is aware of one's experiencing X.

One might propose that the foregoing case falsifies Moderate Internalism too. It provides a situation where, although one has a nondoxastic perceptual awareness of an apparent blue book, neither the proposition that one sees a blue book nor the proposition that one seems to see a blue book is occurrently probable for one; for one has no awareness of one's perceptual awareness of an apparent blue book. Apart from the latter, second-order awareness, the propositions in question will be at best coincidentally true relative to all one is aware of, and so will not be occurrently evidentially probable for one. Thus one might use the foregoing case to reject Moderate Internalism along with Moderate Externalism.

Moderate Internalism needs revision if it is construed to allow that in the proposed example it would be occurrently probable for me that I see a blue book or even that I seem to see a blue book. Neither of the latter propositions is occurrently probable for me in that example. The needed revision is that Moderate Internalism identifies the nonpropositional evidence basis for a proposition such as that one sees a blue book, or that one seems to see a blue book *only if* the relevant posited psychological state is itself presented in the contents, of which one is aware, of one's psychological states. Thus we must revise Moderate Internalism to clarify that a proposition affirming one's being in a psychological state is occurrently probable for one only if one is aware of one's apparently being in that state. But the suggested example does not count against Moderate Internalism if we consider only the proposition that *there is* a blue book, since (a) in that case there is the required awareness of an apparent blue book, and (b) that proposition does not affirm one's being in a psychological state.

One might propose that we need Radical Internalism to identify the basis for the occurrent probability of propositions that affirm the existence of one's psychological states, propositions such as that I *see* a blue book, and that I *seem to see* a blue book. On this proposal, one might try to explain the basis of occurrent evidential probability via two principles: (a) Radical Internalism, regarding propositions that affirm one's being in a psychological state, and (b) Moderate Internalism, regarding propositions that do not do so. This dualism of explanatory principles might seem initially plausible, since the propositions affirming one's being in a psychological state are relevantly different from those that do not affirm this. The occurrent probability of the former requires a kind of second-order awareness not required by the occurrent probability of the latter. Yet I believe we can formulate a unified principle that draws on the two versions of Internalism in question while preserving the strengths and avoiding the weaknesses of both versions. This formulation requires some preliminary discussion.

Specifically, we now must face two important issues. The first concerns the kind of awareness required by Moderate and Radical Internalism; the second concerns how *non*propositional awareness states can make propositions evidentially probable. My treatment of these issues will explain how a certain sort of experience can be an unconditional truth indicator, i.e., an evidential probability-maker in and of itself. It will also lead to a unified version of probability internalism.

a. Modes of awareness

The awareness relevant to Moderate and Radical Internalism must be essentially nonconceptual to enable those views to avoid the defects of the views criticized in §2.2. Nonconceptual awareness is just awareness that does not essentially involve the application or the consideration of a concept. I take a concept to be a classificatory item, such as a class term (perhaps only in a language of thought), that can be a constituent of a proposition.[21] Following C. I. Lewis (1926, 1929), I take an empirical concept to be the sort of psychological classificatory item that an agent can directly impose on what is presented in his sensory or perceptual experience. Thus the sort of low-level structural organization provided, for instance, at the level of one's retinas is *not* conceptual in my sense.

If the awareness relevant to Internalism were essentially conceptual, we would be faced with questions about the evidence basis for its essential conceptual component. An evidence basis for the

---

21 I shall not here pursue the important question of what exactly constitutes the semantic significance of a concept: e.g., exemplars, necessary and sufficient correctness-of-application conditions, justification conditions, or probabilistic relations between instances and certain features. See Moser (1988a) and Appiah (1986) for arguments against an appeal to justification conditions. On the other options, see, for example, Smith and Medin (1981, 1984) and the essays in Neisser (1987a) and in Scholnick (1983). See also Weitz (1988) for an overview of prominent traditional philosophical positions on concepts.

80

application of a concept is something indicating that the application is correct. Concepts are of course neither true nor false, and thus the evidence relevant to concept application is not a *truth* indicator. Rather, such evidence is a *correctness-of-application* indicator. Just as propositions require a nonpropositional evidence basis, so also the components of an awareness state that essentially involve concept application require a nonconceptual evidence basis. The reasons for the latter requirement are directly analogous to those presented in §2.2 regarding propositions.

A conceptual awareness state need not be propositional. It need not involve propositional predication, i.e., the sort of predication that has subject and predicate terms and is a truth-bearer. A conceptual awareness state might involve only nonpropositional, objectual categorization. For example, I might categorize an image as being red without forming an actual judgment that is a truth-bearer. (Here I dissent from Russell's view [1912, p. 54] that nonconceptual items can be constituents of a proposition.) If an awareness state is essentially nonconceptual, then it is also essentially nonpropositional. Propositional items essentially involve predication, and thus have conceptual constituents. So if the awareness relevant to Internalism is essentially nonconceptual, we should be free from the problems of §2.2. But what exactly is nonconceptual awareness?

The sort of nonconceptual awareness most appropriate to Moderate and Radical Internalism is *direct attention attraction*, where one's attention is directly engaged, if only momentarily, by the more or less determinate features of certain presented contents. Such attention attraction, being nonconceptual, does not itself essentially involve one's predicating something of the presented contents; yet of course it can be accompanied by such predicating. And such attention attraction is different from mere sensory stimulation, since it essentially involves direct awareness, albeit nonconceptual awareness, of what is presented in experience.

Direct attention attraction is also different from one's *focusing* attention on something, where one at least implicitly predicates the feature of individuality or of isolatability of what is presented in experience. Attention-focusing, as various psychologists have stressed, essentially involves psychological *selection* of some sort.[22]

22 For useful overviews of relevant psychological literature on such selective attention, see Johnston and Dark (1986), Hirst (1986), and the essays in Parasuraman

Such selection essentially involves a form of conceptualization, since it essentially involves a form of objectual categorization. Attention attraction is *not* thus selective; and so in ordinary English we use the passive voice to characterize it, whereas we use the active voice to characterize attention-focusing. In essence, direct attention attraction is one's being directly psychologically "affected" by certain contents in such a way that one is psychologically *presented* with those contents.

For current purposes I take the notion of psychological *presentation* to be conceptually basic. This notion is familiar from, and receives elucidation in, various foundationalist writings.[23] Russell used the notion of presentation to clarify his famous notion of acquaintance: "to say that S has acquaintance with O is essentially the same thing as to say that O is presented to S" (1911, pp. 202–3). But I do not identify my notion of presentation with Russell's notion of acquaintance, because (a) Russell's notion allows for one's being acquainted with objects of which one is not currently aware (p. 203), and (b) Russell's notion seems to rely on a notion of selective attention (1914a, p. 131).[24] On my notion of presentation, one is presented with nonconceptual contents only if one is directly aware of those contents; and the directness of such awareness consists in its not essentially involving awareness of any other contents. Presentation, as I understand it, essentially involves direct nonconceptual noticing, but does not essentially involve conceptual noticing *as* or noticing *that*.

I prefer to talk of direct *attention attraction* now, because we need to safeguard against any suggestion that the awareness relevant to Internalism is conceptual. Direct visual attention attraction occurs when an object directly *appears* to one. For example, my looking at the sun now is accompanied by my attention's being directly

---

and Davies (1984). On the physiological basis for selective visual attention, see Wurtz, Goldberg, and Robinson (1982) and Robinson and Petersen (1986). Psychologists as well as philosophers have neglected the contrasting notion of attention *attraction*.

23 See, for example, Lewis (1946, pp. 172–4) and, more recently, Van Cleve (1985, pp. 94–7) and Moser (1985, Chap. 5; 1988c). See also the extensive discussion in Brentano (1924, esp. pp. 78–80, 201–5, 315–21). Brentano finds the notion of presentation to be suggested by Descartes's notion of *ideae*. On Descartes's influential notion of perceptual acquaintance, see Yolton (1984, Chap. 1).

24 On the details of Russell's notion of acquaintance, see Chisholm (1974) and White (1981).

attracted by, or presented with, a bright yellow circular item. But not all cases of one's *looking at* an object, even in ideal conditions of illumination and perspective, involve one's attention's being attracted by that object. Sometimes one has no awareness of what one is looking at, such as when one's attention is altogether distracted by something else. For most of us, I suspect, the relevant notion of psychological presentation or direct attention attraction is adequately defined ostensively, by an appeal to common experiences. In §4.2 I shall clarify this notion further by defending it against some likely objections. For now we can achieve some clarification by relating the relevant sort of nonconceptual awareness to a brief taxonomy of experience.

An experience is an event or state of awareness that is either perceptual or nonperceptual. A perceptual experience is an event or state of awareness essentially having as an object a sensory item or feature such as a shape, color, sound, odor, taste, or some combination thereof, or even some subjective, merely ostensible analogue of one of the foregoing items or features, e.g., a merely apparent shape.[25] Here we may also include items of "inner sense" such as pains and other feelings (e.g., being nervous and being anxious).

A perceptual experience is either conceptual or nonconceptual. A conceptual perceptual experience is an event of awareness that essentially has as an object not only a sensory item or feature, but also a concept, i.e., a classificatory item that can be a constituent of a proposition. Typically a conceptual perceptual experience has as an object a concept that semantically involves a sensory item in the sense that it denotes, connotes, or is defined by a sensory item. Consider, for instance, my conceptual taste experience, of a lemon, that this is a sour lemon, where 'this' refers to the lemon in question. This experience is conceptual as well as perceptual. It is conceptual because it is propositional; i.e., it essentially has as an object the proposition *that this is a sour lemon*, where 'this' is defined denota-

---

25 As I noted above, my talk of sensory *items* and *features* aims to be neutral on the issue of the ontological status of sensory contents. Thus we should not construe this talk as taking a stand on the debate involving sense-datum and adverbial theories of sensory and perceptual contents. The adverbial theorist would need to translate this talk, perhaps following Ducasse (1951) and Cornman (1975b), into talk of specific *kinds* of objectless sensing. But since such translation is often grammatically cumbersome, I shall persist in the ordinary talk of sensory items and features.

tively via the lemon in question. And it is perceptual because it essentially has as an object a sensory item. But I shall not assume that a conceptual perceptual experience must have as an object a concept that semantically involves a sensory item. Nor shall I assume that one's having a conceptual perceptual experience requires one's *being aware* of one's considering or applying a concept.

A conceptual perceptual experience, then, essentially has as an object a conceptual item of some sort, such as a proposition. But such an experience need not involve an act of *judging* that something is the case. It might involve only one's *entertaining* that something is the case, where such entertaining is an event of considering and not judging. Or it might involve only objectual categorization where one is not psychologically related to an actual proposition. Thus we should not define a conceptual perceptual experience as a belief that requires a dispositional state resulting from assenting. (See §1.1 on believing as such a dispositional state.) A conceptual perceptual experience need not involve a dispositional state of any sort, and it need not involve assenting or judging. However, direct attention attraction is an essential ingredient of any conceptual perceptual experience. An essential awareness component of a conceptual perceptual experience is direct attention attraction by a sensory item or feature. Without such an awareness component, perceptual experience would be perceptually empty.

A *non*conceptual perceptual experience is also an event or state of awareness that essentially has as an object a sensory item or feature. But it does not essentially have a conceptual item as an object. Such a nonconceptual experience is a psychological event or state of attention attraction essentially related only to a nonconceptual sensory item or feature, such as a shape, color, sound, odor, taste, or some combination or merely ostensible analogue thereof. It is thus, in essence, judgment-free and concept-free. A nonconceptual perceptual experience would occur, for example, if (but not only if) one's attention were directly attracted by a sensory item but (a) one did not have the time to categorize, or to consider a categorization of, that item (perhaps owing to one's attention's being immediately attracted by something else) or (b) one did not have the conceptual capacity to categorize, or to consider a categorization of, that item.

Clearly our *describing* a nonconceptual experience or the object thereof requires our formulating a judgment about it. But this does

84

not mean that the *having* of such an experience is essentially conceptual. The describing of an experience is one thing, and the having of it, another. And there is no reason to think that the having of an experience, construed as nonconceptual attention attraction, essentially involves the describing either of the experience itself or of what is experienced. Thus we apparently have a viable notion of nonconceptual perceptual experience that contrasts with the notion of conceptual perceptual experience.

A *non*perceptual experience is also an event or state of awareness, but it is essentially related only to a nonsensory item, such as a proposition, a constituent of a proposition (e.g., a concept), or a relation between concepts. A nonperceptual experience is either conceptual or nonconceptual. A conceptual nonperceptual experience is an event of awareness that essentially has a conceptual item as an object, but does not essentially have a sensory item as an object. Consider, for example, my current awareness of the proposition that $2 + 3 = 5$. This awareness, I presume, does not essentially involve an awareness of a sensory item. On one plausible view, this awareness has as its only object a conceptual item in a language of thought. This awareness is, in any case, a propositional *non*perceptual experience. But, again, we should not assume that an experience is propositional only if it involves an act of judging that *P*.

A *non*conceptual nonperceptual experience contrasts with an experience of the former sort. It is an event of awareness, or attention attraction, that essentially has only a nonconceptual nonsensory item as its object. Likely candidates for nonconceptual nonsensory items are relations of inclusion and exclusion between concepts, psychological states such as thinking, believing, remembering and intending, and nonconceptual mathematical items. Whatever the actual ontological status of such items is, they are neither sensory nor conceptual. My awareness simply of my remembering something, for instance, is not an awareness of a sensory item; and it is not conceptual, since it is not an awareness of a conceptual item. Even if the *object* of my remembering is conceptual, we can distinguish between a state or event of remembering and its object. My awareness simply of the state or event of remembering would be a nonconceptual nonperceptual experience of attention attraction. And the same is evidently true also of one's awareness simply of one's thinking. Perhaps more needs to be said to make the present

85

notion obvious, but we now have a beginning sketch of a notion of nonconceptual nonperceptual experience that contrasts with the aforementioned notion of a conceptual nonperceptual experience. This sketch serves my purposes of contrast.

On my proposed taxonomy, *every* experience, whether perceptual or not, essentially involves a psychological state or event of direct attention attraction, or presentation. Perceptual and nonperceptual experiences differ because of the kinds of items to which they are essentially related; and the same is true of conceptual and nonconceptual experiences. One virtue of my taxonomy is that it preserves a univocal basis for experience, viz., direct attention attraction understood as psychological presentation. This is indeed a virtue, since the experiences of the various sorts identified are all *experiences*. My taxonomy aims to clarify somewhat the notion of nonconceptual awareness that will play a central role in my account of unconditional evidential probability-makers.

Before returning to questions about evidence, we should acknowledge two important issues about nonconceptual awareness. First, is such awareness physically possible for humans? I have suggested that it is conceptually possible, and now I want to suggest that it is physically possible as well. Evidently it is conceptually coherent to suppose that a human has his attention directly attracted only by a sensory item, while failing to categorize, and even to consider to categorize, this item. And this supposition seems to be compatible with the known laws of physics. For instance, it seems quite compatible with the known laws of physics to suppose that I have my attention directly attracted only by a sensory item, but fail to categorize, and even to consider to categorize, this item because of lack of time. Both categorization and the consideration of categorization take time. But I might not have the required time if I cease to exist immediately after my attention's being attracted by an item, or if my attention is distracted immediately after its being attracted by the item in question. Thus nonconceptual awareness seems to be physically as well as conceptually possible.[26]

26 Incidentally, I am not alone in my endorsement of the possibility of nonconceptual perceptual awareness. Psychologists who endorse the possibility of such awareness include Brentano (1924), Goldstein and Scheerer (1941, pp. 2–3), Harnad (1987), and Neisser (1987b). Like-minded philosophers include Lewis (1946, Chap. 7), Price (1950, pp. 124–5), Ducasse (1951, Chap. 13), Chisholm (1957, Chap. 10), Cornman (1975b, Chaps. 2, 8), Jackson (1977), Dretske (1979; 1981, Chap. 6),

I shall not pursue the empirical issue whether if a normal human has his attention directly attracted by something, then *as a causal result* he considers or applies a categorization. Nothing in my account of experience requires a rejection of such a causal connection between attention attraction and categorization. The claim that direct attention attraction *causally* involves some sort of categorization does not entail the claim that such attention attraction *essentially* involves categorization. Yet I have doubts about a universal causal connection between the two, especially if we consider humans in general. These doubts *perhaps* receive some confirmation from recent psychological work on visual agnosia, where brain-damaged patients are unable to identify visually presented items even though their visual functioning, being otherwise sound, seems to involve visual attention attraction.[27] But again I need not reject the causal connection in question. My account denies only that direct attention attraction essentially involves categorization.

The second issue concerns the role of nonconceptual attention attraction in a conceptual perceptual experience. The relevant question is: does the conceptual component in a conceptual perceptual experience ever alter the essential, internal qualities of the presented objects of the nonconceptual attention-attraction component of the experience? For instance, does one's applying the concept *red* to a presented red item ever alter the redness of that item, perhaps by making it more vivid? My answer to these questions is no, on the assumption that concept application alters at most one's *conception* of presented nonconceptual sensory items. Since the latter items are essentially nonconceptual, they have their essential features independently of conceptual items. Their essential, internal features do not depend in any essential way for their existence, or for their being presented, on concept application. Thus I take conceptual experiences to be simply additive. They essentially have a nonconceptual attention-attraction component *and* a conceptual component. But there seems to be no reason to think that the noncon-

Evans (1982, pp. 122–6, 151–60, 226–31), Peacocke (1983, Chap. 1; 1986; 1988), Van Cleve (1985), and Alan Goldman (1988, Chaps. 5–6). However, none of these theorists uses the notion of direct attention attraction to elucidate the notion of nonconceptual awareness. (But Brentano [1929, p. 19] does mention this notion in passing in a discussion of Descartes.)

27 Some of the relevant psychological work on agnosia is discussed in Jason Brown (1972, Chaps. 18–21), Hecaen and Albert (1978, Chap. 4), and Bauer and Rubens (1985, pp . 188–209).

ceptual component, including its nonconceptual object, is essentially a function of the relevant conceptual component. This consideration will be important to my account of evidence. It does not conflict in any way with the claim, supported by Scheffler (1982), Hardin (1988, pp. 105–8), and others, that one's conceptual discriminations can *causally* influence what perceptual contents are presented to one. (Scheffler and Hardin apparently think they are supporting more than a causal connection, but I remain doubtful.)

We now have an adequate beginning account of the sort of non-conceptual awareness relevant to Internalism. (In §4.2 I shall elaborate further on the notion of nonconceptual awareness when I reply to certain recent anti-foundationalist objections.)

b. Unconditional probability-makers

Returning to the topic of evidential probability, we should recall the earlier conclusion that only the nonconceptual component of an experience can be an unconditional probability-maker. A nonconceptual experience is relevantly different from a proposition and a propositional attitude, since it is not essentially related to a propositional object in need of a probability-maker. A nonconceptual experience essentially has only a *non*conceptual object. Thus a nonconceptual experience does not raise the troublesome considerations mentioned in §2.2 regarding propositions and beliefs as candidates for the evidence basis of evidential probability. So such an experience is an ideal candidate for an unconditional probability-maker, i.e., a truth indicator in and of itself.

But what about a conceptual experience that is not propositional? Is it also relevantly different from a proposition in need of a probability-maker? Its nonconceptual component is relevantly different from a proposition, but its conceptual component is not. A conceptual experience, as characterized above, includes a conceptual item as an essential ingredient. And if that item essentially involves the application of a concept, it needs an evidence basis in the sense that it requires a correctness-of-application indicator. It requires an evidence basis for the same reason that any evidentially probable proposition does: it cannot provide its own. Thus the only sense in which a conceptual perceptual experience can provide unconditional evidence is the sense in which its *non*conceptual component can provide such evidence.

A nonconceptual experience is, then, the best candidate for being an unconditional probability-maker. It can serve such a role because, being nonconceptual, it does not need a further probability-maker. Its being a probability-maker does not derive from another probability-maker. Indeed, a nonconceptual experience is not *the kind of thing* that can be supported by an evidential probability-maker. For it is not conceptual; and an evidential probability-maker necessarily indicates that a proposition is true, or at least that a concept application is correct.

But *how* can a nonconceptual experience, being *non*conceptual, make a proposition evidentially probable to some extent? In other words, how can such an experience be a minimal evidential probability-maker for a proposition? The first step of my answer claims that the *subjective nonconceptual contents* of such an experience do the actual probability-making. One reason for this claim is that one always has an awareness of such contents while having the relevant experience, even if one is not aware of the experience itself (i.e., the event or state of experiencing). This obviously is an important consideration for an account of *occurrent* evidential probability. We now must distinguish subjective nonconceptual contents both from *objective* nonconceptual contents and from a mere *state* (or event) of experiencing or being aware.

Objective contents of an experience exist independently of that experience. The relevant experience is not essential to the existence of such contents. For instance, part of the objective contents of my seeing a bicycle is the physical bicycle itself. But objective contents need not entail the existence of something independent of an experiencer, such as a bicycle. Consider, for example, my experience of this: my being aware of an apparent bicycle. Part of the contents of this experience, viz., the contents consisting of my being aware of an apparent bicycle, is objective in the relevant sense. For I can be aware of an apparent bicycle without my having a second-order experience of this awareness. But my being aware of an apparent bicycle does not entail the existence of anything independent of me. The subjective nonconceptual contents of this latter awareness state, as well as of my seeing a bicycle, are provided by an *apparent* bicycle.

We can characterize subjective nonconceptual contents ontologically either in the familiar adverbial manner suggested by Ducasse (1951) and Cornman (1975b) or in the equally familiar sense-datum terms proposed by Moore (1903), Russell (1912), and Jackson

(1977). But whichever characterization we prefer, such contents do not exist independently of an experience. This does not mean that we must identify subjective nonconceptual contents with a state of experiencing or being aware. Experiencing is a state or an event that can be related to various subjective contents. Its subjective contents are what it is related to, either adverbially or as its sense data, on a particular occasion. Thus let us not confuse subjective nonconceptual contents either with a state of experiencing or with objective contents.

We can specify ontological identity conditions for subjective non-conceptual contents. An adequate criterion for *token* identity is simply this: subjective contents C and subjective contents $C^\star$ are token-identical if and only if necessarily if a person has C, then that person has $C^\star$ also. Regarding *type* identity, matters are less straightforward. Yet we can make do now with this criterion: C and $C^\star$ are type-identical if and only if C and $C^\star$ exemplify all the same internal purely qualitative properties, including internal qualitative relational properties. Internal purely qualitative properties of C and $C^\star$ are attributes essential only to the presented quality of C and $C^\star$; they are the attributes that make a difference only to the presented quality of C and $C^\star$. They do not include properties such as that of "being self-identical" or "being token-identical to C." The difficult question of the conditions for items' exemplifying common properties is a general ontological issue that faces virtually all theories, and that we need not pursue here.[28]

I have noted that my talk of subjective nonconceptual contents does *not* take a stand on the ontological debate concerning direct perceptual realism. Such talk is solely for *epistemological* purposes. We need it to avoid begging important questions against the Humean justification skeptic who claims that one's justified beliefs extend only to what one *apparently* experiences. According to such a skeptic, an inference from a claim about what one apparently experiences to a claim about what one actually experiences, in the sense that the contents of the experience are ontologically independent of that experience, is gratuitous apart from a justification of some sort. Thus if we begin our theory of evidence with the claim that one experiences actual physical objects, or even actual awareness states,

---

28 For useful discussions of this issue, see Butchvarov (1966, Chap. 4; 1979, Chap. 7), Price (1969b, Chap. 1), and Armstrong (1978, Chaps. 7, 8).

the Humean skeptic could object quite plausibly that we have simply *assumed*, in a question-begging manner, that there are actual physical objects or awareness states experienced by one. The Humean skeptic finds such an assumption to be evidentially gratuitous.

Since it is an essential task of a nonskeptical theory of justification to challenge the Humean skeptic, we need to avoid question-begging assumptions. Thus my talk of *subjective* nonconceptual contents is indispensable for this book's epistemological purposes. So in advance of the challenge to the Humean skeptic in §3.5, my talk of nonconceptual experiential contents must use a qualifier such as 'apparent' or 'subjective' to avoid gratuitous commitment to objective contents.

I assume that the skeptic in question has no qualms about talk of *subjective* nonconceptual contents, mainly because the leading justification skeptics from Sextus to Hume to Popper evidently have no such qualms. Relevant skeptical doubts arise when and only when one posits objective contents, contents that have a life of their own apart from one's experience thereof. In fact, justification skeptics often use the existence of subjective contents to make their case that we are not justified in positing objective contents. For example, justification skeptics sometimes argue that their skepticism derives support from the absence of a relevant difference between certain allegedly objective contents and certain subjective contents.

I assume also that the justification skeptic is not bothered by my talk of one*self* or of my*self*. This talk does not connote anything ontologically contentious. The self, for current epistemological purposes, is whatever undergoes the relevant (apparent) experiences that even the skeptic acknowledges: it is just the (apparent) experiencer. This view aims to be compatible with the Humean claim that the self has no life apart from its (apparent) experiences. It allows that the self is essentially determined by a set of (apparent) experiences. Thus we presumably have not yet offended the Humean justification skeptic whom we must challenge later.

Yet this question still remains: *how*, or *in virtue of what*, is a proposition made evidentially probable to some extent by one's direct attention attraction by subjective nonconceptual contents? My rough preliminary proposal is this: one's subjective nonconceptual contents can make a proposition, *P*, evidentially probable to some extent for one in virtue of those contents' *being explained for one* by *P* in the sense that *P* is an essential part of an explanation for one of why those contents exist, or equivalently, why those contents occur as they do. When a proposition is an essential part of such an explanation for one, I shall say, for ease of expression, that it explains the contents in question for one, while granting that it may do so in a partial, incomplete way. Propositions can be essential parts of an explanation for one, since they can provide one with answers to explanation-seeking why-questions.

Subjective nonconceptual contents' being explained for one by a proposition is not sufficient for those contents' making that proposition *evidentially more probable than its denial* for one. Both a proposition and its denial (or at least a proposition entailing its denial) can individually explain one's subjective contents. For example, one's contents consisting of an apparent blue book might be explained for one by the proposition that there is a blue book before one as well as by the proposition that one is simply hallucinating or dreaming. But before considering, in §3.1, the conditions for a proposition's being more probable than not, we need to specify the conditions for a proposition's being evidentially probable *to some extent* due to subjective nonconceptual contents. Let us now leave open the possibility that the extent to which a proposition is made evidentially probable is measurable only comparatively or qualitatively, and not in any informative way by real numbers.

My rough preliminary proposal was that one's subjective nonconceptual contents can be an evidential probability-maker for a proposition for one in virtue of those contents' being explained for one by that proposition. This proposal requires certain important qualifications and clarification of, among other things, the key notion of an *explanation for one*. The latter clarification involves a twofold task, requiring comment on the notion of *explanation* and on the notion of explanation *for one*.

Nonepistemic explanation. Being nonpropositional, one's subjective nonconceptual contents do not themselves explain anything. But they can be explained by a proposition. In fact, both an experience *state* (or event) consisting of attention attraction and the *contents* of such an experience can be explained by a proposition. A general explanation-seeking why-question pertinent to an experience state is: why does this experience state exist at this time? And a corresponding question relevant to the contents of an experience is: why do these contents exist, or occur as they do? An explanatory answer to one of these questions need not be an answer to the other also, but let us not pursue that matter. Let us rather focus on the notion of an explanation of *the subjective nonconceptual contents* of an experience. For first, as suggested earlier, one always has an awareness of the subjective nonconceptual contents of one's current experiences, but the same is not true of the experience states themselves. And second, one must have an awareness of one's *occurrent* evidential probability-makers, as I argued in §2.3.1.

We now need a notion of explanation that does not itself presuppose either the notion of epistemic justification or the notion of evidential probability. Otherwise my account of evidential probability will involve a vicious conceptual circle. Here is an appropriate notion: one thing explains another when and only when the former makes it, to some extent, *understandable why* the latter thing is as it is. Applying this notion to my preliminary story about evidential probability, we can say roughly that a proposition *explains* certain subjective nonconceptual contents if and only if it makes it, to some extent, understandable why those contents are as they are, or equivalently, why those contents occur as they do.

We can simplify matters by characterizing the modal notion of understandability as follows: a proposition makes certain subjective contents' occurring as they do understandable to some extent if and only if anyone who accepts that proposition as a direct result of being presented with those contents will thereby understand why those contents occur as they do. This understanding will be due to one's thereby *having an answer to a why-question* concerning those contents, viz., a question why those contents occur as they do. Thus the relevant explanations are essentially answers to why-questions of a certain sort.[29] We soon shall see some examples that illustrate this point.

My notion of explanation is *non*epistemic in the sense that it does not require the concept of knowledge, justification, or evidential

29 My approach to explanation via why-questions is not altogether new. For discussion of the relation of *scientific* explanations to why-questions, see van Fraassen (1980, Chap. 5) and Bromberger (1966); and for relevant critical discussion, see Teller (1974), Belnap and Steel (1976, Chap. 2), Achinstein (1983, pp. 181–5), Salmon (1984, pp. 101–11), and Temple (1988). However, I am not here endorsing the details of those accounts. None of those theorists relies on a notion of explanation to analyze the concept of evidential probability. In fact, this promising strategy is widely overlooked by contemporary epistemologists and philosophers of science alike.

probability. It requires instead the notion of a proposition that answers a why-question about one's subjective contents. The relevant notion of *understandability to some extent* is thus also nonepistemic. Yet the latter notion does allow for comparative assessments of the extent of understanding provided by the acceptance of propositions. On my view, *any* positive extent of understanding regarding the occurrence of subjective contents requires understanding, or having an answer to a question, why the contents occur as they do. But we must allow not only for one proposition's providing more understanding than another, but also for one explanation's being better than another in virtue of providing better understanding, or better answers to questions, why subjective contents are as they are.

We cannot replace the notion of understandability, or of answering a why-question, by a notion of logical entailment. For an explanation can have a *non*demonstrative connection between its explanans and explanandum. For instance, an explanans might include a statement of the form 'Most *a*'s are *b*'s'. Nor need an explanation be true; a false proposition can be an answer to an explanation-seeking why-question. However, I shall not pursue a general account of the conditions under which a proposition is an answer to a why-question.[30] Such an account is a goal for philosophical semantics. For current purposes, we can proceed with our intuitive sense of a particular proposition's being an answer to a particular why-question. Finally, an explanation need not explain subjective experiential contents of a *visual* sort. There can be explanations of subjective contents that are either visual, auditory, olfactory, tactile, gustatory, kinesthetic, or pain-related.

We can characterize explanation-seeking why-questions by means of distinctions between several prominent senses of 'explanation'. They are: (a) explanation of *what* something is or means, (b) explanation of *how* something functions or of *how* something looks, (c) explanation of *which* of a set has a certain feature, and (d) explanation of *why something is as it is*. Only this last sense pertains to the aforementioned why-questions that determine whether something is an explanation and how good it is. A why-question for current purposes is thus a question why certain sub-

---

30 For contributions to such an account, see Hiz (1962, 1978), Harrah (1963, Chaps. 7, 8), Belnap and Steel (1976, Chaps. 1, 3), and the essays in Kiefer (1983).

jective nonconceptual contents are as they are, or equivalently, why such contents occur as they do. To avoid certain technical complications, I shall restrict my attention to *non*disjunctive explanation-seeking why-questions.

Regarding my subjective contents consisting of an apparent blue book, two obvious why-questions are: why is there an apparent book here (where 'here' refers to part of my visual field), and why is this apparent book apparently blue?[31] Any such question concerning the existence of an actual feature of subjective nonconceptual contents is a relevant why-question for purposes of determining (a) whether something is an explanation relative to those contents, and (b) how good it is from an explanatory point of view. Also relevant, as we shall see in §3.5, are questions why certain features do *not* actually occur in one's subjective contents. But there are why-questions with false presuppositions, and these are not relevant to my subsequent account of evidence. For instance, the question why there is an apparent six-toed demon presented to me now rests on a false presupposition, and thus will turn out to be irrelevant on my account. When I speak of why-questions *about* certain contents, I mean why-questions that do not rest on false presuppositions concerning those contents.

My notion of an explanation *for one* relativizes an explanation to a person, but does so with a weak requirement. We can understand this relativity via the following principle: a proposition, *P*, is an explanation for one of one's subjective nonconceptual contents, *C*, if and only if *P* explains *C* and one understands *P*. I here rely on a notion of understanding that is nonepistemic, that requires at most one's having mere true beliefs, for instance, about the truth conditions for *P*. (For relevant discussion, see Moser [1988a].) A less demanding principle is this: *P* is an explanation for one of *C* if and only if *P* explains *C* and *P* is understand*able* by one in the sense that one would understand *P* upon considering it. The latter principle is less appropriate than the former, since it will commit

---

31 Incidentally, it is not obvious that one can be visually presented with an apparent blue *book* at a particular time. Some philosophers would argue that one can be visually presented only with certain *apparent parts* of an apparent book, such as an apparent front cover and an apparent spine, at a particular time. I shall not try to settle this matter, since it does not significantly affect my account of evidence. We can easily reformulate my account to concern, at the start, apparent parts of apparent books instead of apparent books. But for ease of expression I shall persist in my talk of apparent books.

us, in conjunction with the account under development, to the view that a proposition can be evidentially probable for one when one does not even understand it.

Understandability for one is a feature of many propositions that one has neither thought of nor would think of in the ordinary, or even the extraordinary, course of one's life. Even if quantum theory were understand*able* by Newton in the relevant sense, he did not actually understand it; and this, on my account, precludes its having been evidentially probable for him. What is evidentially probable *for one*, on my account, is limited to what one understands. (Here I agree with Chisholm [1977, p. 13] and Heidelberger [1979].) One's simply having evidence that *would* make a proposition probable for one if one understood it is insufficient for that proposition's actually being evidentially probable for one. Thus I prefer the first of the foregoing two principles. As we shall see, we need the first principle's relativizing of explanation to what one understands to prevent the subsequent account of probability-makers from being too liberal toward the propositions evidentially probable for one. The motivation for it now, in light of the consideration about Newton, is simply that it is initially implausible to say that a proposition is evidentially probable for one when one does not even understand it.

My notion of an explanation for one is clearly not equivalent to the notion of one's *giving* an explanation (of certain subjective contents). The latter notion, unlike the former, requires that one somehow have an explanation in mind. But this requirement is too demanding for a proposition's merely being probable (or justifiable) to some extent for one relative to one's subjective nonconceptual contents. My notion is obviously much weaker. It requires only, in the present context, that one understand a proposition that is, and *can* be used by one as, an explanation of one's subjective nonconceptual contents. A worry that my proposed notion is too weak might arise from a confusion of (a) the conditions for a proposition's being merely evidentially probable, or justifi*able*, for one and (b) the conditions for a proposition's being actually justified for one. But, as we shall see more clearly in §3.2.2, we need to shun that confusion. What is minimally evidentially probable for one need only be what is, from among the propositions one understands, epistemically justifi*able* to some extent on the basis of one's overall evidence. This view preserves the essential modal component of what is evidentially prob*able*, and it restricts the bearers of evidential probability for one to what one actually understands.

Thus far, then, my account proposes this: the notion of noninferential epistemic justification (specifically, justifiability) should be analyzed in part via the notion of unconditional evidential probability; the latter notion should be analyzed in part via the notion of explanation of subjective nonconceptual contents; and this latter notion should be analyzed in part via the notion of making understandable, or providing an answer, why certain subjective nonconceptual contents occur as they do. Some philosophers construe the notion of explanation as requiring an epistemic notion, such as the notion of epistemic probability. (See, for example, Putnam [1983c, pp. 291–8] and Chisholm [1980, p. 562].) But for my purposes such a strategy has things backwards. To develop my account further, we need to clarify the basic notion of a proposition's being evidentially probable to some extent. And then we need to clarify the stronger notions of a proposition's being evidentially more probable than its denial, and a proposition's having maximal evidential probability. However, we need to postpone the latter two tasks until §§3.1 and 3.2, when the basic notion of a minimal evidential probability-maker is sufficiently clear.

I have suggested that a proposition is *evidentially probable to some extent* for one relative to one's subjective nonconceptual contents if and only if that proposition is evidentially probable for one, but is not necessarily evidentially more probable than its denial, relative to those contents. My rough preliminary thesis was that a proposition, *P*, can be evidentially probable to some extent for one relative to one's subjective nonconceptual contents in virtue of *P*'s explaining those contents for one, even if *P* does not explain those contents better than does every contrary proposition one understands. This thesis gives a rough initial portrayal of a proposition's being unconditionally evidentially probable to some extent. Now we need to remove the roughness via clarification of the notion of better explanation and the notion of a contravener.

Better explanation and contraveners. We need to introduce two preliminary notions to clarify the relevant notion of better explanation. The first is the notion of a *gratuitous entity*. From an explanatory viewpoint, a gratuitous entity relative to explained subjective nonconceptual contents C is an item posited by an explanation of C that is not itself represented in C by means of any corresponding feature, i.e., by means of any feature that represents some of the explanatory item's own features. Thus a gratuitous explainer relative to C is an explainer not represented in C by means of any corresponding feature. This notion of a gratuitous explainer is central to the plausible idea that one explanation is better than another if, other things being equal, the first does not posit gratuitous items whereas the second does. We shun gratuitous explainers whenever possible when we are after correct empirical explanations, because they are arbitrary from the standpoint of the empirical data needing explanation. Their arbitrariness consists of course in their not being constrained at all by the relevant empirical data.

By way of example, my current experience only of an apparent blue book is better explained by the physical-object proposition that there is a blue book here than by the proposition that a Cartesian demon is stimulating my brain in a certain way. Even if those explanatory propositions answer the same why-questions about my subjective nonconceptual contents, only the Cartesian proposition posits a gratuitous item in answering those questions. A Cartesian demon is *not* represented in my experience by means of any of its own features, whereas a blue book is: by hypothesis I now experience only an apparent blue book. We shall return to this important matter in the discussion of justification skepticism in §3.5. At that point I shall clarify further my notion of a gratuitous explainer.

The second preliminary notion is that of comparative informational specificity. Let us say that a proposition, P, is informationally more specific than a proposition, Q, if and only if P logically entails Q, but is not logically entailed by Q. Consider a case where two explanations are on a par with each other regarding the answering of why-questions and the positing of gratuitous entities, but where one of the explanations is more specific than the other. For instance, consider a proposition, P, having the form 'a is F', that is an explanation of contents C, and a proposition, Q, that is the existential generalization on P, or instead of Q, a nonredundant disjunction, $(P \lor R)$, where R does not entail P. Even if P and Q, or P and $(P \lor R)$, are equals regarding answering why-questions about C and positing gratuitous entities, P nonetheless is the better explanation, owing to its being more specific.

We now can introduce the following notion of a decisively better explanation, in order to clarify my initial portrayal of minimal evidential probability:

> One proposition, *P*, is a *decisively better explanation* of subjective contents *C* than is another proposition, *Q*, if and only if (i) *P* explains *C*, and (ii) either (a) *P* answers all the explanation-seeking why-questions about *C* answered by *Q*, but posits fewer gratuitous entities and fewer kinds of gratuitous entities than *Q* does, or (b) while positing no more gratuitous entities or kinds of gratuitous entities than *Q* posits, *P* answers all the explanation-seeking why-questions about *C* answered by *Q*, and still others, or (c) *P* and *Q* answer the same why-questions about *C* without either positing more gratuitous entities or kinds of gratuitous entities than the other, but *P* is informationally more specific than *Q*.

Here I assume that the comparative goodness of an explanation of subjective contents is basically a function of how the explanation answers why-questions about those contents.[32] Yet my principle concerns only a special sort of explanatory goodness: decisive goodness. This sort of goodness, I shall propose, is conceptually relevant to various notions of evidential probability.

One might object to my principle on the ground that there can be cases where *P* is a better explanation of contents *C* than is *Q* even though *P* fails to answer *all* the why-questions *Q* answers about *C*. Perhaps my principle could handle such cases if we add this disjunct to its clause (ii): (d) while positing no more gratuitous entities or kinds of gratuitous entities than *Q* posits, *P* answers *more* nondisjunctive why-questions about *C* than *Q* answers. (We need the qualifier 'nondisjunctive' to avoid the potential problem that every explanation of *C* answers an infinite number of disjunctive why-questions about *C*.) This objection suggests this weaker notion of a better explanation:

> One proposition, *P*, is a *nondecisively better explanation* of subjective contents *C* than is another proposition, *Q*, if and only if (i) *P* explains *C*, and (ii) while positing no more gratuitous entities or kinds of

---

32 I shall not assume now that the comparative goodness of an explanation is also a function of an explanation's being integrable in a comprehensive theory. Such an assumption risks circularity now, as it apparently requires constraints concerning evidential probability or at least best explanation on the comprehensive theory in question. Nor is it obvious to me that the better of two explanations must be integrable in a comprehensive theory. A related, more general issue: could not one's experience provide evidential probability and epistemic justification for numerous basically unrelated propositions, but fail to lend itself to a comprehensive coherent explanation? I think so, even though many coherence-oriented theories seem to rule this out in principle.

gratuitous entities than Q posits, P answers more nondisjunctive explanation-seeking why-questions about C than Q answers.

One might object that P could answer more why-questions about C than Q answers while P answers only the relatively *unimportant* questions and Q answers the relatively *important* questions. This objection seems to have some intuitive appeal, but of course it succeeds only if accompanied by clarification of the relevant notion of importance. Given my aim to analyze the notion of evidential probability, I obviously cannot use a notion of importance that presupposes the notion of evidential probability; nor can I plausibly use a notion of *pragmatic* importance.[33] And since there are no other obviously relevant notions of importance, it is not altogether clear what the objection means, or how it bears on my aim.

Perhaps we can allay some worries by acknowledging that non-decisively better explanation is not, on my view, an independent determinant of comparative evidential probability. There is not, on my view, any significant logical connection between (a) P's being a nondecisively better explanation of contents C than is Q and (b) P's being evidentially more probable than Q relative to C. However, I do hold that there is a significant connection between (b) and P's being a decisively better explanation of C than is Q. We can appreciate this connection only after we consider the notion of contravening.

Typically, evidential probability-makers are defeasible. They typically can fail to be such probability-makers for a particular proposition in certain circumstances, specifically when one's experience includes a contravening feature. (The *possible* exceptions are the experiential probability-makers for such "Cartesian" propositions as that I exist, that I think, and that I am aware.) Two basic notions of contravening are essential to the notion of an unconditional evidential probability-maker. We cannot define these notions without circularity via the notion of a probability-maker,

33 Here I dissent from Cornman (1980, Chaps. 1, 8, 9), who explicitly relies on nonevidential pragmatic considerations in his explanatory foundationalist account of epistemic justification. In agreement with most justification skeptics, I fail to see how pragmatic considerations can be essential to the notion of *epistemic* justification. One obvious problem is that what is pragmatic for one need not be supported by one's evidence. (Incidentally, I also find that Cornman's account does not properly acknowledge the role of explanation and nonconceptual experience in *non*inferential justification.)

100

since the latter notion presupposes the notion of contravening. Thus for definitional purposes we need to speak of a proposition's being *contravened as an explanation* for a person.

Let us begin to explain the role of contravening via specific subjective nonconceptual contents. The first kind of contravening, *indirect* contravening, is familiar from everyday experience. Suppose that C is my subjective nonconceptual contents consisting of an apparent blue book, and that P is the proposition that there is a blue book before me. Suppose also that P explains C for me. But assume further that I have as part of my overall subjective contents an apparent light source generating a hologram of a blue book before me. Let $C^\star$ be that part of my contents. $C^\star$ is *negatively relevant* to C in a sense to be specified momentarily. In such a case P is indirectly contravened as an explanation of C for me if P does not itself explain $C^\star$ and does not play an essential role in an explanation of C and $C^\star$ for me (in the sense that for every such explanation for me that entails P, the proposition that P answers no why-questions about C and $C^\star$ beyond those answered when P is omitted).

But when in general are subjective nonconceptual contents $C^\star$ negatively relevant to other subjective nonconceptual contents C? That is, when, in order to be evidentially probable relative to C, must an explanation of C either itself explain $C^\star$ or play an essential role in such an explanation? This principle gives the answer:

> S's subjective nonconceptual contents $C^\star$ are *negatively relevant* to his subjective nonconceptual contents C, relative to a proposition's (P's) explaining C, if and only if (i) there is an explanation, E, for S of such contents that entails either (a) that in the present case not both C and $C^\star$ are objectively veridical (i.e., representative of objective contents), or (b) that in most cases for S not both C-type and $C^\star$-type contents are objectively veridical when they occur together, or (c) that $\sim P$, or (d) that a certain information-source, I, is a source of truth in most cases concerning C-type contents and I affirms, at least by implication, that $\sim P$, and (ii) E is a decisively better explanation of C and $C^\star$ than is every contrary explanation S has.

When S's contents $C^\star$ are negatively relevant in this sense, S's explanation of C, if it is to be evidentially probable for S relative to C, must play an essential role in an explanation for S of $C^\star$ too. The hologram example illustrates this point. We shall see in §2.5 that subjective contents need not be occurrent, but need only be retrievable from memory in a certain way, to play a role in contravening and probability-making. At that point it will become clear that the sort of occurrent evidential probability essential to occurrent justifiability requires the absence of nonoccurrent as well as occurrent uncontravened contravening.

My talk of *objectively veridical* contents connotes *objective* contents of the sort illustrated earlier. That is, it connotes contents that make up, at least in part, how things are independently of one's corresponding experiences thereof. Since the familiar apparent bent stick in the bathtub is not really a bent stick in the bathtub, one's contents consisting of such an apparent bent stick are not altogether objectively veridical in the relevant sense. But my account does not presuppose that some of our subjective contents actually are objectively veridical.

My hologram example assumes that the relevant indirect contravening is itself uncontravened. This means that there is *no additional part* of my overall subjective nonconceptual contents relative to which P does play an essential role in an explanation of C and $C^\star$ for me. Such uncontravened indirect contravening precludes the probability-making efficacy of subjective nonconceptual contents relative to certain explanatory propositions. Thus in the foregoing example P would lack evidential probability for me, given its failure to play an essential explanatory role for me. The role of such contravening in evidential probability introduces a certain total evidence requirement on such probability. For, given the relevance of indirect contravening, any feature of one's subjective nonconceptual contents is potentially relevant to the evidential probability of an explainer. But of course this does not mean that one is always presented with subjective contents that are actually negatively relevant to other contents one has. It is a separate issue whether indirect contravening is ever-present.

Two other examples illustrate indirect contravening. Consider first the case of Ann, a perceptual psychologist who wrote her doctoral dissertation on visual illusions. Ann can explain in detail why she, along with the rest of us, visually experiences the familiar illusory pool of water on the road ahead during summertime driving. Specifically she can explain that this illusion is one of many peculiar effects due to changes in the refractive index of the atmosphere. Ann's explaining the apparent pool of water in this way is decisively better for her, relative to her overall experiential contents, than is any other such explanation she has, including the explanation that there is actually a pool of water ahead. The latter explanation faces a serious problem from Ann's experiencing (apparently) dry pavement whenever she reaches the place where she expects the familiar pool to be. While driving along a country highway one summer day, Ann again seems to see an apparent pool ahead. Nothing in this visual experience itself indicates that the apparent pool is illusory; in this respect Ann's illusory experience is typical. Yet the proposition that there is a pool ahead is not evidentially probable for Ann. This proposition has been indirectly contravened for Ann, relative to her overall contents, by the decisively better explanation she has.

One might object that my example of Ann involves superfluous details. On this objection, Ann need not have the better alternative explanation of her contents consisting of an apparent pool of water on the otherwise dry road ahead. (Call the latter contents 'C-type contents'.) It is sufficient, one might propose, that Ann's having C-type contents has always been accompanied by her having an experience of (apparent) dry pavement on the road ahead. But I doubt that such constant conjunction itself can provide a contravener. Echoing Hume, we must ask why one should think that past constant conjunction by itself affects the probability of propositions based on current experience. I propose that such constant conjunction bears on probability for one only insofar as it figures in the explanatory value for one of a proposition relative to one's experiential contents.

Consider next the case of Mary the magician. Betty knows Mary well, and the best explanation of Betty's interactions with Mary involves the proposition that Mary is a truth-teller concerning matters magical. During Betty's first viewing of Mary's new magic show, Betty seems to see a priceless painting cut in half. But Mary assures Betty that she has just witnessed some fancy trickery, and that the painting remains intact. Nothing in Betty's visual experience of the apparently severed painting indicates that the painting is really intact; in this respect Betty's experience of the magic show is typical. But the proposition that the painting is severed is not evidentially probable for Betty. This proposition has been indirectly contravened for Betty, relative to her overall experiential contents, because of the explanatory value for her of the proposition that trustworthy Mary has testified that the painting remains intact.

The second kind of contravening, *direct* contravening, is also easy to illustrate. Suppose that one has subjective nonconceptual contents consisting of an apparent blue book, and that those contents are explained for one by the well-known Cartesian hypothesis that an evil demon is causing one's subjective contents. Recall that an explanatory item is gratuitous if and only if it is not itself represented in the explained subjective contents by means of a corresponding feature. The Cartesian hypothesis posits an evil demon that causes one to have certain subjective nonconceptual contents, such as those consisting of an apparent blue book. But if such a demon is not itself represented in one's explained subjective contents by means of a corresponding feature, it is gratuitous relative to those contents. And if it is thus gratuitous, the Cartesian hypothesis is directly contravened relative to one's subjective contents.

Direct contravening is itself uncontravened when one has no subjective nonconceptual contents relative to which the initially contravened explainer is *not* gratuitous. Thus once again the role of contravening introduces a certain total evidence requirement on evidential probability, since it provides for the potential relevance of any feature of one's subjective nonconceptual contents. When direct contravening is itself uncontravened, it precludes the probability-making efficacy of subjective nonconceptual contents relative to certain explanatory propositions for a person. In such a case, a proposition such as the Cartesian hypothesis lacks evidential probability even to some extent for one, and thus is at most a mere *possibility*.

But why exactly do I banish gratuitous explainers from the realm of empirical evidential probablity? For reasons outlined earlier, I take (phenomenal) experiential contents to set the basic constraints on empirical evidential probability. Relative to the constraints of one's experiential contents, no gratuitous explainer is evidentially more supportable than any other, since every gratuitous explainer (by definition) lacks corresponding representation in one's contents. But surely not every gratuitous explainer is evidentially probable for one relative to one's experiential contents. So, I propose, no gratuitous explainer is thus probable. Let us call this 'the multiplicity objection' to gratuitous explainers. In essence, it is: there are no evidentially relevant differences among gratuitous explainers; surely not all such explainers are evidentially probable; so none is. Of course one might object that experience can supply evidence for gratuitous explainers. But this objection must be accompanied by a specific notion of empirical evidence, a notion that avoids the multiplicity problem in a compelling way. I doubt that such a notion is forthcoming.

But what about the evidential probability of atomic theory, for example, specifically its commitment to (currently) unobservable electrons? My account fits with at least three noteworthy positions. First, I could endorse some sort of operationism about electrons, and thereby deny that explanation via electrons is gratuitous. Or, second, I could simply deny that a nonoperationist commitment to electrons is now *empirically* evidentially probable, and allow that such a commitment might nonetheless enjoy some sort of *non*empirical evidential support. Or, third, I might argue that commitment to electrons is probable in virtue of its being an essential part of a general physical theory that is not gratuitous in the way that the Cartesian demon hypothesis is. One could build a plausible case for each of these options, but I shall not digress. Instead I shall be content with my account's compatibility with these options.

The two basic notions of contravening, then, are:

> A proposition, *P*, is *directly contravened* for a person, *S*, as an explanation for him of his subjective nonconceptual contents *C* = *df*. Relative to *C* all the explanatory entities posited by *P* are gratuitous.

> A proposition, *P*, is *indirectly contravened* for *S* as an explanation for him of his subjective nonconceptual contents *C* = *df*. (i) *S*'s contents *C*★ are (a part of) *S*'s subjective contents that are negatively relevant to *C*, (ii) *P* itself does not explain *C*★, and (iii) *P* plays no essential role in an explanation of *C* and *C*★ for *S*, in the sense that for every such explanation for *S* that entails *P*, the proposition that *P* answers no why-questions about *C* and *C*★ beyond those answered when *P* is omitted.

Direct contravening bears directly on the explanatory relation between a proposition and certain subjective nonconceptual contents, whereas indirect contravening does not. Indirect contravening bears on the explanatory relation between a proposition and subjective nonconceptual contents without challenging directly the explanatory relation between them. Such direct and indirect contravenings, *when themselves uncontravened*, undermine the probability-making efficacy of subjective nonconceptual contents relative to certain explanatory propositions.

My refined proposal then is this: one's subjective nonconceptual contents are a minimal evidential probability-maker for a proposition that explains those contents for one when and only when one has no uncontravened direct or indirect contravening of that proposition's explaining those contents. On my account, contravening itself has a basis in one's experience. This is preferable to the various accounts in circulation that allow *mere beliefs* to be defeaters of justification.[34] Mere beliefs can be held for bad reasons or with no supporting evidential reasons, and thus they do not necessarily have the evidential backing needed to be defeaters. Genuine defeaters must themselves be grounded in experience; otherwise they can be created arbitrarily.

A refined notion. We now have this notion of a minimal unconditional evidential probability-maker provided by subjective nonconceptual contents:

> Subjective nonconceptual contents, C, are occurrently a *minimal unconditional probability-maker* for a proposition, P, for a person, S, = df. (i) S is presented with C, (ii) P is an explanation of C for S, and (iii) S has no uncontravened direct or indirect contravening of P's being an explanation of C.

We shall see that this notion underlies all other notions of evidential probability.

Three points further clarify the nature of a minimal unconditional probability-maker. First, such an evidential probability-maker is perspectival in the sense that it is *for a person*. This perspectival feature comes from the fact that subjective nonconceptual contents are person-relative: your subjective contents are yours and not necessarily mine also. Given this feature, your having an unconditional evidential probability-maker for a proposition does not entail my having one for this proposition also. But since two people can have type-identical subjective contents, they can have type-identical unconditional probability-makers for a proposition.

Second, although a minimal unconditional probability-maker is perspectival, it is not belief-dependent. It is false that subjective nonconceptual contents are a minimal probability-maker for a proposition for one only if one believes that they are. In §3.3 I shall distinguish various notions of something's being a probability-

---

34 Two such recent accounts come from Pollock (1974, Chap. 2; 1986, p. 177; 1987) and Harman (1986, Chap. 4).

maker *for a person*. At that point it will become clear that evidential probability-makers do not depend on one's believing that they are probability-makers. Here I simply note that according to the opposite view one's having evidence for a proposition requires one's having *the concept* of a probability-maker; for one must have the concepts constituting the objects of one's beliefs. Surely the former requirement is excessive.

Third, subjective contents' being a minimal unconditional probability-maker for a proposition for one is not epistemically dependent. It does not depend on one's knowing, or even one's justifiably believing, that the contents are a probability-maker for the relevant proposition. Subjective contents' being a minimal probability-maker for an understood proposition for one requires only that (a) one be presented with those contents, (b) an explanation relation (of the sort mentioned earlier) obtain between the contents and the proposition, and (c) one have no uncontravened contravening of that proposition's explaining those contents. I shall return to this claim in §3.3 to provide the needed support. Yet I note here that according to the opposite view that affirms epistemic dependency, one's having an unconditional probability-maker requires one's having the concept of such a probability-maker. This, I have suggested, is an implausible requirement.

We now have a fairly straightforward notion of a minimal unconditional probability-maker. This notion will enable us to complete the earlier discussion of Probability Internalism.

c. Internalism unified

The following principle represents a central thesis of Moderate Probability Internalism:

> MPI. A proposition of the form *that there is an X* is occurrently unconditionally probable to some extent for S if and only if (i) S is presented with an apparent X, (ii) S understands the proposition in question, and (iii) S has no uncontravened contravening of that proposition's explaining his subjective contents consisting of an apparent X.

This principle concerns only occurrent evidential probability due solely to nonconceptual experience, i.e., *unconditional* or *noninferential* evidential probability. This principle assumes that a proposition of the form 'that there is an X' (where 'X' can denote a

107

physical object) is *an explainer for S* of his subjective contents consisting of an apparent *X*, so long as he understands that proposition. If *S* does not understand a particular proposition, it is not an explainer *for him*; nor is it then evidentially probable *for him*.

Two considerations add to the plausibility of MPI. First, when it is satisfied, *S* has occurrent experiential evidence for the proposition that there is an *X*, because of his being presented with an apparent *X*. Second, when MPI is satisfied, *S* has no uncontravened contravening of the relevant proposition's being an explanation of the relevant subjective contents. I find it difficult to think of anything else, beyond the conditions of MPI, that might plausibly be required for a proposition, such as a physical-object proposition, of the form 'that there is an *X*', to be occurrently evidentially probable to some extent.

We now can begin to challenge the extreme probability skeptic who claims that no physical-object propositions are minimally evidentially probable for us. We can challenge such a skeptic to explain what else can plausibly be required for the minimal evidential probability of a physical-object proposition. Apparently it is now the burden of the extreme probability skeptic to show that there is a plausible notion of minimal evidential probability whose requirements are not met by the satisfaction of MPI. To my knowledge, no probability skeptic has even suggested such a plausible notion.

Alternatively, the skeptic might accept MPI, but object that it is never satisfied. Here the skeptic's likely strategy is to show that uncontravened contravening is ever-present. But it is not at all clear how this can be shown, or even that this can be shown. So let us leave the probability skeptic at bay until his challenge can be made more plausible in §3.5. At that point we shall see that it is really the probability skeptic who faces a serious challenge.

Recall that Moderate Internalism in its initial form needed revision. The problem was that propositions that affirm one's being in a psychological state are occurrently unconditionally probable for one only if one's apparently being in that state is presented to one. For such propositions to be occurrently evidentially probable for one, one must satisfy a condition of second-order awareness suggested by Radical Internalism. Thus let us consider:

RPI. A proposition of the form *that S experiences (or, seems to experience) an X* is occurrently unconditionally probable to some extent for *S* if and only if (i) *S* is presented with an apparent *X*, (ii) *S* is

108

presented with his apparently being aware of an apparent X, (iii) S understands the proposition in question, and (iv) S has no uncontravened contravening of that proposition's explaining his subjective contents consisting of his apparently being aware of an apparent X.

This principle does not conflict with MPI, since it concerns the occurrent probability of only a special kind of proposition: a proposition that affirms that one is in a particular psychological state. Indeed, all the considerations that can be adduced in favor of Moderate Internalism apply *mutatis mutandis* to RPI.

To emphasize the compatibility of RPI and MPI, we can formulate a general principle of evidential probability internalism that accommodates both RPI and MPI:

> *Awareness Internalism*: A proposition, P, occurrently is unconditionally evidentially probable to some extent for S if and only if (i) S is presented with what is posited by P, (ii) S understands P, and (iii) S has no uncontravened contravening of P's explaining what is presented to him.

Awareness Internalism unifies the internalism of RPI and MPI. Regarding a proposition of the form 'There is an X', let us say that S is presented with what is posited by that proposition if and only if S is presented with an apparent X. And regarding a proposition of the form 'S sees (or, seems to see) an X', let us say that S is presented with what is posited by that proposition if and only if S is presented with an apparent X *and* with his apparently seeing (or, seeming to see) an X. These notions enable us to rely on Awareness Internalism to talk about probability internalism *in general*, without focusing on the differences between the principles MPI and RPI.

Awareness Internalism does *not* imply that a proposition is unconditionally probable for one only if one has actually drawn an inference from subjective contents to an explanation provided by that proposition. Yet whenever one satisfies Awareness Internalism, there will be an inference to an explanation that one *can* draw from the subjective contents of one's awareness state (e.g., there being an apparent X) to the relevant proposition (e.g., that there is an X). We thus can talk of the *inferential basis* of evidentially probable propositions, in the sense that when Awareness Internalism is satisfied, an inference to an explanation *can* be drawn regarding such propositions. Yet one need not actually draw such an inference simply for a *proposition* to be evidentially probable for one. To stipulate otherwise is to make the conditions for evidentially probable propositions excessive. This point will become clear, if it is not already, in §§3.3 and 3.4. For now, we should simply recall that minimally evidentially probable propositions need only be justifi*able* to some extent; they need not be justifiedly believed or even actually justified.

Awareness Internalism identifies how there can be the *non*propositional, nonconceptual probability-makers needed in light of the argument of §2.2. A special virtue of Awareness Internalism is that it ties down the minimal unconditional probability of propositions to the subjective contents of one's awareness states. It thereby avoids the familiar coherentist problem of neglecting the role of experience in evidential probability.

Another virtue of Awareness Internalism is that it allows physical-object propositions to be evidentially probable solely on the basis of experience. Awareness Internalism does not require subjective *beliefs* about what one *seems* to perceive. This is desirable if only because people rarely have such subjective beliefs. Thus Awareness Internalism is psychologically more realistic than traditional versions of foundationalism. Awareness Internalism allows also for derivative, propositional probability-makers, and even for nonoccurrent probability-makers, as we shall see in §§2.4 and 2.5. In addition, Awareness Internalism lays the basis for a straightforward foundationalist account of justifying epistemic reasons, as we shall see in §3.2. The major conclusion now, however, is that we can recommend Awareness Internalism over Moderate and Radical Externalism.

We can draw three additional important lessons from my account of unconditional probability-makers. First, we should not identify unconditional evidential probability either with subjective, belief-dependent probability or with the sort of "objective," experience-independent probability familiar from various statistical, frequency, and propensity interpretations. (In §3.2 I shall apply this lesson to familiar lottery-style examples.) Second, it is doubtful that evidential probability is usefully measurable by real numbers.[35] But this doubt, as we shall see in Chapter 3, does not preclude comparative or qualitative assessments of such probability. Third, contrary to a familiar claim of C. I. Lewis (1946, 1952), evidential probability

---

35 Additional support for my doubt about the numerical measurability of evidential probability has been provided by Pollock (1983; 1986, Chap. 4).

does not require a basis of certainty; instead, it requires a basis in what is presented in experience. The best way to show that minimal evidential probability does not require certainty is to explain how there can be minimally evidentially probable propositions that do not depend on any proposition that is certain. This chapter has explained not only how there can be such propositions, but also how unconditional evidential probability supervenes on a nonconceptual evidence basis. Thus we no longer should think of such probability as depending on certainty or as being purely propositional.

In concluding this section, I should answer an objection that William Alston (1988, p. 271) has raised against my Awareness Internalism. Alston claims that my Internalism "has the crushing disability that one can never complete the formulation of a sufficient condition for justification." Alston's argument for this claim runs as follows:

> ... suppose that we begin by taking condition C to be sufficient for the justification of S's belief that P. But then we must add that S must be aware of C (i.e., the satisfaction of condition C) in order to be justified. Call this enriched condition $C1$. But then $C1$ is not enough by itself either; S must be aware of $C1$. So that must be added to yield a still richer condition, $C2$. And so on ad infinitum.

The flaw in this argument is simple but fatal. The argument fails to distinguish between (a) awareness of *the evidence required for justification* and (b) awareness of *a sufficient condition for justification*. Clearly my Awareness Internalism requires awareness only of the evidence required for occurrent evidential probability and justification. It does not require awareness of the satisfaction of a sufficient condition for occurrent probability and justification. My Internalism also provides for a clear distinction between (c) the evidence required for unconditional occurrent probability and (d) a sufficient condition for such probability. The evidence itself consists of what is presented to one, and the sufficient condition in question involves not only such evidence, but also one's understanding the relevant proposition, and the absence of uncontravened contravening. The clear distinction between (a) and (b), as well as between (c) and (d), undercuts Alston's objection to Awareness Internalism.

Let us turn now to *derivative*, propositional evidential probability-makers.

2.4 Internalism and derivative probability-makers

Even if subjective nonconceptual contents provide the only unconditional evidential probability-makers, there can be *derivative* probability-makers that are propositional. Derivative probability-makers can be provided by believed propositions and by propositions to which one assents. (Propositions to which one assents are not necessarily propositions one believes, since the former do not necessarily involve a dispositional belief state of the sort characterized in §1.1.) Let us say, as an initial portrayal, that a *derivative probability-maker* depends for its being a probability-maker on another probability-maker.

An example will help. Suppose that I have (a) a propositional experience whereby I judge that this lemon is sour, (b) a propositional experience whereby I judge that that lemon is sour, and (c) a similar propositional experience regarding each of the ten lemons I have randomly sampled, where each of these experiences involves my judging that the relevant proposition is true. Assume also that each of the propositions in question is supported, in the absence of contravening, by my subjective nonconceptual contents consisting of an apparent sour lemon. Taken together, the propositional objects of the experiences in question can be a derivative minimal probability-maker for me for the proposition that all lemons are sour. And this latter proposition, when genuinely affirmed or believed by me in such a case, can be a derivative minimal probability-maker for me for the further proposition that the untested lemon in my hand is sour. (I use 'genuinely affirm' to connote assent in the sense of §1.1.)

Thus a genuinely affirmed or believed proposition can be a derivative probability-maker for a proposition if it is supported ultimately by another probability-maker, viz., an unconditional probability-maker. In fact, a derivative probability-maker requires such support to terminate a potentially endless regress of required derivative probability-makers. Without the availability of such support for derivative probability-makers, the argument of §2.2 will threaten us with extreme probability skepticism.

Let us turn now to the exact conditions for an occurrent derivative probability-maker that is supported directly by an unconditional probability-maker. A derivative probability-maker is occurrent for one when the relevant propositional object is present to one's aware-ness, i.e., when one is aware of the relevant proposition. We now can introduce the following notion of an occurrent basic proposi-tional probability-maker (where 'basic' means simply 'basic *relative to other propositions*' and not 'unconditional'):

> A proposition, P, that is an object of S's believing or assenting is occurrently a *minimal basic propositional probability-maker* for a prop-osition, Q, for S = df. (i) P is present to S's awareness, (ii) there is a minimal unconditional probability-maker for P for S, (iii) S un-derstands Q, (iv) P logically entails Q, or P either explains or is explained by Q; (v) if P is disjunctive and explains Q, then P does not explain Q only because Q is explained by a disjunct inessential to P's having an unconditional probability-maker, or if P is dis-junctive and explained by Q, then Q does not explain P only because Q explains a disjunct inessential to P's having an unconditional prob-ability-maker, and (vi) S has no uncontravened contravening re-garding (iv).

A basic propositional probability-maker, P, for one must be grounded in one's experience in the sense that P is directly supported by an unconditional probability-maker from one's experience. This requirement preserves the central role of experience in evidential probability. We can say that a basic propositional probability-maker is *doubly occurrent* when it is occurrent for one *and* when its sup-porting unconditional probability-maker is also occurrent for one (in the sense specified in §2.3.2b).

My proposed notion allows for an occurrent basic propositional probability-maker in a case where (a) there is an unconditional probability-maker for P for me, (b) P logically entails Q, (c) I consciously affirm that P and understand Q, and (d) I have no uncontravened contravening of P's entailing Q. The notion of con-travening relevant to (d) is simply this:

> P's logically entailing Q is contravened for S = df. There is an ex-planation for S of his subjective nonperceptual contents that (a) en-tails that P does not entail Q, and (b) is decisively better than every contrary explanation S has for those contents.

This notion of contravening obviously assumes that subjective con-tents need not be perceptual, but can be the contents of a *non*per-ceptual experience as characterized in §2.3.2a. Apparent conceptual relations of inclusion and exclusion between concepts are paradigm instances of subjective contents that are nonperceptual in the relevant sense. Such relations are the sorts of contents whose explanation is directly relevant to the contravening of an entailment relation for a person.

But my notion of an occurrent basic propositional probability-maker does not restrict the relation between P and Q to logical entailment; it explicitly allows for *non*demonstrative explanatory relations also. My underlying assumption is twofold. First, a (possibly conjunctive) proposition, P, that provides support for an inductive generalization, Q, can be an occurrent basic propositional probability-maker for Q for one when (a) one consciously affirms that P and understands Q, (b) P is supported by an unconditional probability-maker for one, and (c) one has no uncontravened contravening of Q's explaining P. In such a case, the probability-making relation derives in part from Q's being an explanation of P for one.[36]

Clause (v) of my definition meets a potential problem from disjunctive explainers and explained propositions. It prevents a disjunction's being able to derive probability via explanatory considerations about one of its disjuncts that has no basis in experience.

The sorts of contravening relevant to explanatory relations between propositions are directly analogous to the direct and indirect contravening characterized in §2.3.2b. P's being explained by Q is *directly* contravened for S if and only if Q is directly contravened as an explanation of P for S. And P's being explained by Q is *indirectly* contravened for S if and only if Q is indirectly contravened as an explanation of P for S. The only relevant difference between these notions of contravening and the earlier notions is that now we need to construe explanatory gratuitousness (in the case of direct contravening) and negative relevance (in the case of indirect contravening) relative to *the truth of a proposition* as well as to nonconceptual contents. Such a construal is, however, quite natural; it raises no special complications.

Thus we now need to talk about what is gratuitous relative to situations that are minimally sufficient for propositions' being true. And whereas I characterized negative relevance in §2.3.2b as a re-

---

36 In accord with this view, Gilbert Harman has argued at length that inductive inferential relations between propositions are explanatory relations. See, for example, Harman (1965, 1970, 1973, 1980). See also Thagard (1988).

lation between parts of one's subjective nonconceptual contents, we now need to expand that characterization as follows:

> S's subjective nonconceptual contents C are *negatively relevant* to a proposition, P, relative to a proposition's (Q's) explaining P, if and only if (i) there is an explanation, E, for S of C and P that entails either (a) that in the present case it is false both that C is objectively veridical (i.e., representative of objective contents) and that P is true, or (b) that in most cases for S it is false both that C-type contents are objectively veridical and that P is true, or (c) that ~Q, or (d) that a certain information-source, I, is a source of truth in most cases concerning C-type contents and I affirms, at least by implication, that ~Q, and (ii) E is a decisively better explanation of C and P than is every contrary explanation S has.

This characterization is straightforwardly analogous to the earlier notion of negative relevance.

The second of my two earlier-mentioned assumptions is that a proposition, P, can be an occurrent basic propositional probability-maker for Q for one when (a) one consciously assents to P and understands Q, (b) P is supported by an unconditional probability-maker for one, (c) P explains Q for one, and (d) one has no un-contravened contravening of P's explaining Q. Once again, the relevant sorts of contravening are straightforwardly analogous to the direct and indirect contravening characterized in §2.3.2b.

My remarks about explanation in §2.3.2 are also generally applicable now. But as I suggested, there is a minor difference. Whereas the earlier definition involves the notion of explanation of subjective nonconceptual contents, I now rely also on the notion of explanation *why a proposition is true*. Since the latter notion is not unusual at all, and in fact follows the earlier notion without complication, we need not pursue it here. Let it suffice to say that everything said in §2.3.2b about explanation why subjective contents occur can be used, *mutatis mutandis*, to clarify the notion of explanation why a proposition is true.

Not all derivative probability-makers need be *basic* propositional probability-makers. There can be occurrent *non*basic derivative probability-makers in this sense:

> A proposition, P, that is an object of S's believing or assenting is occurrently a *minimal nonbasic propositional probability-maker* for a proposition, Q, for S = df. (i) P is present to S's awareness, (ii) there is a minimal propositional probability-maker for P for S that ultimately depends (for its being a probability-maker) on, or is iden-

tical to, a minimal basic propositional probability-maker for S, (iii) S understands Q, (iv) P logically entails Q, or P either explains or is explained by Q, (v) if P is disjunctive and explains Q, then P does not explain Q only because Q is explained by a disjunct inessential to P's having a probability-maker, or if P is disjunctive and explained by Q, then Q does not explain P only because Q explains a disjunct inessential to P's having a probability-maker, and (vi) S has no uncontravened contravening regarding (iv).

The key feature of such a nonbasic probability-maker is that its proximate supporting probability-maker is *not* an unconditional probability-maker, but is another *propositional* probability-maker. This latter supporting probability-maker must itself either be a basic propositional probability-maker or have a probability-making ancestry that ultimately leads back to a basic propositional probability-maker. Nonbasic propositional probability-makers are thus supported in part by other propositional probability-makers: this is what makes them *non*basic. My remarks about contravening apply straightforwardly to the notion of a nonbasic probability-maker. And as before, we can say that a nonbasic probability-maker is *doubly occurrent* when it *and* its probability-making ancestors are occurrent.

The dependency relation mentioned in my notion of a nonbasic probability-maker need not be direct. Not all nonbasic probability-makers need be directly dependent on basic propositional probability-makers. But at least indirectly all nonbasic probability-makers do depend on basic probability-makers, as all theorems at least indirectly depend on axioms. Indirect dependency occurs when a basic probability-maker, B, makes probable a nonbasic probability-maker, $N1$, and $N1$ makes probable a further nonbasic probability-maker, $N2$, but B does not itself make $N2$ probable.

Let us now identify some salient features of minimal evidential probability-makers in general. First, there can be a minimal evidential probability-maker for a proposition that is false, as when one's subjective nonconceptual contents are explained for one by a false proposition in the absence of contravening. A minimal probability-maker need not make probable a proposition that is actually true. As we shall see in Chapter 3, this allows for the possibility of epistemically justified *false* belief.

Second, a minimal probability-maker need not be a conclusive epistemic reason, in either a logical or a causal sense of 'conclusive'. Yet if it is conclusive, then if it obtains (or is true), the proposition whose probability is thereby provided must be true (in either a logical or a causal sense of 'must'). On the other hand, if a minimal probability-maker is not conclusive, then its obtaining (or being true) does not require, either logically or causally, the truth of the proposition thereby supported.

Third, the relation of *being a minimal evidential probability-maker* is irreflexive and asymmetric. Nothing is a minimal probability-maker of itself, and no minimal probability-maker has its probability provided by something for which it itself is a probability-maker. In §3.2.3, I shall clarify why irreflexivity and asymmetry are features of justifying probability-makers. And I shall then consider the issue whether transitivity, transmissibility through logical entailment, and deductive consistency are features of justifying probability-makers.

Having characterized the key features of minimal evidential probability-makers, we now have a general characterization of a *minimal epistemic reason*. For a minimal epistemic reason is just a minimal evidential probability-maker. A minimal *non*conceptual epistemic reason is a minimal *unconditional* probability-maker. And a minimal *propositional* epistemic reason is a minimal *derivative* probability-maker. A minimal unconditional epistemic reason, being essentially nonconceptual, is neither true nor false. And a minimal derivative epistemic reason, being essentially propositional, is either true or false.

We need to turn now to the notion of a minimal *non*occurrent probability-maker.

2.5   Nonoccurrent probability-makers and memory

We have been considering occurrent probability-makers, i.e., probability-makers that are in a sense present to awareness for the person for whom they make propositions probable. In the case of an unconditional probability-maker, occurrence requires that the relevant nonconceptual contents be present to one's awareness. In the case of a derivative probability-maker, occurrence requires that the relevant proposition be present to one's awareness.

But evidential probability-makers need not be occurrent. Propositional knowledge can be nonoccurrent inasmuch as the evidence satisfying its justification condition can be nonoccurrent. It is possible for justifying evidence to be nonoccurrent in the sense that one can dispositionally have such evidence for a proposition even though the relevant evidence is not now present to one's awareness. For example, one might dispositionally have justifying evidence for the proposition that snow is white even though one is currently aware only of a throbbing toothache, and so is not aware of evidence for the proposition that snow is white. Such nonoccurrent justification requires an evidential probability-maker, since all justification does; but it does not require an occurrent probability-maker. Nonoccurrent justification requires only a nonoccurrent probability-maker.

The notion of a nonoccurrent, dispositional probability-maker is roughly analogous to the notion of a dispositional belief sketched in §1.1. Put very roughly, the idea is that a probability-maker is nonoccurrent for one if and only if it was occurrent for one, but is now only retrievable from memory for one in a specified way. My notion of one's nonoccurrently having evidence differs from the notion of one's being *merely disposed* (or merely able) to have a probability-maker; for my notion requires that a dispositional probability-maker actually *have been occurrent* for one at a time. (Compare here the analogous distinction in §1.1 between a dispositional belief and one's being merely disposed to have a belief.) By requiring that nonoccurrent probability-makers must have been occurrent, we avoid confusion of one's actually having a nonoccurrent probability-maker and one's being merely disposed (or able) to have such a probability-maker. Without such a requirement, there is no easy way to avoid such confusion.

Let us ask first whether, and if so how, there can be a nonoccurrent probability-maker due to one's subjective nonconceptual contents. Specifically, could the apparent blue book constituting my present subjective contents provide me with a nonoccurrent unconditional probability-maker? If so, how? There seems to be an important sense in which subjective nonconceptual contents no longer presented to one could continue to provide a probability-maker for one. My being presented with an apparent blue book, for example, might be interrupted by my being presented with the apparent ringing of a doorbell, yet the former contents could still make it probable (to some extent) for me, in a nonoccurrent manner, that there is a blue book. The evidential probability for the latter proposition is not necessarily lost by the possibly split-second interruption in the subjective contents presented to me.

Clearly, subjective nonconceptual contents are not themselves a dispositional state. So their being nonoccurrent is not their being a dispositional state. But subjective contents can be nonoccurrent owing to their being *the nonoccurrent object* of a dispositional state, such as a memory-state. Thus let us ask how subjective contents can be a nonoccurrent probability-maker because of (a) their having been an occurrent probability-maker and (b) their now being retrievable from memory in the absence of uncontravened contravening. (I shall not pursue the issue whether what is retrievable must be token identical, rather than a merely type-identical analogue, to what was occurrent; if only for ease of expression, I shall proceed as if there is token identity. But my subsequent account does not require an assumption of token identity.)

We can clarify my notion of retrievability via the following principle, which is analogous to my characterization of the dispositional state of believing in §1.1:

> *S*'s subjective nonconceptual contents *C* are *retrievable from memory* for *S* if and only if as a nondeviant result of *C*'s having been presented to him, *S* is in a dispositional state whereby he will recall *C* in any circumstance where he sincerely and understandingly answers the question whether he remembers *C*.

As with the account of believing in §1.1, let us not pursue familiar questions about the possibility of deviant causal chains. Instead let us proceed with the intuitive notion of a well-behaved causal connection. My characterization assumes that one's recalling certain subjective contents at a time entails one's being presented with those contents at that time. Given the familiar phenomenon of our recalling visual images when asked to remember,[37] we may plausibly suppose that subjective contents are indeed retrievable from memory in basically the sense specified. The actual neuronal function of storing such contents is of course a complicated empirical matter that we need not pursue here.[38]

---

37 Considerable empirical evidence for such images can be found, for example, in Shepard and Cooper (1982) and in Kosslyn (1980). See also the essays in Pinker (1985).
38 On this matter, see Lynch (1986), Black, Adler et al. (1987), and Squire (1987). A less technical discussion can be found in Changeux (1986, Chap. 5).

My appeal to retrievability from memory raises two noteworthy questions. The first question is whether this appeal faces problems from the fact that there are many different questions about one's remembering contents C but only some of these questions would prompt one's recalling C. As Feldman (1988) has suggested, we apparently should not say that C is retrievable in the relevant sense when just any question about C would prompt recall. C might not be relevantly retrievable in cases where only very informative probing questions about C would prompt recall. What, then, determines the set of relevant questions?

We have at least two straightforward options. On the one hand, we might say that there is no way to specify general necessary and sufficient conditions for the set of relevant questions. This option implies that the relevant notion of retrievability is inherently vague, and that our notion of nonoccurrent evidence is correspondingly vague. On the other hand, we might take an approach suggested by my principle of retrievability: relative to particular contents C, there is a single straightforward question that basically determines whether those contents are relevantly retrievable. This is the single question whether one remembers C. Such a question, I assume, must describe C just in terms of its essential features; and it must be understood as requiring that one actually recall C if its correct answer is to be affirmative. On this option, C is relevantly retrievable for one if and only if such a single question would prompt, via a nondeviant causal chain, one's recalling C in any case where the other conditions of my principle above are satisfied. Thus this option does not involve merely temporal considerations about prompting.

I prefer my single-question option to the vagueness option, mainly because the notion of nonoccurrent evidence does not seem to be inherently vague. Apart from my single-question option, I know of no criteria for relevant questions that avoid a threatening slippery slope to the vagueness option. The single-question option is not as demanding as it might initially seem. It obviously allows that there can be numerous questions that prompt one's recalling certain contents. Thus it also allows that there can be various dispositional states that generate one's recalling those contents. The point of the single-question option is simply that there is just one question about certain contents that basically determines whether those contents are relevantly retrievable.

The second likely question about my appeal to retrievability is whether I am uncritically assuming that memory is reliable, or that the objective reliability of memory plays an essential role in non-occurrent justification. The answer of course is no. My notion of retrievability makes no assumption about the reliability of memory; it presupposes no answer to the question whether the deliverances of memory are typically or even sometimes objectively veridical. My appeal to retrievability is solely for purposes of characterizing the possible *nonoccurrence* of one's evidence. The feature of non-occurrence does not itself require the reliability, in any sense, of the deliverances of memory. So far as my account of nonoccurrence goes, memory can be highly *un*reliable. Thus I am not begging questions against the memory skeptic.

Now if certain subjective contents are retrievable from memory in basically the way suggested, then these contents can be a non-occurrent probability-maker for one. Specifically, we have this notion of a nonoccurrent minimal probability-maker due to nonoccurrent subjective nonconceptual contents:

> *S*'s (nonoccurrent) subjective nonconceptual contents *C* are *nonoc-currently a minimal unconditional probability-maker* for *S* for a proposition, *P*, at a time, *t*, = *df*. (i) *C* was occurrently a minimal unconditional probability-maker for *S* for *P* at a time before *t*, but is not occurrently such a probability-maker for *S* at *t*, (ii) *C* is retrievable from memory for *S* at *t*, and (iii) if *S* recalled *C* at *t* while everything other than *C*'s not being present to *S* remained the same, then *C* would be an occurrent minimal probability-maker for *S* for *P* at *t*.

When one has a nonoccurrent minimal unconditional probability-maker for a proposition, one will not have an uncontravened con-travening of that proposition's relation to its supporting evidence. For if one now recalled subjective nonconceptual contents that pro-vide a nonoccurrent probability-maker for one for *P* (while every-thing else stayed as it was), then those contents would now provide an occurrent probability-maker for one for *P*. This entails that one now has no uncontravened contravening of *P*'s relation to its sup-porting evidence. (Contravening itself can be nonoccurrent also in the way suggested; but I shall not digress on this straightforward point.)

If we reject the possibility of nonoccurrent probability-makers, we shall face the view that nothing can be unconditionally evidentially probable for one beyond what is made probable by one's meager contents of the moment. Such a view threatens to preclude justified belief, and thus knowledge, concerning everything but the instantaneously perceived present. My notion of nonoccurrent probability enables us to avoid such a dire threat. (But I am not yet ruling out justification skepticism.)

Some elaboration on my previous example will clarify the notion of a nonoccurrent probability-maker. (We need to restrict the example to subjective contents to avoid begging questions against the skeptic, but for stylistic reasons let us drop some of the needed modifiers.) Sitting at my desk, I am presented with subjective contents consisting of an apparent blue book. But suddenly my attention is distracted by a loud doorbell. Before I can move, my friend Jones enters the room and tells me that the door was unlocked. I have not relocated myself in relation to my desk; I have only directed my eyes upward toward my visitor, who is now standing in front of my desk. Naturally, the distraction from the doorbell and the visitor has interrupted my awareness of an apparent blue book. What should we say about evidential probability in such a case?

Before the interruption, let us suppose, my contents consisting of an apparent blue book provided an occurrent probability-maker for me for the proposition that there is a blue book. Suppose also that the contents in question are retrievable from memory for me, and that if I were to recall those contents now (while all else remained the same), they would now, once again, provide an occurrent probability-maker for me for the proposition that there is a blue book. Thus I have no uncontravened contravening of that proposition's relation to its supporting evidence. So it would be implausible to suppose that the proposition that there is a blue book has lost all its evidential probability for me simply because of the momentary distraction. More generally, an example of the current sort makes it implausible to suppose that minimal probability-makers *must* be occurrent. Such an example lends credibility to the possibility of *non*occurrent minimal probability-makers.

But let us ask what sort of proposition can be made probable by subjective contents, consisting for instance of an apparent blue book, that are retrievable from memory. I have suggested that a present-tense proposition, such as that there *is* a blue book, can be made evidentially probable, if only nonoccurrently, by such contents. And I have suggested that one's recalling such contents can make *occurrently* probable the same present-tense proposition in the specified circumstances.

One might object that I am guilty of a confusion of tenses, on the ground that the only proposition possibly made probable in the specified circumstances is a past-tense proposition, such as that there *was* a blue book. But the objection seems misplaced. In the circumstances specified above, there is no contravening of the explanatory relation between my subjective contents and the present-tense proposition that there is a blue book. For instance, in those circumstances, it is not part of my subjective contents that the apparent blue book in question is apparently falling into a shredder, or that it apparently is being tossed into the fireplace. And in the absence of such contravening, there is no compelling reason to restrict a nonoccurrent probability-maker to a past-tense proposition. One consideration supporting this point is that it evidently is part of the meaning of 'blue book', in contrast to 'apparent blue book', that whatever that term designates does not cease to exist just because one looks away. Thus we may plausibly suppose that a proposition affirming the current existence of a blue book need not lose its minimal evidential probability simply in virtue of a probability-maker's ceasing to be occurrent.

The minimal unconditional probability of a *past-tense* proposition, such as that there *was* a blue book, requires the presence of subjective contents that are explained by a past-tense proposition in the absence of uncontravened contravening. One simple example will illustrate such contents. Suppose I experience the apparent familiarity of, or alternatively my apparently recalling, certain subjective contents such as those consisting of an apparent blue book. In certain cases the contents of such an experience might be explained, in the absence of uncontravened contravening, by the proposition that there *was* a blue book before me at an earlier time. Of course such an experience by no means guarantees that there actually was a blue book before me. Yet this does not threaten my general point that past-tense propositions can derive evidential probability from their being uncontravened *past-tense* explainers.

Not only subjective nonconceptual contents can be retrievable from memory. *Propositional* contents can also be retrievable. And this provides for the possibility of a nonoccurrent propositional probability-maker. Thus let us ask how there can be a nonoccurrent

123

derivative probability-maker due to a proposition one believes. I shall explain how a believed proposition that is supported ultimately by an unconditional probability-maker can be a derivative probability-maker for one even when one is unaware of that proposition.

Suppose I believe that all lemons are sour, but I am currently unaware of this believed proposition. Suppose also that this believed proposition is supported ultimately by an unconditional probability-maker due to my subjective contents consisting of apparent sour lemons. In this case I need not be currently aware of the believed proposition for it to provide me with a probability-maker for the proposition that the untested lemon in my hand is sour. For by hypothesis, (a) the proposition that all lemons are sour entails the proposition, which I understand, that the untested lemon in my hand is sour, (b) the former believed proposition is nonoccurrently probable for me owing ultimately (and perhaps in part) to various subjective contents, and (c) I have no contravening of the former believed proposition's explanatory relation to the proposition that the untested lemon in my hand is sour. In such a case the proposition that the lemon in my hand is sour can be probable to some extent for me even if its derivative probability-maker is nonoccurrent. My merely ceasing to be aware of the believed proposition that all lemons are sour does not necessarily preclude that proposition's being a probability-maker for me for the proposition that the lemon in my hand is sour.

We can say of the present case something directly analogous to what I have said about nonoccurrent unconditional probability-makers. (But I shall not bother with the obvious details of the analogy.) So long as one's derivative probability-maker was occurrent for one, and is now retrievable from memory in the absence of uncontravened contravening, it can be a nonoccurrent probability-maker for one. Thus we should not assume that one now must be aware of a proposition for it now to provide a derivative evidential probability-maker. Nor should we assume that the subjective contents on which a derivative probability-maker ultimately depends need be occurrent. Such subjective contents need only be nonoccurrent in the sense I have suggested. The rejection of this view apparently commits us to an implausible probability solipsism of the moment, and thereby raises serious problems for the possibility of evidentially probable belief in persisting physical objects. But I am not yet making a commitment to justified physical-object beliefs.

It seems clear that the sort of occurrent evidential probability essential to occurrent justification and knowledge requires the absence of nonoccurrent as well as occurrent uncontravened contravening. Thus I doubt that we can make good sense of occurrent justification and knowledge if we neglect nonoccurrent phenomena. Accordingly, my talk of uncontravened contravening in the earlier principles of occurrent probability should be construed to connote nonoccurrent as well as occurrent contravening.

2.6 Conclusion

We now have a general account of occurrent and nonoccurrent probability-makers that make propositions evidentially probable to some extent. Such probability-makers do not necessarily make propositions evidentially more probable than not. Thus they do not necessarily make propositions sufficiently probable to satisfy the justification condition for propositional knowledge. But they do give propositions an epistemic status beyond that of mere possibility. They are thus *minimal* evidential probability-makers. They are also minimal truth-indicators and minimal epistemic reasons. This chapter assumes that minimal evidential probability-makers only make a proposition *justifiable* to a degree. In §3.2.2 I shall relate this modal notion of justifiability to the stronger notion of a proposition's actually being *justified*.

Armed with this chapter's account of minimal epistemic reasons, we can turn to the topic of justifying epistemic reasons, i.e., reasons satisfying the justification condition for propositional knowledge. In doing so, we shall find a way to challenge the sort of justification skepticism that has been in circulation at least since Hume's day. And we shall consider the merits of a foundationalist account of epistemic justification. The question of how my account of evidential probability-makers is itself justified must wait until §6.3. Sufficient unto Chapter 3, as we shall see, are the complications thereof.

3

Justifying epistemic reasons

The account of minimal epistemic reasons in Chapter 2 does not characterize reasons that satisfy the justification condition for propositional knowledge. In this sense Chapter 2 does not provide an account of justifying epistemic reasons. This chapter builds on Chapter 2 to provide the needed account of justifying epistemic reasons. In doing so, this chapter also defends a version of epistemic foundationalism, and challenges justification skepticism concerning physical-object propositions. In addition, this chapter explains what it is for a person to *have* a justifying epistemic reason, and what exactly is required by the evidential basing relation for propositional knowledge. For the most part, this chapter presupposes familiarity with the main distinctions and arguments of Chapter 2.

Clearly a proposition is epistemically justified for one only if it is evidentially more probable than its denial for one. But this platitude raises two important questions. When is a proposition evidentially more probable than its denial for a person? And is a proposition's being thus probable sufficient for its satisfying the justification condition for propositional knowledge? These and related questions motivate the next two sections. I shall formulate my answers to these questions via principles of *occurrent* probability, while simply acknowledging that the analogues for nonoccurrent probability are readily available in light of §2.5.

3.1 Justification and overbalancing probability

Chapter 2 laid the basis for a straightforward notion of a proposition's being evidentially more probable than its denial. This section characterizes this notion.

3.1.1 Unconditional overbalancing probability

My rough initial proposal is this: a proposition, *P*, can be unconditionally more probable than its denial for one in virtue of *P*'s being, in the absence of contravening, a decisively better explanation for one of one's subjective nonconceptual contents than is every contrary explanation for one (i.e., every explanation for one that entails *P*'s denial). When *P* is evidentially more probable than its denial for one, relative only to one's subjective nonconceptual contents, one has an *overbalancing* unconditional probability-maker for *P*.

Put more explicitly, the relevant notion concerning occurrent evidential probability is:

> *S*'s subjective nonconceptual contents *C* are occurrently an *overbalancing unconditional probability-maker* for a proposition, *P*, for *S*, inasmuch as *C* occurrently makes *P* *evidentially more probable than* $\sim P$ for *S* = df. (i) *S* is presented with *C*, (ii) *S* understands some proposition contrary to *P*, including $\sim P$ itself, (iii) *P* is a decisively better explanation of *C* for *S* than is every contrary proposition *S* understands, including $\sim P$ itself, and (iv) *S* has no uncontravened contravening regarding (iii).

Clause (i) needs no special comment, given the discussion in §2.3.2a. Clause (ii) prevents clause (iii)'s being satisfied by default from *S*'s lack of understanding (although it is of course hard to imagine one's understanding *P* without one's understanding $\sim P$). Given (ii), we may say that the proposition that Jones committed the crime has an overbalancing unconditional probability-maker for *S* only if this proposition is a better explainer for *S* than is the contrary proposition that Jones did not commit the crime, but somebody else did. Clause (iii) on its intended interpretation entails that *P* is actually an explanation of *C* for *S*.

In §2.3.2 we saw characterizations of the notions of an explanation, a decisively better explanation, and an uncontravened contravener of a proposition's being an explanation for one. Yet we should briefly rehearse the notion of a decisively better explanation, and clarify the notion of uncontravened contravening in the definition above.

Recall that an explanation of subjective nonconceptual contents is an answer to a question why those contents occur as they do, and that a proposition, P, provides an explanation *for one* only if one understands P. Recall also the following characterization of a decisively better explanation:

> One proposition, P, is a *decisively better explanation* of subjective contents C than is another proposition, Q, if and only if (i) P explains C, and (ii) either (a) P answers all the explanation-seeking why-questions about C answered by Q, but posits fewer gratuitous entities and fewer kinds of gratuitous entities than Q does, or (b) while positing no more gratuitous entities or kinds of gratuitous entities than Q posits, P answers all the explanation-seeking why-questions about C answered by Q, and still others, or (c) P and Q answer the same why-questions about C without either positing more gratuitous entities or kinds of gratuitous entities than the other, but P is informationally more specific than Q.

Given this characterization, P's being a decisively better explanation than Q is basically a function of how P answers why-questions in comparison to Q. But P's being a better explanation of C than is Q does *not* entail that Q is actually an explanation of C. This allows for P's being a better explanation of C than is its denial in cases where $\sim P$ is not an explanation of C at all. Regarding clause (c) of condition (ii), I proposed in §2.3.2b that P is informationally more specific than Q if and only if P logically entails, but is not logically entailed by, Q. We saw that the motivation for (c) comes from cases where relevant explanations are provided by existential generalizations and nonredundant disjunctions.

The basic idea of uncontravened contravening is familiar from my account of minimal probability-makers. But we now need an additional complication. Overbalancing unconditional probability for P for one requires that one not have an uncontravened contravening of P's being a decisively better explanation of the relevant subjective contents for one than is every contrary proposition one understands. This requirement is actually twofold. First, P must not be directly contravened for one as an explanation of one's relevant subjective contents. Second, P must not be indirectly contravened for one as an explanation of the relevant contents that is decisively better than every contrary proposition one understands.

The notion of *direct* contravening requires no news, given §2.3.2b. An example comes from a situation where the Cartesian evil-demon hypothesis provides an explanation of one's subjective contents that is decisively better than every contrary proposition one understands. If in such a situation the Cartesian hypothesis nonetheless posits only gratuitous entities relative to one's subjective contents, it will have been directly contravened for one as an explanation of those contents. When such contravening is itself uncontravened, it precludes subjective contents' being an overbalancing probability-maker for a proposition that decisively is a better explanation of those contents than is every contrary proposition one understands.

Direct contravening is itself uncontravened when one has no subjective contents relative to which the initially contravened explainer is not gratuitous. In such a case of uncontravened contravening, an explainer such as the Cartesian hypothesis does not gain any evidential probability whatsoever from the relevant subjective contents. In such a case that sort of explainer has at best the evidential status only of a *possibility*.

The relevant notion of *indirect* contravening requires that we recall the notion of *negative relevance* introduced in §2.3.2b:

> S's subjective nonconceptual contents $C\star$ are *negatively relevant* to his subjective nonconceptual contents C, relative to a proposition's (P's) explaining C, if and only if (i) there is an explanation, E, for S of such contents that entails either (a) that in the present case not both C and $C\star$ are objectively veridical (i.e., representative of objective contents), or (b) that in most cases for S not both C-type and $C\star$-type contents are objectively veridical when they occur together, or (c) that $\sim P$, or (d) that a certain information source, I, is a source of truth in most cases concerning C-type contents and I affirms, at least by implication, that $\sim P$, and (ii) E is a decisively better explanation of C and $C\star$ than is every contrary explanation S has.

When S's contents $C\star$ are negatively relevant in this sense, P will have overbalancing probability for S relative to C only if P plays an essential role in an explanation also of $C\star$ for S that is decisively better than every contrary proposition S understands. Let us say that P does not play an essential role in an explanation of contents C and $C\star$ for S that is decisively better than its understood contraries if and only if for every such explanation for S that entails P, the proposition that P answers no why-questions about C and $C\star$ beyond those answered when P is omitted. Let us also recall that my talk of *objectively veridical* contents connotes objective contents of the sort characterized in §2.3.2. It connotes contents that make up, at least in part, how things are independently of one's corresponding experiences thereof.

We can easily formulate an example of indirect contravening of

129

an explanation decisively better than its understood contraries. Consider a case where my subjective contents C consist of an apparent blue book, and where the proposition that there is a blue book here (call it 'P') is decisively a better explanation for me of C than is every contrary proposition I understand, including the proposition that there is *only* a laser beam generating a hologram of a blue book here. The latter contrary proposition, we might assume, is inferior owing to its positing an explanatory item that is gratuitous *relative to C alone*, viz., a laser beam. (See §2.3.2b on gratuitous explainers.)

Suppose also that in such a case I have as part of my overall subjective contents an apparent light source producing a hologram of a blue book here. By hypothesis, this part of my contents (call it '$C\star$'), which is negatively relevant to C, is not decisively better explained by P than by every contrary proposition I understand. (The latter assumption is natural given that P does not explain $C\star$ at all.) And for any other explanation I have of C and $C\star$ that entails P, the proposition P answers no why-questions about C and $C\star$ beyond those answered when P is omitted. My explanation of $C\star$ might be simply that there is a laser beam generating a hologram of a blue book here. In such a case, P does not play an essential role in an explanation of C and $C\star$ that is decisively better than its understood contraries. That is, P can be dropped from my explanation of C and $C\star$ without explanatory loss. In such a case, the explanation that there is *only* a hologram of a blue book here would be decisively better than the explanation that there are both a blue book and a hologram of a blue book here.

Thus we have a case where an explanation decisively better than its understood contraries relative to certain subjective contents is indirectly contravened due to certain other, negatively relevant contents. When such contravening is itself uncontravened, it undermines one's subjective contents' being an overbalancing probability-maker for a proposition that is decisively a better explanation of those contents than is every contrary proposition one understands. Indirect contravening of an explanation decisively better than its understood contraries is itself uncontravened when this is the case: there is no additional part of one's subjective contents relative to which the initially contravened explainer plays an essential role in an explanation that is decisively better than the explanation from every contrary proposition one understands. So a proposition's being a decisively better explanation of certain contents than are its understood contraries is not logically sufficient for its having overbalancing evidential probability.

In sum, the new notion of indirect contravening is this:

> A proposition, *P*, is *indirectly contravened* for *S* as a decisively better explanation for him of his subjective nonconceptual contents *C* than is every contrary proposition he understands = *df.* (i) *S*'s contents *C*★ are (a part of) *S*'s subjective contents that are negatively relevant to *C*, (ii) *P* itself does not explain *C*★ decisively better than does every contrary proposition *S* understands, and (iii) *P* plays no essential role in an explanation of *C* and *C*★ for *S* that is decisively better than the explanation from every contrary proposition *S* understands, in the sense that for every such explanation for *S* that entails *P*, the proposition that *P* answers no why-questions about *C* and *C*★ beyond those answered when *P* is omitted.

This notion of indirect contravening is straightforwardly analogous to the notion in §2.3.2 of indirect contravening of *an explanation* of one's subjective contents.

3.1.2 Derivative overbalancing probability

Parallel to the *derivative* minimal probability-makers of §2.4, there can also be derivative overbalancing probability-makers. These are *propositional* overbalancing probability-makers, and they are either basic or nonbasic. Let us begin with a characterization of those that occurrently are basic (where their basicness is only relative to *other propositions*, and does not entail their being unconditional):

> A proposition, *P*, that is an object of *S*'s believing or assenting is occurrently an *overbalancing basic propositional probability-maker* for a proposition, *Q*, for *S* = *df.* (i) *P* is present to *S*'s awareness, (ii) there is an overbalancing unconditional probability-maker for *P* for *S*, (iii) *S* understands *Q*, (iv) either (a) *P* logically entails *Q*, or (b) *P* decisively better explains *Q* than does every contrary proposition *S* understands (where *S* understands some proposition contrary to *P*, including ~*P* itself), or (c) *P* is decisively better explained by *Q* than by every contrary proposition *S* understands (where *S* understands some proposition contrary to *Q*, including ~*Q* itself), (v) if *P* is disjunctive and explains *Q*, then *P* does not explain *Q* only because *Q* is explained by a disjunct inessential to *P*'s having an unconditional probability-maker, or if *P* is disjunctive and explained by *Q*, then *Q* does not explain *P* only because *Q* explains a disjunct inessential to *P*'s having an unconditional probability-maker, and (vi) *S* has no uncontravened contravening regarding (iv).

The distinctive feature of an overbalancing *basic* propositional probability-maker is that it is supported just by an overbalancing *unconditional* probability-maker, and on that basis makes another proposition evidentially more probable than not for a person. I have already explained most of the key notions in the proposed definition. But the sorts of contravening relevant to clauses (iv) and (vi) deserve brief additional comment.

The requirement of clause (vi) that there be no uncontravened contravening regarding (iv) is of course variable in the sense that it depends on *P*'s actual evidential relation to *Q*. If, on the one hand, the relevant relation is that of *P*'s entailing *Q*, the following notion from §2.4 applies:

> *P*'s logically entailing *Q* is contravened for *S* = *df.* There is an explanation for *S* of his subjective nonperceptual contents that (a) entails that *P* does not entail *Q*, and (b) is decisively better than every contrary explanation *S* has for those contents.

(In §2.3.2a I illustrated the notion of subjective nonperceptual contents via apparent conceptual relations of inclusion and exclusion.) On the other hand, if the relevant evidential relation is explanatory, we need to consider both my notion of direct contravening of an explanation and my notion of indirect contravening of an explanation decisively better than its understood contraries. Clause (vi) is variable in this sense.

Thus my notion of an overbalancing basic propositional probability-maker does not restrict the relation between *P* and *Q* to logical entailment, but provides also for *non*demonstrative explanatory relations. The two possibilities suggested in §2.4 apply here too. First, a proposition, *P*, that provides support for an inductive generalization, *Q*, can occurrently be an overbalancing basic probability-maker for *Q* for one when (a) one consciously assents to *P* and understands *Q*, (b) *P* is supported by an overbalancing unconditional probability-maker for one, and (c) one has no uncontravened contravening regarding *Q*'s explaining *P* decisively better than does every contrary proposition one understands. In such a case, the overbalancing probability-making relation derives in part from *Q*'s being a decisively better explanation of *P* for one than is every contrary proposition one understands.

The sorts of contravening relevant here are analogous to the direct and indirect contravening I characterized in connection with overbalancing unconditional probability-makers. Thus P's being decisively better explained by Q for S than by every contrary proposition S understands is *directly* contravened for S if and only if Q is directly contravened as an explanation of P for S. And P's being decisively better explained by Q for S than by every contrary proposition S understands is *indirectly* contravened for S if and only if Q is indirectly contravened as an explanation of P for S that is decisively better than every contrary proposition S understands. (See §2.4 on how to understand negative relevance and explanatory gratuitousness relative to the truth of a proposition.)

The second anticipated possibility is that a proposition, P, can occurrently be an overbalancing basic propositional probability-maker for Q for one when (a) one consciously assents to P and understands Q, (b) P is supported by an overbalancing unconditional probability-maker for one, and (c) one has no uncontravened contravening regarding P's explaining Q decisively better than does every contrary proposition one understands. Once again, the relevant sorts of contravening are analogous to the direct and indirect contravening pertinent to overbalancing unconditional probability-makers.

The related notion of an overbalancing *non*basic probability-maker is:

> A proposition, P, that is an object of S's believing or assenting is occurrently an *overbalancing nonbasic propositional probability-maker* for a proposition, Q, for $S = df.$ (i) P is present to S's awareness, (ii) there is an overbalancing propositional probability-maker for P for S that ultimately depends (for its being an overbalancing probability-maker) on, or is identical to, an overbalancing basic propositional probability-maker for S, (iii) S understands Q, (iv) either (a) P logically entails Q, or (b) P explains Q decisively better than does every contrary proposition S understands (where S understands some proposition contrary to P, including $\sim P$ itself), or (c) P is decisively better explained by Q than by every contrary proposition S understands (where S understands some proposition contrary to Q, including $\sim Q$ itself), (v) if P is disjunctive and explains Q, then P does not explain Q only because Q is explained by a disjunct inessential to P's having a probability-maker, or if P is disjunctive and explained by Q, then Q does not explain P only because Q explains a disjunct inessential to P's having a probability-maker, and (vi) S has no uncontravened contravening regarding (iv).

The distinctive feature of such a nonbasic overbalancing probability-maker is that its supporting overbalancing probability-maker is propositional. If the latter supporting probability-maker is not itself basic, it at least has a probability-making ancestry that ends with an overbalancing basic probability-maker. Thus nonbasic overbalancing probability-makers need not be directly dependent upon basic overbalancing probability-makers; there can be indirect dependency relations between the two. The preceding remarks about contravening and overbalancing basic probability-makers also apply straightforwardly here.

Derivative and unconditional overbalancing probability-makers can be *non*occurrent in the sense specified in §2.5. If it is plausible to suppose that minimal probability-makers can be nonoccurrent, then the same is true of overbalancing probability-makers. But the parallel notion of a nonoccurrent overbalancing probability-maker does not require separate attention here; this notion should be obvious in light of §2.5.

We should not generalize on the notions of an overbalancing probability-maker to imply that for *any* two explanations, P and Q, of contents C for S, if P is decisively a better explanation of C for S than is Q, then in the absence of uncontravened contravening, P is evidentially more probable than Q for S. If P and Q are logically consistent, P might be evidentially no more probable than Q for S despite P's explanatory superiority over Q for S. Suppose 'P' stands for 'Jones committed the crime' and 'Q' stands for 'Someone committed the crime'. Even if P has explanatory superiority over Q for S, Q ordinarily will have evidential probability for S at least to the extent that P does. An inference from explanatory superiority, in the absence of uncontravened contravening, to greater evidential probability is valid only when the decisively better explanation does not logically entail the inferior explanation.

3.1.3 The insufficiency of overbalancing probability

We now can explain why overbalancing probability-makers do not necessarily satisfy the justification condition for propositional knowledge. Suppose I have an overbalancing probability-maker for the proposition that there is a blue book here, owing to my visual and tactile subjective contents. In such a case the proposition that there is a blue book here would be evidentially more probable than not for me. For instance, that proposition would be evidentially more probable for me than the contrary proposition that there is *only* a hologram of a blue book before me. But suppose also that

I have an overbalancing probability-maker, relative to other subjective contents, for the proposition that there are not both a blue book and a hologram of a blue book here. In such a case, if the proposition that there is a blue book here is to be epistemically justified for me, it must be evidentially more probable for me than not only the contrary proposition that there is *only* a hologram of a blue book here, but also the proposition that there is at least a hologram of a blue book here.

The proposition that there is a hologram of a blue book here does not entail the denial of the proposition that there is a blue book here. More to the point, causal overdetermination of one's subjective contents involving an apparent blue book is a logical possibility. So the two propositions in question are not contrary explanations. Thus my having an overbalancing probability-maker for the proposition that there is a blue book here does not entail that I have an overbalancing probability-maker for the denial of the proposition that there is a hologram of a blue book here. Yet there is a sense in which these two propositions can compete.

Let us say that two propositions are *probabilistic competitors* for one if both are explainers for one of certain of one's subjective contents, and one has an overbalancing probability-maker for the proposition that they are not both true. Thus the proposition that there is a hologram of a blue book here is a probabilistic competitor for me against the proposition that there is a blue book here when two conditions are satisfied: (a) both propositions explain for me my subjective contents consisting of an apparent blue book, and (b) I have an overbalancing probability-maker for the proposition that there are not both a blue book and a hologram of a blue book here. Yet we should not assume that *all* the different explanations of certain contents compete with each other. An explanation, P, for example, does not compete with the disjunctive explanation ($P \lor Q$). The important point, however, is that since an overbalancing probability-maker for P does not necessarily make P evidentially more probable than all its probabilistic competitors, such a probability-maker does not necessarily satisfy the justification condition for propositional knowledge.[1]

1 For the same reason, a *counter*balancing probability-maker does not necessarily satisfy the justification condition for knowledge. Such a probability-maker makes a proposition, P, evidentially probable to some extent, but only *evidentially as probable as its denial*, for one. In its unconditional form, such a probability-maker involves

Let us turn now to probability-makers that do necessarily satisfy the epistemic justification condition.

3.2   Justification and maximal probability

Philosophers commonly use the term 'justifying reason' to connote a reason sufficient for the satisfaction of the justification condition for propositional knowledge. I shall follow that usage in this section. A justifying epistemic reason for a proposition is a justifying evidential probability-maker for that proposition. And a justifying epistemic reason for a *belief* is a justifying evidential probability-maker for a believed proposition. This section explains that there is something special about a *justifying* evidential probability-maker.

For simplicity, let us focus on justifying probability-makers for a particular kind of proposition: a physical-object proposition. And let us assume that a proposition is a physical-object proposition if and only if its being true requires the existence of a physical object. One important reason for focusing on physical-object propositions is that justification skeptics have aimed their attacks consistently, if not mainly, at these propositions. The following account of justifying probability-makers will enable us in §3.5 to challenge the sort of justification skepticism that has troubled epistemology since the time of Hume.

3.2.1   *Unconditional and derivative justifiers*

Let us call an evidential probability-maker that is a justifying reason for P (in the sense that it makes P *justifiable*) a *maximal evidential probability-maker* for P. Such a probability-maker makes P maximally probable in the sense that it makes P more probable than not only its understood contraries but also all its probabilistic competitors. Put more explicitly, the relevant notion regarding an occurrent unconditional probability-maker is:

> Subjective nonconceptual contents C are occurrently a *maximal unconditional probability-maker* for a proposition, P, for a person, S, inasmuch as C makes P *evidentially more probable than not only its*

one's having subjective contents C, of which P is an explanation for one, but P is neither a decisively better nor a decisively worse explanation of C for one than is $\sim P$ or at least some proposition entailing $\sim P$.

(understood) contraries, but also all its probabilistic competitors for S = df. (i) S is presented with C, (ii) S understands some proposition contrary to P, including $\sim P$ itself, (iii) P is decisively a better explanation of C for S than is every contrary proposition S understands and every probabilistic competitor for S, and (iv) S has no uncontravened contravening regarding (iii).

This definition assumes, in accord with §3.1.3, that two propositions are *probabilistic competitors* for one if they both explain certain of one's subjective contents, and one has an overbalancing probability-maker for the proposition that they are not both true.

Perhaps contrary explanations for a person are typically probabilistic competitors for that person, but it is not clear that they must be. For it is not clear that one necessarily has overbalancing probability-makers for the falsity of the simple conjunctions of all one's contrary explanations. But it is clear that not all probabilistic competitors are logically contrary propositions in the sense that every competitor *entails* the denial of another.

The preceding definition, like the notion of an overbalancing probability-maker, relies on the characterization of direct contravening from §2.3.2b. So we need not dwell on direct contravening again.

We now need only a straightforward modification of the previous characterization of indirect contravening:

A proposition, P, is *indirectly contravened* for S as an explanation for him of his subjective contents C that is decisively better than every contrary proposition he understands and every probabilistic competitor for him = df. (i) S's contents $C^\star$ are a part of S's subjective contents that are negatively relevant to C, (ii) P itself does not explain $C^\star$ decisively better than does every contrary proposition S understands and every probabilistic competitor for S, and (iii) P plays no essential role in an explanation of C and $C^\star$ for S that is decisively better than the explanation from every contrary proposition S understands and every probabilistic competitor for S (in the sense that for every such explanation for S that entails P, the proposition that P answers no why-questions about C and $C^\star$ beyond those answered when P is omitted).

This characterization includes no new notions. The example used in §3.1.1 to illustrate indirect contravening of an explanation better than its contraries can, with minor alteration, also illustrate this notion of contravening. The alteration is the additional assumption that P explains C decisively better than do its probabilistic competitors as well as its understood contraries.

137

Let us consider an example of indirect contravening that focuses on probabilistic competitors regarding negatively relevant contents. Suppose that my visual subjective contents C consist of an apparent blue book, and that the proposition that there is a blue book here (call it 'B') explains those contents decisively better than do its probabilistic competitors and its understood contraries. Suppose also that my further (partly auditory) subjective contents C^*, which are negatively relevant to C in the sense of §3.1.1, include an apparent *hollow-sounding* booklike object. Now C and C^* are explained for me by the proposition that there is a book facsimile here (call it 'F'). In fact, F is a probabilistic competitor for me against the explanation provided by B. But B and F are not contraries. There could be a book inside a book facsimile here, or a book facsimile inside a book here, or even a book connected to a book facsimile in such a way that they look, feel, and sound like a single book.

Let us assume also that B is a decisively better explanation of C and C^* than is every contrary proposition I understand, including the contrary propositions that $(F \& \sim B)$. Conceivably B is decisively better than $(F \& \sim B)$, given the exceptionally fine booklike features of my subjective contents. This assumption does *not* entail that B is a decisively better explanation of C and C^* than is F, since these two propositions are not contraries. It is possible that there is at least a book here, *and* that there is at least a book facsimile here too.

Thus we can suppose that B is not a decisively better explanation of C and C^* than is the competing explanation F. That is, B and F might be only equally good explanations of C and C^*, even if B is decisively better than all its understood contraries and F is better than all its understood contraries. In such a case, B would be indirectly contravened for me as an explanation of C that is decisively better than all its probabilistic competitors and understood contraries. This contravening itself would be uncontravened given this condition: there is no additional part of my subjective contents relative to which the initially contravened B plays an essential role in an explanation decisively better than that provided from every contrary proposition I understand and every probabilistic competitor for me. In a case of such uncontravened contravening, B would not have sufficient evidential backing to satisfy the justification condition for propositional knowledge. That is, B would not have maximal evidential probability relative to C.

The significance of indirect and direct contravening to maximal evidential probability provides for a certain total evidence requirement on such probability. It implies that any part of one's subjective contents is potentially relevant to the maximal probability of a proposition. This implication is desirable, since a proposition having maximal evidential probability for one should have that probability relative to all one's subjective contents. Thus my account accommodates the familiar plausible view that a justified proposition for one must be justified relative to all one's evidence. As in §§2.3–2.5, my account assumes that relevant contravening can be nonoccurrent as well as occurrent.

Parallel to the *derivative* overbalancing probability-makers of §3.1.2, there can also be derivative maximal probability-makers. These are *propositional* probability-makers, and they are either basic or nonbasic. We can characterize maximal basic probability-makers in their occurrent form as follows (where their basicness is relative only to other propositions):

> A proposition, P, that is an object of S's believing or assenting is occurrently a *maximal basic propositional probability-maker* for a proposition, Q, for S = df. (i) P is present to S's awareness, (ii) there is a maximal unconditional probability-maker for P for S, (iii) S understands Q, (iv) either (a) P logically entails Q, or (b) P explains Q decisively better than does every understood contrary and every probabilistic competitor for S (where S understands some proposition contrary to P, including ~P itself), or (c) P is explained by Q decisively better than by every understood contrary and every probabilistic competitor for S (where S understands some proposition contrary to Q, including ~Q itself), (v) if P is disjunctive and explains Q, then P does not explain Q only because Q is explained by a disjunct inessential to P's having an unconditional probability-maker, or if P is disjunctive and explained by Q, then Q does not explain P only because Q explains a disjunct inessential to P's having an unconditional probability-maker, and (vi) S has no uncontravened contravening regarding (iv).

We can briefly portray a maximal basic probability-maker by saying that it is supported directly by a maximal *unconditional* probability-maker, and on that basis makes another proposition maximally evidentially probable.

The preceding definition requires no substantially new notions. I have explained the notion of a probabilistic competitor in §3.1.3; and the relevant notions of contravening are directly analogous to the previous accounts concerning contravening of maximal unconditional and overbalancing probability-makers. (See §2.4 on how to understand negative relevance and explanatory gratuitousness relative to the truth of a proposition.) Here I simply note that whenever there is a maximal unconditional probability-maker supporting *P*, *direct* contravening will be excluded in the sense that *P* will not then be a gratuitous explainer for one.

In addition to maximal basic probability-makers, there can also be maximal *non*basic probability-makers. We can characterize their occurrent species as follows:

> A proposition, *P*, that is an object of *S*'s believing or assenting is occurrently a *maximal nonbasic propositional probability-maker* for a proposition, *Q*, for *S* = *df.* (i) *P* is present to *S*'s awareness, (ii) there is a maximal propositional probability-maker for *P* for *S* that ultimately depends (for its being a maximal probability-maker) on, or is identical to, a maximal basic propositional probability-maker for *S*, (iii) *S* understands *Q*, (iv) either (a) *P* logically entails *Q*, or (b) *P* explains *Q* decisively better than does every understood contrary or probabilistic competitor for *S* (where *S* understands some proposition contrary to *P*, including ~*P* itself), or (c) *P* is explained by *Q* decisively better than by every understood contrary or probabilistic competitor for *S* (where *S* understands some proposition contrary to *Q*, including ~*Q* itself), (v) if *P* is disjunctive and explains *Q*, then *P* does not explain *Q* only because *Q* is explained by a disjunct inessential to *P*'s having a probability-maker, or if *P* is disjunctive and explained by *Q*, then *Q* does not explain *P* only because *Q* explains a disjunct inessential to *P*'s having a probability-maker, and (vi) *S* has no uncontravened contravening regarding (iv).

The proximate maximal probability-maker for such a nonbasic probability-maker is of course not an unconditional probability-maker; it is, rather, another maximal *propositional* probability-maker. Thus this sort of probability-maker is *not* basic relative to all other propositional probability-makers. Since there are no new notions in the foregoing definition, we need not go into its components.

Maximal probability-makers need not be occurrent. Both derivative and unconditional maximal probability-makers can be non-occurrent in the way characterized in §2.5. Thus we can make sense of the common supposition that one has justification for a belief even though one is not now entertaining one's relevant justifying evidence. But we need not devote special attention here to non-occurrent maximal probability-makers. Instead we now need to pursue less familiar matters.

3.2.2 Justifiability and justifiedness

The notion of a *justifying* probability-maker hides the crucial but widely neglected ambiguity between (a) a probability-maker that makes a proposition *actually justified* for one and (b) a probability-maker that makes a proposition *merely justifiable* for one. We can initially characterize the notion of making-justified as follows: *evidence E makes P justified for S* if and only if *E* is a maximal probability-maker for *P* for *S*, and *S* has associated *E* and *P* in a certain way (a way to be specified below). Using this rough characterization, we can say this about justifiability: *evidence E makes P justifiable for S* if and only if *E* is a maximal probability-maker for *P* for *S* and *P* would be justified for *S* were *S* to associate *E* and *P* in a certain way while everything else remained the same. This claim, although not a definition, usefully links the notions of justifiability and justifiedness. My account of course does *not* define the notion of justifiability via the notion of justifiedness. Instead it defines 'justifiability' via the notion of one's having a maximal probability-maker, and then uses the latter notion in its definition of 'justifiedness'.

The difference between a merely justifiable proposition and an actually justified proposition consists in one's having associated a maximal probability-maker and a proposition in a certain way in the case of a justified proposition. Philosophers have rarely given attention to this important difference. Yet if we neglect it, we nonskeptics shall risk commitment to the existence of a proposition that is justified for one even though one never has been aware of a relation of evidential support between the proposition and one's evidence. In such a case a proposition might be justifi*able* for one, but it cannot plausibly be said to be actually justified. Thus we cannot plausibly ignore the distinction at hand.

We now need to characterize the association relation crucial to an actually justified proposition. Regarding a proposition, *P*, that is justified for *S* on evidence *E*, this relation in its occurrent form can be characterized as follows:

> *S* occurrently satisfies an association relation between *E* and *P* = *df*. (i) *S* has a *de re* awareness of *E*'s supporting *P*, and (ii) as a nondeviant result of this awareness, *S* is in a dispositional state whereby if he were to focus his attention only on his evidence for *P* (while all else remained the same), he would focus his attention on *E*.

An association relation's being satisfied *non*occurrently in connection with *P* and *E* can be understood roughly along the lines of §2.5. That is, *S* does not satisfy the association relation occurrently, but he did at some past time, and as a nondeviant result he is now in a dispositional state whereby if he were to attend only to his evidence for *P* (while all else remained the same), *S* would thereby attend to *E*.

I shall remain somewhat uncommitted on what exactly is needed psychologically for clause (ii) above to be true of one. Yet I see no reason to think that (ii) requires one to have the notion of a maximal probability-maker, even if it requires one to have some minimal notion of evidential support. I am also unconvinced that (ii) requires one to have a *de re belief* about an evidential relation that it holds between *E* and *P*. (On such *de re* belief, see Audi [1986, p. 34].) One problem with requiring such *de re* belief is that it raises difficulties concerning how such belief is itself justified. Presumably, the relevant *de re* belief would itself have to be justified to play an essential role in justified belief that *P*. But does this mean that an additional association relation must be satisfied? If so, must there be yet another justified *de re* belief? The threatening regress is evidently vicious. Fortunately clause (ii) does not itself commit us to a belief requirement that generates such a regress.

We can gain more clarity from several points. First, the required association is not epistemic: it does not itself involve knowledge or justified belief. If it did, a vicious regress would threaten. Second, it is *de re* at least inasmuch as it involves awareness of an actual evidential probability-making relation between *E* and *P*. This evidential relation, in accord with the foregoing account of maximal probability-makers, will be an explanatory relation or a logical-entailment relation. Third, the *de re* awareness of such a relation can be understood via the notion of direct attention attraction introduced in §2.3.2 to clarify the notion of presentation. But we need not rehearse that notion here. Fourth, the required association relation need not be occurrent for there to be a justified proposition for a person. There need only have been an occurrent event of association that resulted, without causal deviance, in the aforementioned sort of dispositional state. This point is important since it allows for a justified proposition for one who is not now aware of either the relevant justified proposition or its justifying evidence.

It allows us to maintain a notion of *non*occurrent justifiedness in light of §2.5.

My characterization of making-justified does *not* imply that P's being justified for one requires one's actually *showing* that P is justified. Nor does my characterization require that one actually believe either the justified proposition P or the relevant justifying evidence. Since E may be nonpropositional, such a requirement would be incoherent. In addition, the association of E and P does not entail that one believes that P, since it does not entail one's assenting, or having assented, to P. (See §1.1 on the assent requirement for believing.)

Without the sort of association required by the making-justified relation, there will be at most a *justifiable* proposition for one relative to a maximal probability-maker. Thus maximal probability-makers are *by themselves* justifying reasons only inasmuch as they make propositions justif*iable*. An additional association relation must be satisfied for maximal probability-makers to make propositions actually justified for a person. Given this distinction, we see that the ordinary talk of a *justifying* reason is crucially ambiguous.

To clarify further the distinction between making-justified and making-justifiable, we can compare it to a distinction between *propositional* and *doxastic* justification.[2] Propositional justification obtains, let us say, when and only when a proposition is evidentially more probable than its understood contraries and its probabilistic competitors for one, relative to one's total evidence. And doxastic justification obtains when and only when three conditions hold: (i) a proposition, P, has propositional justification for one, (ii) one believes that P, and (iii) one's believing that P is based on the evidence that provides propositional justification for P.

Propositional justification thus provides justifiability, but not justifiedness. On my account, evidential probability does not require actual justifiedness to some degree; it requires only justif*iability* to some degree. The satisfaction of the aforementioned relations of making-justified and making-justifiable is sufficient for propositional justification, but not for doxastic justification. Those relations

2 Apparently such a distinction was suggested first by Firth (1978, pp. 217–19). My own characterization of it goes beyond what Firth actually says. For still other characterizations of the distinction, see Goldman (1979, pp. 21–2; 1986, p. 112), Ginet (1983, pp. 32–3), and Alston (1985, pp. 40–1).

are insufficient for doxastic justification, because they do not require that an evidential basing relation be satisfied by a belief. In fact, they do not require a belief at all. Let us say, then, that those relations satisfy the conditions for a proposition's being justified or at least justifiable *for one*, but do not necessarily satisfy the conditions for one's being justified *in believing* a proposition. In §3.4 I shall characterize the distinctive basing condition for the latter, doxastic justification.

My account of maximal probability-makers qualifies as a foundationalist approach to epistemic justification. Epistemic foundationalism states that necessarily if any proposition is justifiable for one on the basis of another proposition, then there is some proposition justifiable for one independently of its evidential relations to other propositions. In this sense, foundationalism states that epistemic justification has a two-tier structure. But contrary to a popular view, foundationalism does *not* require that some proposition is self-justified or self-justifiable (if one proposition is to be justifiable via another). A requirement of noninferential, nonpropositional justification is *not* a requirement of self-justification. A proposition's noninferential justification can derive from its relation not to itself, but to the subjective nonconceptual contents of one's experience.

If one has a maximal unconditional probability-maker for a proposition, P, then P is noninferentially justifiable for one. For P's justifiability does not then depend on the justifiability of another proposition. In fact, P's supporting evidence is then altogether nonpropositional. In this sense, noninferential justification is nonpropositional on my account. Propositions that are thus noninferentially justifiable can provide the propositional foundations for the justification of all other justified propositions. So I have characterized the former propositions as maximal *basic* propositional probability-makers. And I have characterized the justifying propositions made justifiable via such basic propositions as maximal *nonbasic* propositional probability-makers. Thus I have tried to clarify the traditional foundationalist thesis that every justified proposition is either a noninferentially justified proposition or an inferentially justified proposition supported by a noninferentially justified proposition. Of course my earlier definitions concern only justifi*able* propositions; but to provide corresponding notions of a justified proposition, we need only add the relevant association relation.

My version of foundationalism has at least two noteworthy advantages over various traditional versions. First, it does *not* require incorrigible or indubitable beliefs; and second, it does *not* require that the justification of physical-object beliefs be based on the justification of *beliefs* about what one *seems* to perceive. My version is thus epistemically more modest and psychologically more realistic than the traditional foundationalism represented by C. I. Lewis (1946), for example. I shall further clarify and defend the foundationalist element of my account in Chapter 4.

3.2.3 *Some logical matters*

Let us now return to the issue, anticipated in §2.4, whether the relation of being a justifying, maximal probability-maker for *P* is reflexive, symmetric, or transitive. First, neither unconditional nor derivative maximal probability-makers are reflexive, i.e., self-justifying. Unconditional maximal probability-makers cannot be self-justifying, since they cannot be justified *in any way*. Being nonconceptual, they are not the *kind* of thing susceptible to epistemic justification: they cannot be true or false, or correct or incorrect. Derivative maximal probability-makers are not self-justifying either, because, as I argued in §2.2, propositional probability-makers cannot be probability-makers in and of themselves. That is, their being probability-makers depends on unconditional, *non*propositional probability-makers. Thus I have designated propositional probability-makers as *derivative* probability-makers.

Second, neither unconditional nor derivative maximal probability-makers are symmetric. That is, it is false that necessarily if *X* is a justifying, maximal probability-maker for *P*, then *P* is a justifying, maximal probability-maker for *X*. For once again unconditional probability-makers are not the kind of thing susceptible to epistemic justification. And it is false that necessarily if a propositional probability-maker, *P*, is a justifying, maximal probability-maker for *Q*, then *Q* is a justifying, maximal probability-maker for *P*. If *Q* depends for its being justifiable on *P*, *P* will not be able to depend for its being justifiable on *Q*. In other words, if *Q* does

145

not have its justifiability independently of P, Q will not be able to provide the justifiability for P. More generally, the relevant defining relations of *being an explainer, being explained,* and *logical entailing* are not symmetric.

Third, maximal probability-makers are not transitive in the way specified by this principle: necessarily, if X is a justifying, maximal probability-maker for P for S, and P is a justifying, maximal probability-maker for Q for S, then X is a justifying, maximal probability-maker for Q for S. Given this principle, my foundationalist account of maximal probability-makers would imply that all justified propositions are *non*inferentially justified via nonpropositional experiences. We can see this by letting X in that principle be a nonpropositional experience. Inferential justification then becomes superfluous. But since it is not superfluous on my foundationalist account, we should question the transitivity principle in question.

In §2.4 we saw an example that apparently falsifies the transitivity principle. Suppose my subjective nonconceptual contents C, consisting of various apparent sour lemons, make justifiable for me on explanatory grounds the generalization that all lemons are sour (call it 'G'). Suppose also that G makes justifiable for me, via an entailment relation, the proposition that the untested lemon in the refrigerator is sour (call it 'U'). Even though C makes G justifiable for me, and G makes U justifiable for me, C does not itself make U justifiable for me. At least, nothing in my account enables us to say that C itself makes U justifiable for me. After all, C itself does not stand in an explanatory relation to U; nor does C stand in an entailment relation to U. Hence the foregoing transitivity principle apparently fails.

Another basic issue is whether justifying, maximal probability-makers are transmissible through entailment in this sense: necessarily, if there is a justifying, maximal probability-maker for P for S, and P logically entails another proposition, Q, then P is a justifying, maximal probability-maker for Q for S. We can approach this issue via the foregoing characterizations of derivative maximal probability-makers.

Let us ask whether we can imagine a case where: (i) there is a justifying, maximal probability-maker for P for S, (ii) P entails Q, but (iii) there is an uncontravened contravening of (ii) for S. Condition (iii) would be satisfied in certain cases where S has an explanation of his subjective nonperceptual contents that entails that

146

P does not entail Q, and where that explanation is decisively better than every contrary explanation S has for those contents. Or, to use the terminology of §3.1, condition (iii) would be satisfied in cases where S has an overbalancing probability-maker for the proposition that P does not entail Q. Given the possibility of such cases, we should deny that maximal probability-making is transmissible through entailment in the sense specified. Or, at the very least, we now can demand of proponents of transmissibility an explanation why it would be impossible in such cases for S to have uncontravened contravening of the sort suggested. The mere fact that (a) there is a justifying, maximal probability-maker for P and (b) P entails Q does not provide for such an impossibility.

A simple way to salvage the foregoing transmissibility principle is to revise it to include the condition that S have a justifying, maximal probability-maker for the proposition that P entails Q. This condition excludes the troublesome sort of contravening. Thus maximal probability-making is transmissible through entailment if the relevant entailment relation is itself supported by a maximal probability-maker.

A less demanding way to save the transmissibility principle does not require that one have a probability-maker for the relevant entailment relation. Instead it requires (a) that one simply not have an uncontravened contravening of that relation and (b) that one understand the relevant entailed proposition. This requirement also excludes the troublesome sort of contravening, and it saves the transmissibility principle. Thus we have this principle: necessarily, if (i) P is justifiable for S, (ii) P logically entails another proposition, Q, (iii) S understands Q, and (iv) S has no uncontravened contravening of (ii), then P makes Q justifiable for S. This principle will seem implausible if, and apparently only if, we neglect my distinction between justifiability and actual justifiedness.

My account of justifying reasons implies that high statistical probability is not logically sufficient for justifying evidential probability. We can illustrate this point via a familiar lottery case. Consider a fair one-hundred ticket lottery, where I justifiedly believe that just one ticket will win, and where I hold a single ticket. The statistical probability of my ticket's winning is of course 1 percent, and its statistical probability of losing, 99 percent. If high statistical probability were sufficient for epistemic justification, then in such a lottery case the proposition that my ticket will lose would be epistemically justified, or at least justifiable, for me. If the statistical probability of 99 percent is not sufficiently high, we could easily change the example to involve one million, or even one trillion, tickets. The moral of the story would not thereby change. However high the statistical probability of my ticket's losing, such probability is not sufficient for epistemic justification. The reason for this is simple: in the typical lottery case, the proposition that one ticket, such as my ticket, will lose is a probabilistic competitor against the proposition that all the other tickets will lose.

Specifically, in the imagined case the proposition that my ticket will lose is a probabilistic competitor against the proposition that the other ninety-nine tickets will lose. That is, I have an overbalancing probability-maker for the proposition that it is false that my ticket will lose *and* the other ninety-nine tickets will lose. The latter probability-maker derives from the fact that I justifiedly believe that one ticket will win. The proposition that my ticket will lose is no better explanation of my evidence relevant to the lottery than is the proposition that the other ninety-nine tickets will lose. So I do not have a maximal probability-maker for the proposition that my ticket will lose. Thus the proposition that my ticket will lose is not epistemically justified or justifiable for me.

This result is desirable. If we suppose that high statistical probability is sufficient for epistemic justification, we face the problem that it is perfectly arbitrary where we draw the line to distinguish sufficiently high from insufficiently high statistical probability. Should we draw the line at 66 percent or at 95 percent? There is no nonarbitrary answer to such a question. A better approach to evidential probability comes from my proposed account of maximal probability-makers. This account implies that high statistical probability is *not* sufficient for epistemic justification.

Some philosophers have used lottery-style examples to illustrate that one can have a set of justified contingent propositions that is logically inconsistent in the sense that all its members cannot be true.[3] (For relevant discussion see Foley [1979; 1987, Chap. 6] and Klein [1985].) But now we can see that such examples are incon-

---

3 The qualifier 'contingent' is important. If we consider noncontingent propositions too, the possibility of one's having a set of justified inconsistent propositions is virtually automatic, for it seems clear that a necessarily false proposition can be justified for one. When a necessarily false proposition is justified for one, it is of course false that all the propositions justified for one can be true.

clusive if they assume, as they appear to assume, that high statistical probability is sufficient for epistemic justification.

One might propose, however, that an inconsistent lottery-style proposition – call it 'I' – can be justified for one in virtue of its explanatory power for one. Suppose I is inconsistent in the sense that its conjuncts cannot all be true. Could I still be justified for one in virtue of its being a decisively better explanation of one's evidence E than is every understood contrary and probabilistic competitor for one? I suspect not.

It seems that whenever I explains E for one, there will be a consistent explanation, C, of E for one, and I will not be decisively better than C for one. C results from revising I in a way minimally adequate to remove its inconsistency. The inconsistent I entails a contradiction, and thus provides in effect contradictory answers to a single why-question. Either these contradictory answers are essential to I's explaining E or they are not. If not, I's inconsistency apparently is not essential to its explaining E. If they are essential, and if I is basic, then one can have subjective contents whose decisively better explanation for one is provided by an inconsistent proposition. But this seems impossible, given the plausible assumption that one's subjective contents cannot be both F and $\sim F$ in the same respect. On this assumption, C would prevent I from being decisively better for one. For while preserving the consistent explanatory features of I, C would avoid the gratuitous explanatory component due to one conjunct of the implied contradiction. (A directly analogous argument applies to the assumption that I is a nonbasic explainer.)

On my account a contingent proposition, P, is justified for one only if either (a) P is a decisively better explanation for one of one's subjective nonconceptual contents or of a proposition grounded thereon than is every contrary proposition one understands, including $\sim P$, or (b) P is decisively better explained for one by a proposition satisfying (a) than by every contrary proposition one understands, or (c) P is entailed by a proposition satisfying (a) or (b). Regarding (a), if P is a decisively better explanation for one than is every contrary proposition, Q, one understands, then Q of course is not a decisively better explanation than P is for one. And I have just raised doubt that P itself could consist of an inconsistent set of conjuncts, i.e., a set all of whose conjuncts cannot be true. Here my account reduces the issue of justified inconsistent contingent propositions to the question whether there could be an inconsistent contingent proposition that is a decisively better explanation for one than is every understood contrary and probabilistic competitor for one. If my doubt is sound, the latter question deserves a negative answer. And if the propositions satisfying (a) must be consistent, there is no reason to think that alternatives (b) and (c) will allow for justified inconsistent contingent propositions. Thus my account calls into question the possibility of justified inconsistent contingent propositions.

Some philosophers, following Kyburg (1970b), have also used lottery-style examples to argue that the set of justifiable propositions is not closed under conjunction. But my account indicates otherwise, given a certain qualification. Suppose the propositional members of the following set are individually justifiable for me: $\{P1, P2, \ldots, Pn\}$. Is the following conjunctive proposition thereby justifiable for me also: $(P1 \& P2 \& \ldots \& Pn)$? My account enables us to reformulate this question as a question about explanation and entailment relations.

Suppose being *best* for one entails being decisively better than every understood contrary and probabilistic competitor for one. We then have this question: if $P1-Pn$ individually (a) are best explanations for me of my relevant evidence, or (b) are best explained for me by propositions satisfying (a), or (c) are entailed by propositions satisfying (a) or (b), then does $(P1 \& P2 \& \ldots \& Pn)$ also satisfy one of (a)–(c)? Call the latter conjunctive proposition 'C'. Regarding (a), *if* I understand C, then it is a best explanation for me if its individual conjuncts are. For given my preceding remarks on the consistency of best explanations, the mere conjoining of best explainers does not decrease their explanatory efficacy. Similarly regarding (b), *if* I understand C and the conjunction of the propositions that individually best explain C's conjuncts, C will also be best explained for me. Specifically, C will be best explained for me by the conjunction of the propositions that individually best explain its conjuncts. And regarding option (c), if the conjuncts of C are entailed by propositions satisfying (a) or (b), then C of course will be entailed by those propositions too.

Thus it appears that C will be justifiable for one if its individual conjuncts are, so long as (i) one understands C, (ii) in cases where option (b) applies, one understands every proposition essential to C's being best explained for one, and (iii) one has no contravening of the entailment relation between *C*'s individual conjuncts and *C* itself. I assume that there cannot be contravening that applies to *C* itself, but does not apply to some of its conjuncts. Thus I find that the set of justifiable propositions for one is closed under conjunction so long as one satisfies conditions (i)–(iii).

In sum, we now have a fairly clear notion of a justifying reason. A justifying reason is simply a maximal probability-maker. The sort of justification provided by a maximal probability-maker is *epistemic* justification, i.e., the sort of justification required by propositional knowledge. I have distinguished between *unconditional* nonpropositional justifiers, *basic* propositional justifiers, and *nonbasic* propositional justifiers. In doing so, I have emphasized the central importance of the notion of contravening to the notion of a justifying reason. And I have explained how my account accords with epistemic foundationalism.

Let us turn now to the topic of one's *having* a reason, particularly a justifying epistemic reason.

3.3   Having a justifying reason for belief

One's having an epistemically justified belief requires one's *having* a justifying epistemic reason for the relevant believed proposition. I suggested in §1.3 that one can have a justifying reason for a proposition even if one does not actually believe that proposition. In such a case, a proposition is justified, or at least justifiable, *for one*, even if one is not justified *in believing* that proposition.

But what does it mean to say that one *has* a reason, particularly a justifying epistemic reason, for a proposition? Does one have a justifying reason, *X*, for a proposition only if one is thinking about *X*? Or need *X* only be accessible to one in some weaker sense? The considerations about nonoccurrent reasons in §2.5 support the view that one's having a justifying reason at a time does *not* entail one's thinking about that reason at that time. Yet the conditions for one's having a reason deserve attention beyond that given in §2.5.

Let us begin with the notion of one's occurrently having a justifying *non*propositional reason, where such a reason is a maximal unconditional probability-maker as characterized in §3.2. There are at least four noteworthy senses of '*S* occurrently has a justifying nonpropositional reason, *X*, for a proposition, *P*'. They are:

(a) X is occurrently a justifying, maximal probability-maker for P for S (in the sense of §3.2).

(b) X is occurrently a justifying, maximal probability-maker for P for S; and the proposition that X is a justifying reason for P is justified for S on S's total evidence.

(c) X is occurrently a justifying, maximal probability-maker for P for S; and S is justified in believing that X is a justifying reason for P.

(d) X is occurrently a justifying, maximal probability-maker for P for S; and S believes that X is a justifying reason for P.

We might use senses (b)–(d) to generate additional senses, simply by omitting the clause 'X is occurrently a justifying, maximal probability-maker for P for S'. But on such additional senses, S does not necessarily have a justifying reason for P. On such senses S might have only what he *believes* to be, *is justified in believing* to be, or *has evidence to believe* to be, a justifying reason for P. Thus let us overlook such additional senses for now, as we now are concerned with one's having a genuine justifying reason.

Corresponding to senses (a)–(d), there are four noteworthy senses of 'S occurrently has a justifying *propositional* reason, P, for a proposition, Q', where such a reason is a maximal derivative probability-maker as characterized in §3.2. These senses are:

(e) P is occurrently a justifying, maximal probability-maker for Q for S (in the sense of §3.2).

(f) P is occurrently a justifying, maximal probability-maker for Q for S; and the proposition that P is a justifying reason for Q is justified for S on S's total evidence.

(g) P is occurrently a justifying, maximal probability-maker for Q for S; and S is justified in believing that P is a justifying reason for Q.

(h) P is occurrently a justifying, maximal probability-maker for Q for S; and S believes that P is a justifying reason for Q.

Once again we could generate additional senses by omitting the clause 'P is occurrently a justifying, maximal probability-maker for Q for S' from (f)–(h); but, for the reason noted above, we shall not do so.

Let us take (a)–(h), then, as the relevant notions of one's occurrently *having* a justifying reason. We can eliminate all but two of the notions above on the ground that only two are essential to the concept of one's having propositional knowledge.

Clearly one can have propositional knowledge even if one does not have the *concept* of epistemic justification. The propositional knowledge possibly had by many young children, and even by

152

many adults, is not accompanied by one's having the concept of epistemic justification. One's having the concept of justification requires a sort of *epistemological* sophistication that is not found in all possible knowers. This point is compatible of course with the standard view, defended in §1.3, that propositional knowledge requires one's having a justifying reason. One's having a justifying reason is not the same as, and does not require, one's having a *concept* of epistemic justification. But we can eliminate notions (c), (d), (g), and (h) on this ground. For if we assume that occurrent knowledge requires one's having an occurrent justifying reason, and that (c), (d), (g), or (h) determines what it is to have such a reason, we have the view that one's having knowledge requires one's having the concept of epistemic justification.

The key considerations here are (i) that one's genuinely *believing* that X is a justifying reason requires one's having the concept of epistemic justification, since the concept of epistemic justification is a constituent of that believed proposition, and (ii) that (c), (d), (g), and (h) require, for one's having justification, that one believe that X is a justifying reason. Thus notions (c), (d), (g), and (h) are too demanding to provide the notion of one's having a justifying reason that is essential to the concept of propositional knowledge.

The notions (b) and (f) are also too demanding to be essential to the concept of propositional knowledge. If propositional knowledge is justified true belief/assent (which, roughly, is unaccompanied by truths that ultimately contravene one's justification when conjoined to it),[4] then propositional knowledge does not require one's having a justifying reason in the senses (b) and (f). Such justified true belief/assent that P does not require one's having evidence indicating that P is justified; instead it requires that P *be* justified for one. One must have justifying evidence *for P*, but one need not have additional evidence for the epistemic proposition *that P is justified*. Thus to avoid a confusion of levels, we should reject (b) and (f) as candidates for being essential to the concept of propositional knowledge.[5] Another serious problem with senses (b) and

4 We need this parenthetical clause, or at least some variation thereon, to block Gettier-style counterexamples. The present discussion of course does not require a specific resolution of the Gettier problem. I shall provide a straightforward solution to that problem in §6.2.
5 On the general importance of avoiding confusions of epistemic levels, see Alston (1980, 1983).

(f) is that they use the notion of justification *on S's evidence*. This notion presupposes the notion of evidence *that S has*, and thereby threatens circularity in the account of S's having a justifying epistemic reason.

Notions (a) and (e) remain as the concepts of one's having a justifying reason that are required by the concept of occurrent propositional knowledge. It is quite plausible to suppose that these are in fact the required concepts. If, in accord with §3.2.2, we expand these concepts to involve the occurrent satisfaction of the association relation required by actual justifiedness (in contrast to mere justifiability), then they will provide notions of one's occurrently having a reason that provides occurrent justifiedness. Apart from the satisfaction of this association relation, (a) and (e) specify only what it is for a proposition to be occurrently *justifiable for one by a justifying reason one has*. Notion (a) provides the concept of having reasons essential to the concept of occurrent *non*inferential, foundational knowledge, whereas notion (e) is essential to the concept of occurrent *inferential*, nonfoundational knowledge.

At least three points speak in favor of notions (a) and (e). First, in accord with the concept of propositional knowledge, they do not commit one to the excessively demanding view that one's having a justifying reason requires one's having the *concept* of epistemic justification. Second, unlike notions (b) and (f), they do not commit one to a level confusion or to conceptual circularity. And third, it is difficult to think of anything else, beyond the conditions of (a) and (e), that might plausibly be required for one's occurrently having a justifying reason of the sort required by occurrent propositional knowledge. Thus we plausibly can accept (a) and (e) as the notions of one's occurrently having a justifying reason that are required by the concept of occurrent propositional knowledge.

One's having a justifying reason for *P*, in the senses of (a) and (e), is not sufficient for *doxastic* justification, i.e., for one's being justified *in believing* that *P*. Such doxastic justification requires that one's believing that *P* satisfy an evidential basing relation. It requires that one's believing that *P* be appropriately related to one's justifying evidence. For doxastic justification precludes one's believing that *P* solely for the wrong reasons. One's having a justifying reason in the senses (a) and (e) does not require that one satisfy an evidential basing relation. In fact, (a) and (e) do not even require that one believe the relevant justified proposition. So senses (a) and (e) capture only the concept of one's having a justifying reason that is equivalent to the notion of *a proposition's being justifiable for one* by a reason one has. I shall specify the conditions for doxastic justification in §3.4.

Now we can return to the question whether one's having a justifying reason for a proposition, *P*, at a time requires one's thinking about that reason at that time. Clearly one's having such a reason at a time does not require one's thinking about *P* at that time. Sense (a) simply requires that *X* occurrently be a maximal unconditional probability-maker for *P* for one in the sense of §3.2.1; and this does not require one's thinking about *P*. Sense (e) simply requires that *P* occurrently be a maximal derivative probability-maker for *Q* for one, also in the sense of §3.2.1; and this does not require one's thinking about *Q*. Thus neither notion requires one's currently thinking about the proposition made justifiable by the relevant maximal probability-maker.

Similarly, neither notion (a) nor notion (e) requires one's currently thinking about the *justifying*, maximal probability-maker itself. These notions do require one's being presented with the relevant occurrent evidence: subjective nonconceptual contents in the case of (a), and a proposition in the case of (e). But if one's thinking about evidence *E* entails one's formulating judgments about *E*, (a) and (e) are compatible with one's not thinking about *E*. For *E*'s directly attracting one's attention does not entail one's formulating judgments about *E*. Thus given (a) and (e), we evidently should deny that one's occurrently having a justifying reason at a time requires one's thinking about that reason at that time.

Notions (a) and (e) do not give the whole story about having reasons. They tell only the occurrent side of this story. One can have a reason *non*occurrently. We get the nonoccurrent side of the story simply be replacing 'occurrently' in (a) and (e) with 'nonoccurrently'. Thus my account of having reasons fits with the view of §2.5 that justifying reasons can be nonoccurrent, inasmuch as they can be retrievable from memory without being present to one's awareness. My remarks on one's occurrently having a reason have direct analogues to one's nonoccurrently having a reason.

Let us turn now to the evidential basing relation for propositional knowledge.

3.4 The evidential basing relation

Propositional knowledge requires doxastic justification, i.e., one's being justified *in believing* a proposition. Clearly one does not know that P simply when P is justified for one, one believes that P, and P is true. In such a situation one might believe that P solely *for the wrong reason*.[6] Propositional knowledge that P requires that one's believing that P be appropriately related to, or based on, one's justifying reason for P. But *how* must one's believing be based on a justifying reason? This question motivates this section.

We need to distinguish two questions: (i) in *non*inferential knowledge how must one's believing or assenting be based on one's justifying *non*propositional probability-makers, and (ii) in *inferential* knowledge how must one's believing or affirming be based on one's justifying *propositional* probability-makers? Question (ii) will be especially troublesome if we take the basing relation to be a causal relation, and allow abstract entities *alone* to be justifying propositional reasons. For it is not clear how there can be a causal relation between an abstract entity and a belief state or assent state. We can avoid this problem by relying on the sense of 'S has a justifying propositional reason' endorsed in §3.3. Given this sense, the justifying propositional reasons had by S will be propositions *believed* or *assented to* by S. And a belief state or an assent state can stand in a causal relation to another belief state or assent state.

But even aside from the matter of deviant causal chains, mere causal relations between belief states or assent states are insufficient for the evidential basing relation. (Here I agree with Audi [1986] and Alston [1988].) Such causal relations, even if they are direct, do not require that one's believing or affirming be sustained by one's awareness of a relation of evidential support between the relevant proposition and an evidential probability-maker. Mere causal relations between belief states or assent states do not provide for the causal significance of the aforementioned association relation in the evidential basing relation. A version of awareness internalism should provide for the causal significance of that association relation.

6 Of course there could be a case of overdetermination where one believes that P for an unjustifying reason *and* for a justifying reason. I deny that such a case of overdetermination automatically prevents one from knowing that P.

Thus let us consider the following answer to question (ii), which aims to improve on standard causal accounts:

S's believing or assenting to P *is based on* his justifying propositional reason Q = *df.* S's believing or assenting to P is causally sustained in a nondeviant manner by his believing or assenting to Q, and by his associating P and Q.

In §3.2.2 I characterized the relevant notion of associating as the sort of association relation that must be satisfied for a proposition to be actually justified, rather than merely justifiable, for one.

I have used the notion of causal *sustaining* in the foregoing definition, because one's believing that P can be based on one's associating P and Q even if this believing did not causally *originate* from this associating. The important consideration for the basing relation is not the causal *origin* of believing or assenting. It is rather that one *continues* to believe or to assent to P *because* of one's having associated it with one's supporting evidence, which in the case of inferential knowledge is a proposition one believes or assents to. We can understand causal sustenance as follows: barring causal overdetermination, if one had not associated P and Q, and believed or assented to Q, one would not continue to believe or assent to P. The association relation plays a crucial causal role in evidential basing. Its role links one's awareness of the relevant supporting connection (between the supported proposition and its supporting probability-maker) to one's believing or assenting to the supported proposition. One's believing or assenting to the relevant propositional probability-maker also plays a crucial causal role in evidential basing. Its role connects one's commitment to the supporting probability-maker to one's believing or assenting to the supported proposition. Both of these causal components are indispensable to the evidential basing relation.

In answer to question (i) above about noninferential knowledge, we have this notion:

S's believing or assenting to P *is based on* his justifying nonpropositional reason X, consisting of S's subjective nonconceptual experiential contents = *df.* S's believing or assenting to P is causally sustained in a nondeviant manner by his experiencing X, and by his associating P and X.

*Non*inferential propositional knowledge requires the satisfaction of such an evidential basing relation, since the believing or assenting essential to such knowledge must be appropriately related to its relevant nonpropositional evidence. The points above regarding a belief's being based on a propositional reason have obvious analogues applicable to the basing relation and nonpropositional evidence. Since the present definition involves an *experience* as a causal basis, it does not face any special difficulty from its notion of causal sustenance regarding a belief state or an assent state.

We can distinguish occurrent basing from nonoccurrent basing. Occurrent basing obtains when all the relevant relata and connections in the basing relation are present to one's awareness. Otherwise basing is nonoccurrent for one. Fully occurrent knowledge requires occurrent basing, but nonoccurrent knowledge does not.

One point favoring the foregoing two definitions is that it is difficult to think of anything else, beyond their stated conditions, that might plausibly be required for the satisfaction of an evidential basing relation. A special virtue of these definitions is that they avoid over-intellectualizing justification. They allow for one's having doxastic justification without one's having the *concept* of epistemic justification. Thus these definitions are especially generous toward knowers such as children and higher animals outside our species. Indeed, the addition of further requirements to these definitions risks inexcusable unkindness here.

In sum, my account of justifying reasons as maximal probability-makers lends itself to a straightforward causal approach to the evidential basing relation. Having clarified the nature of justifying epistemic reasons, we need now to consider the viability of justification skepticism.

3.5   Against justification skepticism

Justification skepticism comes in many forms. Let us speak of *Humean justification skepticism* as the view that no physical-object propositions are epistemically justifiable for us on the basis of our evidence (where a physical-object proposition is any proposition entailing that there is a physical object).[7] Such skepticism does not

7 Let us not construe this view to presuppose all the details of Hume's own skepticism. On those details, see Stove (1973), Cornman (1980, pp. xi–xix), and Fogelin (1985). Hume's own commitment to Humean skepticism is suggested by his well-

imply that it is logically impossible for physical-object propositions to be justified for us. Its central implication is rather that the evidence we now have is insufficient to provide epistemic justification for any physical-object proposition. According to Humean skepticism, no physical-object proposition is sufficiently epistemically probable, relative to our evidence, to satisfy the justification condition for propositional knowledge.

Humean skepticism has had numerous proponents from Sextus to Hume to Popper.[8] But its proponents are not my main concern. Instead I want to ask whether, and if so how, the nonskeptic can challenge such skepticism. Various nonskeptics from Reid to Moore to Chisholm have simply *assumed* that our commonsense commitments to certain physical-object propositions are justified, and thus that Humean skepticism is false. Chisholm, for example, begins his nonskeptical theory with the "presupposition" that "I am justified in believing certain things [including physical-object propositions] and I am not justified in believing certain other things."[9] Such an approach is simply question-begging against Humean skepticism. Fortunately the nonskeptic has an alternative, non–question-begging approach to such skepticism. I shall explain how my account of justifying reasons enables us to raise a forceful challenge to Humean skepticism.

Suppose I satisfy the conditions for having a maximal probability-maker as follows: (i) I am visually presented with an apparent blue book, (ii) the physical-object proposition that there is a blue book here explains the subjective contents of my experience for me decisively better than does every understood contrary and probabilistic competitor for me, (iii) there is no uncontravened contravening regarding (ii), and (iv) I have associated my subjective contents of an apparent blue book and the physical-object proposition in question in the way specified in §3.2.2.

A skeptic might object that my conditions for a maximal probability-maker fail to require that the supporting evidence *logically*

known remark in the *Treatise* (bk. I, pt. iv, sect. ii) that " 'tis in vain to ask whether there be body or not."

8 On Popper's Humean skepticism, see his (1965, Chap. 10; 1972, Chap. 1). Some other recent proponents include Unger (1975, Chap. 5), Watkins (1984), and Johnsen (1987).

9 See Chisholm (1980, pp. 544–5); cf. Chisholm (1982). Relevantly similar treatment of the skeptic can be found in Armstrong (1973).

guarantee the truth of the relevant physical-object proposition. But such an objection is uncompelling. For admittedly we are trying to capture a notion of epistemic justification that does *not* require truth-entailing certainty or any entailment relation, for that matter. Thus a ground rule for the debate between the skeptic and the nonskeptic is that supporting evidence for contingent propositions need not entail those propositions.[10]

I have suggested that it is difficult to think of anything beyond the conditions specified in §3.2 that might plausibly be required for the (propositional) justification of a physical-object proposition. Thus we now can challenge the justification skeptic to explain what else can be plausibly required for such justification. For it is now the burden of the skeptic to show that there is a plausible notion of such justification whose requirements are not satisfied by the conditions specified in §3.2. This is the first horn of my anti-skeptical dilemma.

Alternatively, the skeptic might accept my notion of justification, but deny that we ever satisfy its conditions. Yet how can one substantiate such a general denial? Can the skeptic support the claim that uncontravened contravening *always* accompanies one's experiences and beliefs? It is not clear how he can. Recall that for a proposition to have unconditional maximal probability for one, it must be a decisively better explanation of one's subjective contents than is every understood contrary and probabilistic competitor for one. Let us say that in such a case of maximal probability, a proposition is a *best* explanation for one. Thus let us ask whether the skeptic can show that a physical-object proposition *never* provides a best explanation for one of the subjective contents of one's experiences. This question leads to the second horn of my anti-skeptical dilemma.

Returning to my example of the proposition that there is a blue book here, we now can identify the skeptic's task as that of showing that that proposition is not a best explanation for me of my subjective contents consisting of an apparent blue book. Specifically, the skeptic must identify an explanation better than, or at least as good as, that provided by the physical-object proposition that there is a blue book here. The noteworthy skeptical explanations are these:

10 This point has been emphasized also by Klein (1981, pp. 12–15, 112–13).

Evil Demon Hypothesis: My subjective contents consisting of an apparent blue book are best explained by the proposition that an evil demon causes me to have such contents.

Berkeleyan Idealist Hypothesis: My subjective contents consisting of an apparent blue book are best explained by the proposition that a divine being causes me to have such contents.

Hallucination Hypothesis: My subjective contents consisting of an apparent blue book are best explained by the proposition that I am simply hallucinating a blue book.

Dream Hypothesis: My subjective contents consisting of an apparent blue book are best explained by the proposition that I am simply dreaming of a blue book.

Reductive Phenomenalist Hypothesis: My subjective contents consisting of an apparent blue book are best explained by the proposition that I am presented with an appearance of a blue book.

Given my conditions for a decisively better explanation (cf. §2.3.2), we can challenge these skeptical proposals and their relevant analogues in short order.

When compared with the foregoing skeptical explanations, the following realist hypothesis provides a physical-object explanation that satisfies the conditions for a decisively better explanation:

Realist Hypothesis: My subjective contents consisting of an apparent blue book are best explained by the physical-object proposition that there is a blue book here.

I shall argue that the physical-object explanation provided by this Realist Hypothesis is decisively superior to the foregoing skeptical explanations. This argument will forcefully challenge any version of justification skepticism involving those explanations. Such skepticism derives whatever plausibility it has from its *actual* explanatory merits; thus we must evaluate it, from an epistemic point of view, in terms of those merits. So the *mere logical possibility* of the skeptical explainers does not lend *epistemic* credibility to justification skepticism concerning physical-object propositions. (My discussion focuses on occurrent justification but can be generalized easily to apply also to nonoccurrent justification.)

The Evil Demon Hypothesis and the Berkeleyan Idealist Hypothesis are relevantly similar in the way they are inferior to the Realist Hypothesis. To account for my subjective contents consisting of an apparent blue book, both of those anti-realist hypotheses posit something that is independent of me and is not represented, in terms of any of its own features, in the contents of my experience. The properties of being rectangular and of being booklike, which are featured by direct analogues in the subjective contents of my experience, are obviously not representative, in *any* straightforward sense, of the features of the Cartesian evil demon or of the Berkeleyan divine being. That is, the posited skeptical explainers are not *themselves* represented at all in my current subjective contents. Thus the explainers posited by those skeptical hypotheses are gratuitous. (In fact, we can plausibly suppose that those hypotheses are gratuitous relative to *all* my subjective contents, past and present.) Consider, too, all the features of the Cartesian evil demon and the Berkeleyan divine being that are not identifiable in my experience by means of corresponding analogues. The Realist Hypothesis, in contrast, does not posit such gratuitous explainers.

So given the conditions of §2.3.2 for a decisively better explanation, the Realist Hypothesis provides a better explanation than either the Evil Demon Hypothesis or the Berkeleyan Idealist Hypothesis. I am not assuming that relative quantitative simplicity of posited explainers is sufficient for a better explanation. My conditions for a decisively better explanation allow for the explanatory *in*feriority of the simpler of two explanations in cases where the simpler account fails to answer the relevant why-questions answered by the more complex explanation. Note also that the skeptical hypotheses under consideration do not have a nongratuitous answer to this simple question: why are there *discrete* features in my current subjective contents? Those skeptical hypotheses cannot appeal of course to discrete physical objects to provide the needed answer.

The Hallucination Hypothesis and the Dream Hypothesis are also similar in the way they are inferior to the Realist Hypothesis. Both of these skeptical hypotheses posit psychological states whose contents are unveridical in the sense that their features do not correspond to the way things really are. But the essential features of such states are not identifiable at all in the subjective contents of my experience. That is, there is no identifiable indication in my present subjective contents of *illusive features due to my hallucinating*

162

or dreaming. I now have no indication whatsoever from my experience that I am simply hallucinating or dreaming. Admittedly I *might* be hallucinating or dreaming now. But so long as there is no identifiable indication of illusive features in my experience, the Hallucination Hypothesis and the Dream Hypothesis will be inferior to the Realist Hypothesis. For in that case those two skeptical hypotheses will fall short of the Realist Hypothesis in the satisfaction of the conditions for a decisively better explanation. Specifically, they will be guilty of positing gratuitous items. The Realist Hypothesis, as ordinarily understood, does not posit items unidentifiable in experience. Thus we should prefer it to the skeptical competitors above. (A directly analogous line of argument applies to a Kantian skeptical hypothesis stating that my own perceptual constitution distorts all my perceptual input.)

We must invoke a different consideration to undercut the Reductive Phenomenalist Hypothesis. For this hypothesis is exceedingly parsimonious in the items it posits. Indeed, its excessiveness on this score is its downfall in the competition with the Realist Hypothesis. That is, the Phenomenalist Hypothesis fails to be an explanation *in any sense* of the relevant subjective contents. For it fails to answer any explanation-seeking why-question concerning those contents. If one asks, for instance, *why* there is an apparent blue book here in my visual field, the Phenomenalist Hypothesis provides only the information that I am presented with an appearance of a blue book. But this information is not an answer in any sense to that why-question; it simply affirms what is queried by that question. And the same is true of the Phenomenalist Hypothesis with regard to any other relevant why-question concerning subjective contents.

Thus given that the features of one's subjective contents need explanation, the Realist Hypothesis is superior to Reductive Phenomenalism. It would be *ad hoc* and unconvincing to object that explanatory considerations are not really relevant to one's subjective contents. For if they are irrelevant here, they cannot nonarbitrarily be invoked elsewhere. And, as I have already suggested, any relevant anti-realist hypothesis depends for its epistemic significance on its actual explanatory success.

Now we can raise the second horn of my dilemma for Humean justification skepticism: it needs to provide an explanation of our

163

subjective contents that is as good as the explanation provided by the Realist Hypothesis. In light of the foregoing considerations, it is doubtful that such an explanation is actually forthcoming.[11]

We have then the basis for a powerful challenge to justification skepticism, once we regard physical-object propositions as potential explainers of one's subjective contents. The foregoing considerations enable us to challenge the Humean justification skeptic with this dilemma: either come up with plausible conditions for justification that this chapter overlooks, or provide an anti-realist explanatory hypothesis that improves on, or at least equals, the Realist Hypothesis. Since Humean skeptics have not accomplished either task, we now have explanatory grounds for recommending the physical-object realism appropriate to my account of justification. Humean skepticism is thus itself a doubtful hypothesis.

My appeal to explanatory considerations here does *not* entail that one has a justified belief only if one actually *draws* an inference to a best explanation of one's subjective contents, where the latter inference requires one's comparing alternative explanations. Yet when one satisfies the conditions for an unconditional maximal probability-maker, there will be an inference to a best explanation that *can be drawn* between one's subjective contents (i.e., there being an apparent X here) and the proposition that there is an X here. We might thus talk of the *inferential basis* of justified propositions, in the sense that when one has a maximal probability-maker for a proposition, an inference to a best explanation *can* be drawn to that proposition. But of course this does not mean that one must actually draw such an inference for a proposition to be justified for one.

3.6 Conclusion

My foundationalist account of justifiers has the distinct advantage of allowing for the noninferential justification of physical-object beliefs. It thus relieves us of the formidable task of deriving all justification from subjective, "seeming-to-perceive" beliefs. And we have seen how my account leads to definite doubts about the viability of justification skepticism concerning physical-object be-

11 Incidentally, this second horn of my dilemma is not altogether new. Somewhat similar anti-skeptical arguments can be found, for instance, in Russell (1912, Chap. 2; 1914b, Chap. 3; 1927, Chap. 20), Ayer (1973, Chap. 5), and Mackie (1976, Chap. 2).

liefs. We have seen that on the basis of this account we can raise a forceful challenge to such skepticism. The availability of this challenge is, I believe, a point in favor of my proposed account of justifying reasons. In addition, we have seen how the proposed account avoids epistemic-level confusions, and is hospitable to knowers such as children and higher non-human animals. Such hospitality is surely a virtue of a theory of epistemic reasons.

But hospitality aside, we have seen numerous other notable virtues of the proposed theory of justifying reasons as maximal probability-makers. For example, we have seen how it avoids the implausible view that high statistical probability is sufficient for epistemic justification. And we have seen how it fits nicely with a causal approach to the evidential basing relation. In §6.3 I shall explain how my foundationalist theory is itself justified.

Overall, then, we now can present this chapter's theory of justifying evidence as a challenger to the various coherentist, contextualist, and reliabilist theories of justification in circulation. Let us turn now to a consideration of such theories and to some likely objections to my foundationalism.

4

Foundationalism and some alternatives

This chapter clarifies the motivation for my foundationalist account of epistemic justification. It anticipates some likely objections, and challenges some prominent alternatives to my account. Specifically, it challenges prominent versions of coherentism, contextualism, and reliabilism; and it answers anti-foundationalist objections from such philosophers as Richard Rorty and Wilfrid Sellars. If the arguments of this chapter are sound, my foundationalist account in Chapters 2 and 3 provides a durable alternative to coherentism, contextualism, and reliabilism.

4.1 Foundationalism is not a mistake

The main likely objections to my foundationalism concern its thesis that the subjective contents of nonconceptual experiences can provide a source of noninferential justification. I shall begin with Richard Rorty's recent anti-foundationalist argument that bears directly on my account.

Following a suggestion from Wilfrid Sellars, Rorty (1979, Chaps. 3, 4) has argued that traditional foundationalism rests on a mistake analogous to the naturalistic fallacy in ethics. After reconstructing Rorty's argument, I shall show that it is unsound, and thus that Rorty has not provided good grounds for his accusation that traditional foundationalism rests on a mistake. I shall also outline the main motivation for my epistemic foundationalism, and argue that Rorty's nonfoundationalist contextualist epistemology itself rests on a mistake. With the tables thus turned, we shall see that my foundationalism escapes Rorty's criticisms.

Rorty claims that epistemology in its standard dress would not have arisen without Locke's "confusion" between "a mechanistic account of the operations of our mind and the 'grounding' of our claims to knowledge" (1979, p. 140). Rorty quotes a remark from Sellars to oppose the sort of confusion allegedly found in Locke: "In characterizing an episode or a state of *knowing* we are not giving an empirical description of that episode or state; we are placing it in the logical space of reasons, of justifying and being able to justify what one says."[1] Following Sellars, Rorty claims that since Locke tried to analyze epistemic facts, such as knowing and justified believing, solely in terms of *non*epistemic facts, he made a mistake analogous to the naturalistic fallacy in ethics. Rorty's central objection to Locke's attempt comes by way of a simple question: why should one think "that a causal explanation of how one comes to have a belief should be an indication of the justification one has for that belief?" (p. 141). Unable to find a plausible answer to this question, Rorty concludes that Locke illicitly confused explanation and justification.

Rorty also provides a diagnosis of Locke's alleged confusion. He claims that Locke, in accord with seventeenth-century philosophers generally, did not think of knowledge as basically a relation between a person and a proposition, and so did not think of knowledge as basically justified true belief. Instead, according to Rorty, Locke followed Aristotle in regarding "knowledge of" as (logically) prior to "knowledge that," and thus he viewed knowledge as basically a relation between a person and an object rather than a person and a proposition. But unlike Aristotle, Locke posited sensory impressions as the causal results of one's "perceiving" physical objects. Such impressions serve as immediate objects of knowledge mediating between the knower and external physical objects.

Thus, following another suggestion from Sellars,[2] Rorty attributes to Locke a confusion between

(a) an impression of a red triangle as *a red and triangular item* that is immediately and noninferentially known to exist and to be red and triangular,

and

(b) an impression of a red triangle as *a knowing that* a red and triangular item exists.

1 Rorty (1979, p. 141). The quote from Sellars comes from his (1963, p. 169). Subsequent page references in this section are to Rorty (1979).
2 See Sellars (1967, p. 211). Cf. Rorty (1979, p. 143). Rorty is actually adapting Sellars's criticism of *Hume's* empiricism.

By confusing (a) and (b), so Rorty's diagnosis goes, Locke neglected the distinction between one's simply *having* an impression of a red triangular object and one's *knowing that* one has an impression of a red triangular object. One could imagine Locke trying to defend his obscuring this distinction by affirming that sensory impressions are "self-intimating" in the sense that whenever they are had, they are known. But Rorty finds that this sort of defense gets Locke into trouble by requiring the existence of a faculty that is aware of, and judges the representational reliability of, the impressions received. The problem is that Locke has no room for such a faculty, as it would introduce a ghost into his Newtonian, machine-like knower (p. 144).

In sum, Rorty takes Locke's mistake to be a confusion between (i) nonpropositional knowledge as the having of a sensory impression and (ii) propositional knowledge as the forming of justified true belief. The major problem of Locke's foundationalism, as Rorty sees it (p. 146), is its failure to explain how propositional "knowledge that" can be based on nonpropositional "knowledge of," i.e., how "knowledge of" can provide an epistemic foundation for "knowledge that."

Locke's effort to found "knowledge that" on "knowledge of" has attracted the support of prominent empiricists at least up through the time of Bertrand Russell. But Rorty claims that there is no reason to support this effort once we understand the basis of Sellars's famous attack on the so-called Myth of the Given.

A distinction between two sorts of awareness underlies Sellars's attack: one's being aware in the sense of one's simply exercising one's ability to respond to stimuli, and one's being aware in the sense of one's giving reasons for, and thereby justifying, what one says. This distinction also underlies the first premise of my reconstruction of Rorty's argument against a foundationalist effort to base "knowledge that" on "knowledge of":

(1) One's simply having a sensory impression of X (e.g., a red triangular object) is just one's exercising one's ability to respond to stimuli; it is at most "knowing what X is like," and is not "knowing what sort of thing X is," which requires the ability to relate the concept of Xness to other concepts in such a way that a claim about X's can be justified (pp. 182, 183).

(2) One can know what red triangularity, for example, is like without knowing that it is different from blue rectangularity, that it is a colored geometrical shape, etc. (p. 184).

(3) One can know that red triangularity is different from blue rectangularity, that it is a colored geometrical shape, etc., while having been blind from birth, and so while not knowing what red triangularity is like (p. 184).

(4) One's having the sort of justification essential to empirical propositional knowledge that X is F requires that one engage in the social practice of showing that appropriate relations hold between the proposition that X is F and certain other propositions supported by the "epistemic authority" of one's social community (pp. 186, 187, 188).

(5) Hence one's knowing what X is like, in the sense of (1), is at most an insufficient and unnecessary causal condition, but is not a justifying ground, for empirical propositional knowledge that X is F (p. 183).

(6) Hence knowledge of X, being knowledge of what X is like, is not temporally prior to knowledge that X is F, but is at most an abstraction from the latter (p. 183).

(7) Hence any empiricist epistemology asserting a nonpropositional foundation for propositional knowledge is "inevitably misguided" (p. 183).

Let us turn now to an assessment of Rorty's anti-foundationalist argument, since it obviously bears on my foundationalism.

Premise (1) is unobjectionable for the purposes of my foundationalism. Its basic claim is that one's merely having a sensory impression is different from one's engaging in the conceptual activity of categorizing that sensory impression as being of a certain sort. The former event of having a sensory impression, X, is just "knowing what X is like" (simply in virtue of having X); but the latter conceptual event is "knowing what *sort* of thing X is," and so requires the categorizing of X.

Rorty, once again following Sellars, holds that "knowing what sort of thing X is" requires an ability to use language, but that "knowing what X is like" is a form of *non*linguistic awareness (pp. 183–5). And he proposes that our attributing nonlinguistic awareness to infants and other non–language-users is just a "courtesy extended potential or imagined fellow-speakers of our language" (p. 190). But premise (1) itself does not entail this controversial proposal.

Premise (2) is also basically unobjectionable. It is equivalent to the plausible claim that it is possible for one to have a sensory impression of red triangularity without one's *knowing that* red triangularity is different from blue rectangularity, or that it is a colored geometrical shape, etc. This latter claim receives support from cases where one responds appropriately to a stimulus of red triangularity while lacking the concepts of blue rectangularity and colored geometrical shape.[3] Clearly if one lacks these concepts, one will also lack the beliefs, and thus the knowledge, that red triangularity is different from blue rectangularity, and that red triangularity is a colored geometrical shape.

Premise (3) is also basically unobjectionable once we acknowledge that a blind person could come to know, perhaps via testimonial evidence from a reliable acquaintance, that red triangularity is different from blue rectangularity, and that it is a colored geometrical shape. Such testimonial evidence would not need to involve the blind person's knowing what red triangularity is like. Consequently, (3) is as unobjectionable as (2).

But premise (4) raises a serious problem: it is question-begging against foundationalism of the sort I proposed in Chapters 2 and 3. Premise (4) implies not only that (a) the sort of justification required by empirical propositional knowledge is a matter of one's *showing* justification to obtain with regard to a proposition, but also that (b) empirical epistemic justification depends on a proposition's being appropriately related to other propositions. A third controversial implication of (4) is that the sort of justification required by empirical propositional knowledge depends on the "epistemic authority" of a social community. Each of these implications of (4) is not only highly controversial but also implausible.

The second implication, viz. (b), is especially relevant to my assessment of argument (1)–(7). (I shall postpone comment on the other two implications until §4.1.2.) What reason do we have to believe that for every empirical proposition, P, the justification of P depends on P's being appropriately related to other *propositions*? Rorty himself nowhere provides the needed reason, and in Chapter 2 I provided grounds for doubting that there is such a reason. Thus Rorty's use of (4) is simply question-begging against my foundationalist thesis stating that the justification of propositions ultimately depends, not on propositions, but on *non*propositional

---

3 Unfortunately Rorty does not provide a positive account of mere response to stimuli, or of the mere having of sensory impressions. But he does claim that such response is nonconceptual "reliable signaling," and that it can be had by rats and amoebas and computers (p. 182). It is not clear though how the latter claim fits with Rorty's aforementioned claim that the attribution of nonlinguistic awareness is just a "courtesy extended potential or imagined fellow-speakers of our language" (pp. 188, 190).

justifiers. Premise (4) is at best a gratuitous assumption of Rorty's anti-foundationalist argument.

But since (4) is gratuitous, Rorty cannot justifiably infer (5), the conclusion that one's knowing what X is like is not a justifying ground for empirical knowledge that X is F. Similarly given the unavailability of (5), Rorty cannot justifiably infer (7), the main conclusion that any epistemology asserting a nonpropositional foundation for empirical propositional knowledge is "inevitably misguided." So Rorty's central argument against foundationalism is at best question-begging and inconclusive.[4] Hence my foundationalism escapes Rorty's argument. Let us turn now to some considerations supporting the foundationalism of Chapters 2 and 3.

One good reason for accepting the foundationalist strategy of ultimately basing the justification of propositions on nonpropositional justifiers is that it provides the most plausible way of terminating a potentially endless regress of justification due to propositions. Since this claim assumes that a foundationalist solution to the famous epistemic regress problem is at least as plausible as any coherentist solution, I shall elaborate on some of the central points of my foundationalist solution.

I construe Locke's thesis that "knowledge that" is based on "knowledge of" as this claim: the justification of empirical propositions is founded ultimately on nonpropositional justifiers, viz., the subjective contents of a nonconceptual perceptual experience. In accord with §2.3.2, let us take one's nonconceptual experience of subjective contents to be a psychological state of direct awareness whereby one's attention is directly attracted by certain phenomenal contents in the sense that one is psychologically presented with those contents. Chapters 2 and 3 explain in detail how one's subjective nonconceptual contents can play a role in the epistemic justification of a proposition. The important point now is simply that since one's subjective nonconceptual contents can be a justifier of

---

4 As for subconclusion (6), Rorty claims (p. 183) that it is a "corollary" of (5). But this claim is false. It is quite consistent for one to accept (5) while denying (6), i.e., while claiming that knowledge of what X is like just happens to be temporally prior to knowledge that X is F. What *is* a corollary of (5) is the claim that knowledge of what X is like is not *logically* prior to knowledge that X is F. But Rorty cannot justifiably infer the latter claim from (5), since so far as Rorty's argument goes, (5) is unjustified.

propositions, but are not themselves in need of epistemic justification (and are not the sort of thing that could be), such contents are a most plausible candidate for what terminates regresses of inferential justification.

But, one might ask, why should we hold that a regress of justification due to propositions must terminate? I treated this question indirectly in §2.2, but now I need to clarify my answer. If a regress of justifiers does not terminate, then either it extends infinitely or it forms a circle of some sort. But it is doubtful that either of these sorts of justificatory regress, infinite or circular, can provide epistemic justification for the proposition at its head. An infinite justificatory regress that is self-contained provides at most an endless chain of *merely conditional* justifiers, i.e., a chain where the head member, M_0, is justified *if* the preceding member M_1 is, and where M_1 is justified *if* M_2 is, and so on *ad infinitum*. As I argued in §2.2.2, it is highly doubtful that such a chain of merely conditional justifiers ever *actually* justifies the proposition at its head.[5]

As for circular regresses of justification, matters are considerably more complicated. So we need to be more detailed.

4.1.1 Two problems for coherentism

A typical objection to circular regresses of justification is that an evidence chain for the head member, M_0, cannot form a circle, since positing a circular evidence chain is equivalent to this claim: M_0 is justified by M_1, M_1 is justified by M_2, . . . , M_{n-1} is justified by M_n, and M_n is justified by M_0. The latter claim, in conjunction with the assumption that epistemic justification is transitive, implies that M_0 justifies itself. But this implication – so the objection goes – indicates that circular evidence chains are unacceptable. The main problem with this sort of objection is that it rests on a false assumption. Most contemporary proponents of circular evidence chains, so-called coherentists, explain regresses of justification in

---

5 For an alternative, *reductio* argument against the conceptual possibility of infinite justificatory regresses, see Cornman (1980, pp. 135–8) and Post (1980, pp. 32–7; 1987, pp. 87–91). We must restrict Cornman's *reductio* to noncircular infinite justificatory regresses in which every member, including the terminal member, is purportedly justified solely by the next member, *and not by any external information*. Similarly my foregoing remarks are restricted to just such regresses. If we neglect this restriction, our anti-infinitist argument will fall prey to objections raised by Sosa (1980a, pp. 11–13). On this matter, see Moser (1985, pp. 107–15).

terms of *non*literal circles, i.e., "circles" of justification involving *non*transitive justificatory relations. Thus they apparently avoid the foregoing objection.

But two serious problems face coherentist approaches to the regress problem. The first problem is a dilemma that assumes that a plausible version of coherentism needs to avoid the sort of externalism I criticized in §2.3.1. My dilemma raises a doubt that coherentism can be conjoined with a plausible version of internalism.

a. A dilemma for internalist coherentism

I shall illustrate my dilemma via Laurence BonJour's (1985) version of coherentism, since it is a straightforward version of internalist coherentism. BonJour has argued at length that only an internalist coherence theory of justification can solve the epistemic regress problem, the problem of explaining how one empirical belief can be justified on the basis of another empirical belief. BonJour's theory is internalist in the minimal sense that it requires that one must have some sort of *access* to the justifiers of one's justified beliefs (1985, pp. 10, 23, 31). And it is coherentist in that it assumes that every justified empirical belief is justified by coherence with the set of one's other beliefs (p. 92). We shall see that this combination of internalism and coherentism generates a fatal dilemma.

BonJour's coherentism relies on the familiar coherentist assumption that the basic source of empirical justification is one's *entire system* of beliefs. On this assumption a particular empirical belief derives its epistemic justification from its cohering with (i.e., sustaining an appropriate inferential relation, such as an explanatory or implication relation to) one's overall belief system. Thus BonJour holds that "the primary justificatory issue is whether or not, under the presumption that I do indeed hold approximately the system of beliefs which I believe myself to hold, those beliefs are justified" (p. 103).

Given its internalism, BonJour's coherentism must also specify the sort of *access* to one's overall belief system that is required. A troublesome question is whether this required access is "cognitive" in BonJour's sense; that is, whether it essentially involves one's *judging* that something is the case, such as that certain beliefs constitute one's overall belief system. If, on the one hand, the access is not cognitive in this sense, then given BonJour's coherentism (and its rejection of the traditional doctrine of givenness), it cannot provide a source of justification (p. 69). And, given BonJour's version of internalism, noncognitive access fails to provide the needed possession of a justifying reason for a justified belief. (I shall discuss the doctrine of givenness in §4.2.) According to BonJour's internalism, an empirical belief, P, is epistemically justified for a person, S, only if S is in *cognitive* possession of a reason making P likely to be true; and "the only way to be in cognitive possession of such a reason is to believe *with justification* the premises from which it follows that the belief [that P] is likely to be true" (1985, p. 32; cf. pp. 43, 123).

Thus BonJour claims that "if a particular belief B is to be justified for a particular person by virtue of possessing [a certain] property, then (if externalism is to be avoided) that person must believe with justification that B does in fact have this property" (p. 80; cf. pp. 31, 50). Such internalism underlies BonJour's rejection of foundationalist solutions to the regress problem, according to which a foundational empirical belief can be justified independently of the justification of any other belief. The rejection of such internalism would leave BonJour and many other coherentists without their main challenge to foundationalism.

If, on the other hand, the required access to one's overall belief system is cognitive in BonJour's sense, an equally serious problem arises. In keeping with BonJour's internalism, suppose that the cognitive access relevant to my justified belief that P is a further belief: the belief – call it 'A_1' – that the members of my overall belief system are B_1, B_2, . . . , B_n, and that P coheres with those members. Given BonJour's internalism, A_1 by itself cannot provide the needed cognitive possession of a justificatory argument for P. For that purpose, according to BonJour (cf. pp. 31, 43, 80, 123), A_1 must itself be justified, since otherwise it would not be a preventive against "epistemic irresponsibility"; that is, it otherwise would fail to preserve the essential connection between justified belief and high likelihood of truth.

Thus there must also be a justificatory argument supporting A_1, an argument whose premises I must believe, according to BonJour's internalism. Call the latter belief (that the relevant premises are true) 'A_2'. Just as A_1 could not provide the needed cognitive possession of a justificatory argument for P, so also A_2, on BonJour's internalism, cannot provide by itself the needed cognitive possession of a justificatory argument for A_1. For this purpose, A_2 must itself be justified. But this means that we need an A_3 in support of A_2, and an A_4 in support of A_3, and so on *ad infinitum*.

So BonJour's internalism leaves us with an infinite regress of required justified beliefs, an endless regress of this form:

A_1: My belief set is B, and P coheres with B.
A_2: My belief set is B, and A_1 coheres with B.
A_3: My belief set is B, and A_2 coheres with B.

$.$

$.$

$.$

This regress *is* endless, since at no point do we arrive at a member that is already justified by an earlier member in the series. Each member in the series is a logically distinct belief. And on BonJour's internalism, each such member requires a logically distinct justifying *and justified* belief concerning its coherence with one's overall belief system.

But it is implausible to suppose that the justification of every empirical belief requires an infinity of additional justified beliefs. A justified belief concerning a proposition's coherence with one's overall belief set is not a *mere disposition to believe*; it is an actual, distinct belief state. (See §1.1 on this distinction.) The formation of a distinct belief state concerning a proposition's coherence with a belief set takes time, given that a belief state requires assenting, which of course takes time. So we have good reason to deny that every justified empirical belief requires an infinity of additional justified beliefs. And even aside from this point, there is, contrary to BonJour's internalism, no reason to think that any of us has, or need have, the sort of endless series of justified beliefs noted above. The members of such a series involve increasingly complex, iterated levels of coherence assessment, and thus require a degree of conceptual sophistication that goes beyond the requirements of simple, non-iterative justification.

One might try to avoid the threat of an endless regress by simply stipulating that the belief providing cognitive access to one's overall belief system does not need justification. BonJour evidently favors this move (1985, pp. 106, 147; 1988). But it is *ad hoc* and troublesome. It is *ad hoc* because its sole purpose is to save BonJour's coherentism from the aforementioned infinite-regress problem generated by its internalism. And it is troublesome for two main reasons. First, it leaves us with the mystery of how justified belief can derive ultimately from *un*justified belief, thereby raising the question whether BonJour's coherentism preserves the essential connection between justified belief and high likelihood of truth. And second, it conflicts with BonJour's anti-foundationalist internalist stricture that a judgmental cognitive state requires justification if it is to play a role in epistemic justification. In relaxing this stricture for his own account, BonJour undercuts the main motivation for his coherentism. For he thereby removes the basis for his rejection of foundationalist solutions to the epistemic regress problem.

We have then a straightforward dilemma for internalist coherentism as developed by BonJour: either its internalism generates an implausible endless regress of required justified beliefs, or it loses its motivation as a coherentist alternative to foundationalism. Both horns of this dilemma are fatally sharp: they imply that BonJour-style internalist coherentism is either implausible or unmotivated.

The general positive lesson of my dilemma is threefold. First, coherentists should drop BonJour's internalist notion of cognitive access in their effort to challenge foundationalist solutions to the epistemic regress problem. Second, internalist coherentists need to identify a type of cognitive access to justifiers that does not itself consist in justified belief. (See §2.3.2 on the basis of my awareness internalism.) Third, it is not at all clear how an internalist version of coherentism can solve the epistemic regress problem.

The key problem here is of course that coherentism acknowledges only propositional belief states and acceptance states as providers of epistemic justification. If a coherentist were to allow for the significance of *non*propositional awareness states to justification, he would be well on the way to avoiding my dilemma, but also to abandoning coherentism. Once one allows for the epistemic significance of nonpropositional awareness, one has departed from the basic coherentist assumption that justification is a function solely of one's beliefs and their interrelations. Thus my dilemma for BonJour-style coherentism evidently provides the basis for a challenge to internalist coherentism in general.

b. The isolation objection

The second serious problem for coherentism is the isolation objection. This objection supports my suggestion that coherentism cannot solve the epistemic regress problem. The basic claim of my isolation objection is simply this: so long as the holding of coherence relations between believed or accepted propositions is sufficient for empirical epistemic justification, such justification can be divorced from one's total empirical evidence. That is, some propositions that are justified on the coherentist account will actually be *un*likely to be true given one's total empirical evidence, including the subjective contents of one's perceptual experiences. So my objection is:

> Epistemic coherentism entails that one can be epistemically justified in accepting a contingent empirical proposition that is incompatible with, or at least improbable given, one's total empirical evidence.

This isolation objection is universally applicable to coherence theories of justification so long as we acknowledge that one's empirical evidence extends beyond the propositions one believes or accepts.

The problem of course is that there is no necessary connection between (a) the holding of coherence relations, however comprehensive, between propositions one believes or accepts and (b) conformity to the subjective contents of one's perceptual experiences. But empirical epistemic justification, by definition, requires that if one has such justification for a proposition, P, then P is likely to be true for one, relative to *all* one's empirical evidence, including the contents of one's perceptual experiences.

Thus to put my isolation objection as a question: why should we grant that a proposition's being coherently related to the other propositions one (coherently) believes or accepts is sufficient for that proposition's being epistemically justified, or even minimally likely to be true, relative to one's total empirical evidence? Cannot one's coherent belief set or acceptance set completely neglect, or even conflict with, what is presented in the contents of one's perceptual experiences? On the basis of these questions, we have good reason to remain suspicious of the justificatory adequacy of coherence relations among believed and accepted propositions. Coherentism in its familiar dress seems not only to neglect the *epistemic* relevance of the contents of one's nonpropositional sensory and perceptual states, but also to allow that one can provide empirical epistemic justification for virtually *any* proposition simply by formulating a coherent belief system into which that proposition fits. These are clearly unacceptable consequences of epistemic coherentism.

Yet let us briefly consider the attempt of BonJour (1985) to salvage epistemic coherentism by means of an *a priori* observation requirement. (Apparently this is the most promising attempt available to the coherentist.) BonJour's observation requirement aims to undercut the objection that coherentism neglects the significance to empirical justification of input from the extra-theoretic world. This requirement basically is that "for the beliefs of a cognitive system to be even candidates for empirical justification, that system must contain laws attributing a high degree of reliability to a reasonable variety of cognitively spontaneous beliefs."[6] This requirement is *a priori*, according to BonJour's coherentism. (But this does not mean that the justification of cognitively spontaneous beliefs derives from something other than coherence.) Beliefs are cognitively spontaneous if and only if their existence is not a result of inference. Thus such beliefs can provide input for a belief system in the sense that they are not derived inferentially from other elements in the system. In fact, BonJour calls such beliefs 'observational beliefs'.

Two serious problems face BonJour's *a priori* observation requirement. First, it is intolerably vague, since it fails to specify what constitutes a "reasonable variety of cognitively spontaneous beliefs." What sort of variety is reasonable? And what is the exact sense of 'reasonable' in BonJour's requirement? If the requirement involves a notion of what is *epistemically* reasonable, it risks circularity; for it plays a role in an explication of the notion of epistemic reasonableness. On the other hand, if the requirement is just that one have a considerable *number* of spontaneous beliefs of different sorts, it will not block my isolation objection. For one's having a great number of such spontaneous beliefs is quite compatible with one's coherent beliefs' neglecting, or being in conflict with, what is presented in one's subjective perceptual contents. Thus we cannot justifiably say that BonJour's theory avoids the isolation objection by preserving the essential connection between empirical justification and what is evidentially probable relative to one's experience.

Second, the observation requirement neglects the special *epistemic* significance of perceptual contents to empirical justification. The requirement does *not* specify that cognitively spontaneous beliefs are justified via their special relation to perceptual contents. Instead

6 BonJour (1985, p. 141). BonJour endorses a similar requirement in his (1976).

178

it assumes that their justification has the same epistemic basis as all other justified beliefs: coherence with the relevant belief system. But this is a serious defect. It is implausible to assume that *all* one's cognitively spontaneous beliefs are evidentially likely to be true so long as they cohere with one's other beliefs. Are such cohering spontaneous beliefs likely to be true even when their only basis is spontaneous conjecture or spontaneous wishful thinking? Surely not. Thus to provide the needed restriction on the set of epistemically relevant spontaneous beliefs, we must introduce a criterion other than coherence. And since the criterion concerns *empirical* justification, we would do well to look to a belief's being supported by the contents of perceptual experience. If we overlook the epistemic significance of this experiential basis, we shall forever be at sea on the coherentist's doxastic raft, with no anchor in the foundation of perceptual experience.

Another noteworthy attempt to avoid the isolation objection comes from Keith Lehrer's coherentism. Lehrer (1988) claims that epistemic justification is a function not only of what one actually accepts, but also of one's "ultrasystem" of accepted propositions. One's ultrasystem is formed by correcting errors in one's acceptance system in two ways: (a) by *weak* correction where we simply delete any error in the acceptance system and any error it entails, and (b) by *strong* correction where we replace any error in the system with the acceptance of its denial, and make such replacements for any error entailed by it. An example will help us determine whether Lehrer's appeal to such an ultrasystem avoids my isolation objection.

Suppose that eliminative materialism about pains is true, and thus that there are no pains, certainly no throbbing pains. And consider the truth-seeking beginning philosophy student, California Jones, who accepts eliminative materialism about pains as a result of hearing some of Paul Churchland's introductory supporting lectures. One night Jones, while eating his own homegrown popcorn, bites into a rusty bolt that had fallen into his cornfield from his old tractor. Jones, as would be expected, apparently experiences a throbbing toothache, since the bolt cracked one of his teeth. (Note that eliminative materialism about pains is by hypothesis true, and thus that by hypothesis there are no throbbing toothaches; accordingly, one's *apparently* experiencing a throbbing toothache does not entail that there is a throbbing toothache.) Yet Jones, let us suppose, does not believe or even accept that he has a throbbing toothache, because he has been convinced by Churchland's eloquent presentation of eliminative materialism about pains.

Jones, accordingly, accepts various true propositions indicating that he does not get throbbing toothaches, and this acceptance is the result of Jones's aiming to obtain truth and avoid error. In addition, the proposition that Jones does not get throbbing toothaches coheres, at least in Lehrer's required sense, with his acceptance system. Yet Jones is acutely aware of his apparent throbbing toothache; it definitely attracts his attention, and it prevents him from finishing his popcorn. But unfortunately Jones, being a beginner at philosophy, has not absorbed enough of Churchland's lectures to account for his apparent throbbing toothache in terms of eliminativism. Jones's commitment to eliminativism consists mainly of these general theses: there are no mental items, all psychological states are physical states, and all talk of mental items is replaceable by talk of physical items. What, then, should we say about what Jones is justified in accepting – aside from obvious lessons about the risks of homegrown popcorn and the dangers of but a little philosophy?

We can make some of the example's assumptions more explicit. We are assuming that the proposition that N [= There are no throbbing toothaches] coheres, at least in Lehrer's required sense, with Jones's acceptance system. That is, we are assuming that Jones accepts that N is, on the basis of his acceptance system, more likely to be true than all its competitors.[7] We can also assume that N coheres with Jones's corrected acceptance system, i.e., his ultrasystem. For we can assume that N and the propositions providing justification for N relative to Jones's actual acceptance system are true. In addition, we can assume that the probabilities determining this coherence are objective in a sense apparently required by Lehrer. Roughly characterized, these probabilities, according to Lehrer (1980b, p. 237), are the probabilities that Jones, given his corrected acceptance system, "would be right" about N. Given these suppositions, we can assume that Jones is justified in accepting that N on the basis of his ultrasystem, the system formed by weak and

7 Lehrer's most recent notion of propositional competition is this: P competes with Q for S on the basis of his acceptance system A if and only if on the basis of A it is more reasonable for S to accept that P on the assumption that $\sim Q$ than on the assumption that Q. See Lehrer (1986, p. 10; 1988, p. 342).

strong corrections in his acceptance system. We now can assume also that Jones is *completely* justified in accepting that N, in the sense that N is justified on Jones's actual acceptance system and on his ultrasystem.

But something has gone wrong. For Jones's apparent throbbing toothache is directly relevant to the justification of his accepting that N. We may call this apparent toothache a *potential underminer* of that justification, since if Jones cannot adequately account for it via an explanation that can incorporate N, then (a) his justification for N will be evidentially defective, and thus (b) he epistemically should refrain from accepting that N. That is, Jones epistemically needs an adequate explanation of his apparent toothache in accord with his eliminative materialism about pains. And if he lacks such an explanation, he epistemically should not accept that N, since his justification for N will then be defective. Jones's accepting that N without such an explanation would be evidentially defective in the sense that it would conflict with, or at least disregard gratuitously, a potential underminer that has not been neutralized. Epistemically justified acceptance is incompatible with such defectiveness. Hence the implication of Lehrer's coherentism that Jones is justified in accepting that N seems wrong.

Put positively, my point is that epistemic justification is a function of (but not only of) what one apparently experiences. The subjective nonpropositional, nonconceptual contents of one's sensory and perceptual experiences are part of one's total empirical evidence, and thereby place constraints on what one is justified in accepting. My California Jones example illustrates just this point.

Thus a coherence theory, such as Lehrer's, that makes justification a function *only* of coherence relations among accepted propositions, even accepted propositions in a corrected ultrasystem, neglects a key constraint on justification. Such a coherence theory allows that one can be justified in accepting an empirical proposition that is improbable relative to one's total empirical evidence. Relative to the subjective contents of Jones's nonbelief experiences, Jones's eliminative materialism about pains (specifically its component N) is not sufficiently probable to be justified. For Jones has no account of how his eliminativism can accommodate the potential underminer due to those experiential contents. Thus my isolation objection seems to apply straightforwardly to Lehrer's coherentism.

Lehrer might reply that his account can accommodate nonpropo-

181

sitional potential underminers in virtue of the fact that people accept propositions concerning what they *apparently experience*. On this reply, Jones accepts that he has an apparent toothache, and this acceptance provides an unneutralized competitor for Jones's view that there are no pains. I am not convinced that this acceptance provides a relevant competitor in Lehrer's sense, but this is not my main problem with the anticipated reply. The main problem is that there is no reason to think that in my example Jones must accept that he has an apparent toothache. As Pollock (1979, 1986) and others have suggested, people rarely even consider propositions about what they *apparently* experience (e.g., what they *seem* to see); and thus it is plausible to suppose that in my example Jones does *not* accept the proposition that he has an apparent toothache. Yet Jones still has the potential underminer due to his nonpropositional sensory contents.

So long as an epistemology fails to acknowledge the *evidential* significance of the subjective nonpropositional contents of one's sensory and perceptual states, it will face serious problems from the isolation objection. And this means that epistemic coherentism, by definition, will always be haunted by the isolation objection.[8]

The foundationalism of Chapters 2 and 3 enables us to avoid both of the serious problems facing coherentism as well as the aforementioned sort of infinite justificatory regress that leaves us with merely conditional justification. On my foundationalism, any regress of inferential justification terminates ultimately with a *non*propositional justifier due to subjective nonconceptual contents, which itself is not in need of any justification. Thus such foundationalism does not neglect the epistemic relevance of one's perceptual contents; nor does it generate an endless regress of justification-requiring items. So to return to Locke's foundationalist strategy, we now can see two distinct advantages of the attempt to found the empirical justification of propositions ultimately on nonpropositional justifiers due to perceptual contents. Far from involving confusion, this foundationalist strategy improves on the shortcomings of epistemic coherentism and infinitism.[9]

8 For additional discussion of my isolation objection to epistemic coherentism, see Moser (1985, pp. 84–102; 1989c).
9 I should reiterate that my nonpropositional justifiers due to perceptual contents are not justified by anything, *including themselves*. A nonpropositional justifier is not the sort of thing susceptible to epistemic justification. Since a nonpropositional

Having clarified the motivation for my foundationalism, let us turn to some key features of Rorty's contextualist alternative to foundationalism.

4.1.2 Against epistemological behaviorism

Epistemic contextualism finds the basis of epistemic justification in a social consensus of some sort.[10] The essence of Rorty's contextualist alternative to foundationalism, his *epistemological behaviorism*, is its aim at "explaining rationality and epistemic authority by reference to what society lets us say, rather than the latter by the former" (1979, p. 174). Rorty's epistemological behaviorism, in accord with premise (4) of his earlier-mentioned antifoundationalist argument, entails this principle:

> EB. One is justified in believing that *P* if and only if one has engaged in the social practice of showing that one's belief that *P* sustains appropriate relations to the other beliefs supported by the "epistemic authority" of one's social community (cf. pp. 186, 187, 188).

This principle is objectionable on at least two counts: it relies on an implausible *showing* notion of justification, and it appeals to the epistemic authority of a social community. Let us briefly consider these two points.

The first flaw in Rorty's epistemological behaviorism is that it runs afoul of the important distinction between one's *having* justification and one's *showing*, or presenting, justification. Nor does it give us any reason to reject this distinction. Contemporary foundationalists typically regard foundationalism as an account of one's having justification for propositions, not of one's showing such justification. Thus it would be irrelevant, if not unfair, to criticize their foundationalism as an account of showing justification. If one's having epistemic justification necessarily involved the showing of evidence, then any foundationalist account relying on subjective nonpropositional justifiers would fail. For one cannot present one's nonpropositional justifiers themselves to another person in any straightforward sense. Of course one might publicly *describe* such

---

justifier can be neither true nor false, and can be neither correct nor incorrect, such a justifier is not even a candidate for epistemic justification.
10 For general discussion of such contextualism, see Moser (1985, Chap. 2), where I assess the contextualism of Annis (1978), Harold Brown (1977), Kuhn (1970), and Wittgenstein (1969).

justifiers, but in doing so one would formulate and present propositions, and thus would not present the nonpropositional justifiers themselves.

Yet one's inability to present one's nonpropositional justification to another person does not entail one's lacking such justification. For it is quite possible that one has justification that one is incapable of publicly presenting. At least, Rorty has given us no reason to deny this possibility. And in overlooking this possibility Rorty's epistemological behaviorism begs a crucial question against the sort of foundationalism I have proposed: the question whether propositional knowledge requires the showing of justification. It seems highly implausible to answer this question in the affirmative.

Another flaw in Rorty's epistemological behaviorism is its appeal to the "epistemic authority" of one's social community. A troublesome question is: how can one's social community have ultimate epistemic authority for oneself? It seems clear that each individual must rely ultimately on his own "epistemic authority" to determine just what it is that his social community agrees on as being true or reasonable. For each individual must rely on his own sensory and perceptual learning processes in finding out what is held in common by the various members of his particular community. One must either read the relevant writings of those community members, or listen, either first-hand or second-hand, to their common claims about what is true or reasonable. But in either case one will be relying ultimately on one's "epistemic authority," at least insofar as one relies on one's own learning processes based on one's own sensory and perceptual experiences.

Rorty's epistemological behaviorism neglects the central importance of the individual's "epistemic authority" in the justificatory process. It is clear that EB above fails to provide for the individual's crucial role in the acquisition of justified belief. The individual's role *is* crucial, since epistemic justification is essentially perspectival, i.e., relative to an individual's evidence. This point is made clear throughout Chapters 2 and 3 of this book.

My concluding proposal is that Rorty's epistemological behaviorism, rather than foundationalism, ultimately rests on a mistake. Epistemological behaviorism rests on a confusion between (i) one's social community's rarely being questioned, and so rarely being shown to be mistaken, with regard to its common knowledge claims, and (ii) one's social community's having epistemic authority

184

for oneself. Clearly (i) does not entail (ii). But Rorty, I suspect, was led to (ii) on the basis of (i). For in developing his epistemological behaviorism, Rorty suggests that it is impossible for our social community to be mistaken in its epistemic assessments (1979, pp. 187–8).

Rorty's guiding assumption appears to be that the very notion of an epistemically justified belief depends on the epistemic rules and decisions of one's social community. But here again Rorty seems to have confused one's *having* an epistemically justified belief with one's *showing* a belief to be epistemically justified. While such showing, in order to be *practically* successful, does require one to conform to certain rules and practices of presenting evidence that are shared by one's fellow discussants, the mere having of justification evidently does not. One's simply having a justified belief does not require one's having any discussants at all; thus it does not require one's satisfying any discussants. At least, Rorty's epistemological behaviorism gives us no reason to think otherwise.

Even if an individual's social community is rarely shown to be mistaken regarding its common knowledge claims (and this is a *big* if), we should hesitate nonetheless to infer that epistemic authority lies in the cognitive decisions of one's social community. For the cognitive decisions of one's social community can, and often do, arise in epistemically unjustified and irrational ways. (Recall, for instance, the notorious Lysenko affair in Soviet biology, or the earlier widespread commitment to racism and sexism in the USA.) Similarly one's social community often lets one say unjustified and irrational things – to return to an earlier remark from Rorty. Social history is replete with unhappy examples of the latter point. It is difficult to formulate clear-cut epistemic principles by means of which one can accurately assess the rationality of one's social community – however 'social community' is defined – but this difficulty does not lend credibility to epistemological behaviorism.

A promising alternative to Rorty's epistemological behaviorism states that epistemic authority lies not in one's social community itself, but rather in *the justifying evidence* possessed by one's social community. On this alternative, we can readily acknowledge the real possibility of a "cognitive rebel" who rationally opposes a socially accepted epistemic assessment with a minority view backed by justifying evidence as characterized in Chapters 2 and 3. Rorty's epistemological behaviorism rules out the real possibility of such a

185

cognitive rebel, and thereby lends support to a sort of epistemo-logical "communityism" that is just as arbitrary as racism. Just as racism is morally repugnant because of its arbitrariness, so also epistemological behaviorism is epistemologically repugnant for a similar reason: it provides no nonarbitrary basis for regarding one's own social community as epistemically authoritative.

In sum, we have seen that Rorty fails not only to show that foundationalism rests on a mistake, but also to provide an adequate, nonarbitrary alternative to foundationalism. Thus if the argument of this section is sound, then it is Rorty's epistemological behav-iorism (and related versions of contextualism), rather than foun-dationalism, that rests on a serious mistake.

4.2   The given is not a myth

My commitment to nonconceptual perceptual contents is a com-mitment to a *given* element in experience, i.e., an element that is not essentially something *taken* to be of a certain sort. This com-mitment to a given element in experience must answer several likely objections. This section faces these objections head on.

Let us begin by characterizing the given in such a way that it obviously is epistemically relevant:

> X is given to a person, S = df. S is immediately aware of X, and X can play a prominent evidential role in the noninferential, im-mediate justification of a foundational belief.

In opposing the so-called Myth of the Given, Wilfrid Sellars is opposing, at the least, the thesis that something is given in the sense specified by this definition.[11] To understand exactly what Sellars is opposing, we should specify the notion of immediate awareness involved in that definition.

Let us assume that one is immediately aware of an object, X, only if one is aware of X in such a way that one need have no propositional or conceptual relations to X, or any other interme-diaries in one's awareness of X. One's having a propositional re-

11 I am not denying that Sellars aims to oppose some other sorts of given too. On the other relevant notions of the given, see Cornman (1972). For evidence that Sellars opposes any doctrine of the given relying on the aforementioned definition, see his (1963, pp. 128, 157, 159). See also Sellars (1973, pp. 616–17; 1979, p. 171).

lation to X is, let us assume, just one's predicating something, such as a property or a relation, of X. And one's having a conceptual relation to X is, let us assume, just one's classifying or categorizing X in accord with some classificatory scheme consisting of certain terms (which might be the members only of a language of thought). Since we plausibly can construe one's predicating something of X as entailing one's classifying or categorizing X under some term, we plausibly can regard one's having a propositional relation to X as entailing one's having a conceptual relation to X. Thus if we can show that one has no conceptual relation to X, we thereby can show that one has no propositional relation to X.

Since one's conceptualizing X in one way rather than in a contrary way (e.g., as F rather than as $\sim F$) requires justification, one's immediate awareness of the given cannot essentially involve conceptualization. On the supposition that immediate awareness of the given essentially involves conceptualization, such awareness will itself require justification. In that case, such awareness will be unable to provide immediate justification for a foundational belief in such a way that a regress of justification-requiring items terminates. One's immediate awareness of the given will then be just another member in a chain of conceptual events requiring justification; it will not then be a terminus of such a chain. So if immediate awareness of the given essentially involves conceptualization, such awareness will be incapable of serving the main foundationalist purpose.

What the proponent of the given needs, then, is a plausible account of *nonconceptual* awareness of the given. I suggested in §2.3.2 that the best candidate for the needed sort of awareness is direct attention attraction whereby one is psychologically presented with certain subjective contents. Although William James once blithely suggested that everyone understands what attention attraction is, it is important to emphasize some of its features. First, it is not a matter of one's categorizing the given under a class term, or any term for that matter. Second, it is not mere sensory stimulation. Clearly one can have one's sensory receptors stimulated by an object, but fail to have one's attention attracted by that object in the sense that one is psychologically presented with, and thus aware of, that object. Thus we should reject the identification of direct visual attention attraction with the purely physical state called 'looking at something'. Direct attention attraction has an ineliminable psychological component: it essentially involves psychological presentation and thus awareness. Yet these considerations do not characterize *what* is given in experience.

As I suggested in §2.3.2, we cannot assume from the start that physical objects are given in experience, if we are to challenge justification skepticism. Thus I suggested for epistemological purposes that what is given are *apparent* physical objects and properties. On this view, talk of immediate awareness of the given does not commit one to an achievement notion of awareness involving one's being psychologically related to mind-independent, external physical objects. On this view, immediate awareness of the given relates one only to apparent physical objects and their properties. Such objects and properties are just the *phenomenal* contents of a nonconceptual awareness state; thus they do not require the existence of mind-independent physical objects. Following adverbial theorists such as Ducasse (1951) and Cornman (1975b), we can think of the apparent physical objects and properties constituting the given as just *the specific character* of some possibly hallucinatory awareness state.[12] But the important point for epistemological purposes is that the given does not transcend the phenomenal contents of such a state.

The first objection to my approach to the given concerns the alleged essential, radical conceptualization of perceptual experience. Proponents of the essential, radical conceptualization of perceptual experience typically rely on an argument of the following sort:

(1) Perceptual experience essentially involves the discrimination of a discrete thing X.
(2) But to discriminate X is to discriminate X as something.
(3) Thus to perceive X is to perceive X as something.
(4) But to perceive X as something is to conceptualize X.
(5) Hence perceptual experience essentially involves conceptualization.

On the basis of such an argument many philosophers have concluded that all perceptual experience is essentially conceptual, and thus that perceptual experience is radically conceptual. Let us call

12 If the adverbial approach to the given can be sustained, we can avoid commitment to the troublesome notion of sense data. For some support for the view that perceptual contents consist of apparent physical objects and their properties rather than sense data, see Firth (1949). We should recall once again, however, that for my epistemological purposes we need not take a stand on the ontological debate concerning direct perceptual realism.

such a view *radical conceptualism*, and its proponents, *radical conceptualists*.[13]

The major problem with the foregoing argument is that premise (1) is false, or at least question-begging. For simplicity I shall focus on visual experience to support this claim. Typically the radical conceptualist countenances only three types of visual process: (a) the purely physical process of merely looking at something, (b) an unconscious "seeing as," and (c) a conscious "seeing as." The process characterized by (a), according to the radical conceptualist, does not provide one with visual perceptual *experience*. But the visual processes characterized by (b) and (c) essentially involve discrimination, and thus differ significantly from the process of merely looking at something. Thus only (b) and (c), according to the radical conceptualist, qualify as processes of visual perceptual experience.

But in assuming that visual perceptual experience requires conscious or unconscious discriminative "seeing as," the radical conceptualist neglects an important kind of nonconceptual experience: visual attention attraction involving visual psychological presentation. As I noted above, visual attention attraction is nonconceptual since it does not require the categorization of anything. And it is important, perceptually as well as epistemically, at least inasmuch as conceptual "seeing as" presupposes it, as I suggested in §2.3.2a.

One noteworthy problem for radical conceptualism, which evidently supports my latter point, is that such a view faces the threat of an imminent endless regress of required conceptual events. According to such conceptualism, if a person, S, is to have a visual perceptual experience of an object, X, S must discriminate X as something, and thus categorize X under some term, F. But it seems that if S is to categorize X under F, S must have some logically prior event of awareness of X; otherwise S may have in his psychological possession nothing whatsoever to categorize under F. Thus it seems that the categorization of X presupposes an awareness of X. Given radical conceptualism, this means that S must have a logically prior event of *conceptual awareness* of X if S is to categorize X under F. But since this prior event of awareness of X is itself conceptual, it also involves categorization of X, and thus presup-

---

13 Proponents of radical conceptualism are legion. Here is a partial list: Armstrong (1961, p. 112), Sellars (1963, pp. 175–6), Rescher (1973, pp. 9–13), Craig (1976), Scheffler (1982, Chap. 2), and Runzo (1982).

poses some logically prior event of awareness of X. For once again, without a logically prior event of awareness of X, S may have in his psychological possession nothing to categorize under F. Moreover, this latter event of awareness will also be conceptual according to radical conceptualism, and thus it will presuppose still another event of conceptual awareness. And the same is true of each member of the resulting endless regress of required events of conceptual awareness.

But of course it is implausible to suppose that every event of perceptual awareness requires an infinity of conceptual events. Since each of our episodic conceptual events occupies a distinct and finite amount of time, and since our events of perceptual awareness occur in a finite amount of time, we should deny that perceptual awareness entails an infinity of conceptual events. Thus we now can challenge the radical conceptualist to explain how we can avoid the threatening regress. Clearly he needs to propose some sort of logical integration of awareness and conceptualization; but the details of such an integration are far from clear. Minimally the radical conceptualist owes us a detailed account of this integration, and an argument for the view that it is indeed a logical integration.

One related problem is that it is quite unclear just what sort of conceptualization is allegedly needed for one's visual experience of a particular item. Suppose that I visually experience the familiar Müller–Lyer illusion, where the bottom line in the illusion looks longer than the top line even though I know that the two lines have the same length. Surely we should not say that my visual experience of this illusion essentially involves my conceptualizing the bottom line as being longer than the top line. After all, I know that the bottom line is not longer. But what then is the conceptualization that is essential to my experience of this illusion? It seems that for any plausible candidates one offers, we can imagine a case where I experience the illusion but lack the relevant conceptualization. This point should make life difficult for the radical conceptualist. (For additional support on this, see Jackson [1977, Chap. 2] and Fodor [1984].)

If we countenance nonconceptual direct attention attraction as a species of experience, we can accommodate the nonconceptual sort of "appearing" or "how something looks" that is suggested by the Müller–Lyer illusion. And we then can avoid the threatening regress identified above. For then we shall be free of the troublesome assumption that every perceptual experience essentially involves conceptualization. The rejection of this assumption does allow us to hold that perceptual awareness *requires* conceptualization in various ways (e.g., causally, psychologically). This rejection entails only that some perceptual awareness does not itself *essentially involve* conceptualization.

One might object in a Kantian vein that direct attention attraction, being nonconceptual, relates one at most to a mere homogenous *this*, and not to determinate perceptual contents having definite (apparent) empirical features. According to this objection, the contents of perceptual experience acquire a determinate nature only via conceptualization, and thus *non*conceptual perceptual contents are *in*determinate in the sense that they do not exemplify definite features. If this objection is correct, nonconceptual attention attraction will be unable to play a central evidential role in the justification of foundational beliefs.

But the anticipated objection is unconvincing, given its reliance on the implausible assumption that the contents of perceptual experience are indeterminate apart from conceptualization. Two main problems face this assumption. First, it entails that all conceptualization of perceptual contents is, in effect, *mis*representation, because such conceptualization attributes *definite* features to the contents of perceptual experience. Given the assumption in question, the conceptualization of perceptual contents as being definite in some way is erroneous. For on this assumption perceptual contents are indeterminate apart from conceptualization. Thus on this assumption all our empirical judgments entailing the determinateness of our perceptual contents are, strictly speaking, false. Moreover, we cannot defend the assumption in question on the ground that one always conceptualizes perceptual contents that already are determinate owing to a prior conceptualization; for we must avoid commitment to the aforementioned sort of endless regress of required conceptual events.

The second problem is that the assumption in question rules out our experiencing perceptual anomalies. That is, it precludes our being aware of perceptual contents that have a determinate nature different from that attributed by our own conceptual activity. On this assumption it will never be true of a perceiver that he experiences perceptual contents exemplifying features that are different from the features he has attributed to those contents via his conceptualization. But this means, contrary to our familiar experiences, that one will never experience perceptual anomalies. I suspect that only a subjective idealist would be content with such an implication.

Another likely objection to my account of the given concerns the so-called ineffability of the given. Numerous philosophers have suggested that since one's immediate awareness of the given is by hypothesis nonpropositional and nonconceptual, it is therefore ineffable. And since one's awareness of the given is ineffable, these philosophers argue, it cannot have any epistemic import.[14]

This objection rests on at least one false assumption: viz., if one's immediate awareness of the given is nonconceptual, it cannot have epistemic import. Chapters 2 and 3 explained how the subjective nonconceptual contents of an awareness state can be a probability-maker, even a justifying probability-maker, for one. And I emphasized in §4.1.1 that the nonconceptual contents of such an awareness state can play a central role in terminating a regress of inferential justification. The latter role saves us from commitment to endless regresses and circles of justification, and thereby provides a solution to the notorious epistemic regress problem. So it is gratuitous to assume that what is nonconceptual is therefore epistemically useless.

Another flaw in the objection at hand is its false assumption that immediate awareness of the given is ineffable. Inasmuch as such immediate awareness is characterizable via the aforementioned notion of direct attention attraction by subjective contents, there is a sense in which it is not ineffable. But perhaps the real worry here is that the given itself is ineffable inasmuch as it is uncharacterizable. Although some foundationalists, such as C. I. Lewis,[15] have spoken paradoxically about the given as being ineffable, I see no reason to agree. In fact, on the basis of the foregoing considerations against radical conceptualism, we evidently have reason to regard the given as having a determinate nature apart from our conceptualization.

In addition, it is quite plausible to suppose in light of my account of the given that one ordinarily can describe the given by means of inspection of one's phenomenal contents. Such a description need not be restricted to those residual sensory qualities often called

14 Some contemporary proponents of this objection are Rorty (1972, p. 650), Michael Williams (1977, pp. 31, 102), Scheffler (1982, pp. 13, 22, 26), and Rescher (1982, pp. 45–6).
15 See Lewis (1926, pp. 206–7; 1929, pp. 52–3). For some relevant discussion, see Firth (1969) and Moser (1988c).

'qualia', since as I suggested above, apparent objects and their properties can be given in experience. Thus in characterizing the given one can speak of apparent objects of various sorts and of apparent features of such objects. Yet we must maintain a clear distinction between the given and its interpretation. An interpretation is introduced when and only when one conceptualizes the given. Thus the given is one thing, and one's interpretation of it, something else.

The next likely objection is that no belief can be justified solely on the basis of the nonconceptual subjective contents that constitute the given. This objection assumes that one will be justified in believing that one sees, or even seems to see, a red square, for instance, only if one has the independent information needed to enable one to distinguish an apparent red square from, say, an apparent blue octagon. Unless one has such information, so the objection goes, one will not be justified in believing anything about the given or on the basis of the given.[16]

The proponent of foundationalism could grant the present claim, but deny that it rules out justification solely on the basis of the given. For it is plausible to hold that the needed information is *semantic* information, i.e., information needed for the understanding, and thus the existence, of one's belief supported by the given. It is also plausible to distinguish the conditions essential to the *justification* of a belief supported by the given from the conditions essential to the *existence* of that belief.[17] Epistemological issues about the justification of a particular belief about the given will presuppose the existence of that belief and thus any conditions essential to that belief's existence. Since the needed semantic information is essential to one's genuinely having a belief supported by the given, we can plausibly deny that one's having such information is essential to the *justification* of that belief; at most it is a condition essential to one's *having* that belief. Mere preconditions of something, *X*, are not necessarily essential to *X* itself.

The final likely objection is simply that one interpretation of experience, such as a perceptual belief, can be justified only by

16 On such a claim, see Sellars (1963, pp. 146–7). This is one of the considerations that led Sellars to introduce talk of "the Myth of the Given."
17 This distinction has been suggested even by philosophers unsympathetic to foundationalism relying on the given. See, for instance, Lehrer (1974, pp. 102–11), Pappas (1982), and Alston (1983, pp. 78–9).

another interpretation of experience, such as another perceptual belief.[18] Yet what we need now, in light of the evidence to the contrary in Chapter 2, is an argument showing that beliefs in general can be justified *only* by cognitive states essentially involving interpretation. It is plausible to suppose that a belief might be *morally* justified, for instance, by its nonbelief consequences. And in the epistemic domain, Chapters 2 and 3 have given us reason to think that foundational beliefs can be justified by the contents of nonbelief perceptual states of seeming to see, hear, smell, taste, and touch. The main conclusion of §2.2 is that we must acknowledge the epistemic significance of the nonbelief presented element in experience. The objection at hand is harmless against this conclusion; in fact, it is simply question-begging against the foundationalism I have defended. This foundationalism explains how the given plays, and must play, a central role in the justification of beliefs about external physical objects. In the absence of further argument to the contrary, then, we may conclude that the given is not a myth after all.

I turn now to another prominent alternative to my foundationalism: epistemic reliabilism.

4.3 Epistemic reliabilism and relevant worlds

Epistemic reliabilism is the widely held view that the epistemic justification of a belief is a function of the reliability of the process that causes that belief. Reliability, broadly conceived, consists in the tendency of a process to produce beliefs that are true rather than false. There are two main variations on epistemic reliabilism: *maximization* reliabilism makes reliability a function of the *number* of true beliefs produced by a process; and *ratio* reliabilism makes reliability a function of the *ratio* of true to false beliefs produced by a process.

One consideration against maximization reliabilism is that the

---

18 This anti-foundationalist objection is common. It is endorsed, for example, by Michael Williams (1977, pp. 31, 102) and by BonJour (1985, p. 69). It appears to be assumed also by Johnsen (1986, p. 605), where it is suggested that the given is suited to play the role of an epistemic foundation only if it is propositional. This suggestion appears to be taken for granted by these three authors. Recently various philosophers, including Sosa (1980a) and Van Cleve (1985), have emphasized the need for argument for such a view.

excessively liberal process of believing *every* proposition one can consider may produce the largest set of true beliefs for one. But whichever version of reliabilism we prefer, we must answer a basic question: what set of possible worlds is relevant to the reliability of a belief-forming process that is justification-conferring? Another, less metaphorical way to put the question is to ask what situations featuring the reliability of a belief-forming process are necessary and sufficient for that process to be a source of justified belief. The argument of this section is that the available answers to this question are inadequate and unpromising, and that therefore epistemic reliabilism is an unacceptable theory of justified belief.

4.3.1 *Three variations on reliabilism*

Let us first consider *actualist reliabilism*, according to which a belief-forming process is justification-conferring if and only if it is reliable *in the actual world*. Such reliabilism is too demanding. Consider the belief-forming process of perception, and suppose that the actual world is inhabited by a deceiving super-neuroscientist who, unbeknownst to us, guarantees that our perceptual processes are unreliable in both the maximization and the ratio sense of 'reliability'. Clearly the *mere existence* of such a deceiver would be insufficient to preclude the epistemic justification of our perceptual beliefs. For from the standpoint of all our justifying evidence (i.e., maximal probability-makers in the sense of §3.2), it still could be maximally probable that our perceptual processes are truth-conducive in the actual world. Thus despite the existence of the deceiver, our perceptual processes could be justification-conferring.

Actualist reliabilism is also too weak. Consider the process of believing in accord with Monday's horoscope, and suppose that this process turns out, contrary to our evidence, to be inerrant. Clearly such a reliable belief process would fail to be justification-conferring, given that our justifying evidence counts strongly against its coincidental reliability. So it is doubtful that actualist reliabilism can solve the problem of relevant worlds.

Obvious analogues of the foregoing two cases count decisively against what may be called *causal reliabilism*, the view that a belief process is justification-conferring if and only if it is reliable in all those worlds *having the same causal laws* as the actual world. But we need not pursue those straightforward analogues.

195

An equally troublesome view is *unrestricted reliabilism*, according to which a belief process is justification-conferring if and only if it is reliable in *all possible worlds*. Such a view is too demanding, since although a process might be unreliable in a bizarre, merely logically possible world, all our justifying evidence (of the sort just mentioned) could indicate that that process is unexceptionably reliable in the actual world. Unrestricted reliabilism is also too weak. Consider a belief process with unrestricted reliability, and suppose that all our justifying evidence indicates that the process in question is highly *un*reliable in the actual world. Given our justifying evidence, that process, although actually truth-conducive, would not be justification-conferring. So unrestricted reliabilism is no real improvement over actualist reliabilism or causal reliabilism. The reliabilist needs an alternative to these three variations. For they neglect the relativity of epistemic justification to one's actual evidence.

4.3.2 Normal-world reliabilism

Let us turn next to Alvin Goldman's recent solution to the problem of relevant worlds.[19] Goldman's reliabilism depends on a rule framework provided by this principle:

> S's believing that P at time t is justified if and only if S's believing that P at t is permitted by a right system of justification rules, and this permission is not undermined by S's cognitive state at t (p. 63).

Goldman's position makes rightness of justification rules a function of the *ratio* of true beliefs produced by the permitted belief-forming processes. Regarding the specific ratio that must be met, Goldman's view is somewhat indefinite. Of course it does require that "a justificationally permitted process must be one that yields a high truth ratio, higher – perhaps appreciably higher – than .50" (p. 103). But beyond this general requirement, Goldman's position is vague, owing to the alleged vagueness in the ordinary concept of justification.

Goldman's criterion for a right system of justification rules can be put simply as follows:

19 Goldman's solution is presented in his (1986, Chap. 5). (All subsequent parenthetical page numbers in this section refer to this book.) Goldman's solution was suggested earlier in his (1979, pp. 17–18).

> A system of justification rules, R, is right if and only if R permits certain belief-forming processes, and the instantiation of these processes would result in a truth ratio of beliefs that meets some specified threshold greater than .50 (p. 106).

Regarding the problem of relevant possible worlds, Goldman endorses what he calls *normal-world chauvinism*, the view that rightness is determined by a sufficiently high truth ratio *in normal worlds*. Normal worlds, on Goldman's account, are possible worlds compatible with our general beliefs about the actual world: worlds consistent with common general beliefs about the sorts of objects, events, and changes that occur in the actual world (p. 107). Thus Goldman's proposal is that, according to our ordinary notion of justification, a rule system is *right* in any world just in case it has a sufficiently high truth ratio *in normal worlds*.

In sum, let us state the core of Goldman's reliabilism as follows:

> A belief-forming process is justified if and only if it is permitted by a system of justification rules that permits only belief-forming processes that are reliable (i.e., have a high truth ratio) in normal worlds.

Goldman concedes that his notion of normal worlds is rather vague, but he finds this acceptable on the ground that our ordinary conception of justification is similarly vague. And he is content with the assumption of his view that the meaning of 'justified' is fixed by our mere (i.e., perhaps false and unjustified) beliefs of a general sort about the world.

Normal-world chauvinism is of course different from the sort of causal reliabilism identified above. Causal reliabilism specifies that a belief process is justification-conferring just in case it is reliable in all those worlds *having the same causal laws as the actual world*. In contrast, normal-world chauvinism states that a belief process is justification-conferring just in case it is reliable in all those worlds *consistent with our general beliefs*. The set of worlds having the same causal laws as the actual world is not necessarily identical to the set of worlds consistent with our general beliefs. Thus these versions of reliabilism are conceptually distinct, since they appeal to conceptually different sets of reliability-determining worlds to determine justification.

It is doubtful that the problem of relevant worlds is adequately handled by normal-world chauvinism. The first troublesome issue suggests that Goldman's requirement for justification-conferring reliability is too demanding. It concerns the assumption that the truth ratio of a belief-forming process is invariant, at least for justification-conferring purposes, across all normal worlds. Recall that normal worlds are possible worlds *consistent* with our general beliefs about the actual world. Such consistency seems not to preserve reliability. For we can conceive of a possible world which is consistent with all our general beliefs about the actual world, but which does not feature the reliability of a particular belief-forming process that is highly reliable in all, or at least almost all, other normal worlds, including the actual world. (Here I follow Goldman in bracketing complications from a potential infinity of normal worlds.) Conceivably the reliability is not featured in the world in question because in that world there is a single, highly limited factor (logically compatible with our general beliefs) that makes the truth ratio of the relevant belief process an even .50. But is this really a possibility for a normal world in Goldman's sense?

The answer depends on what our general beliefs actually *are*, since normal worlds are worlds consistent with such beliefs. The envisaged possibility is genuine, if our general beliefs about belief processes, which determine normal worlds, are of a certain sort. For example, suppose the belief process in question is perception, and assume that we have the (naively optimistic) general belief that perception is reliable in *all* worlds (or even in all worlds where there is perception). Given this hopeful general belief, any world where perception has a truth ratio of .50 would be *ab*normal owing to its being inconsistent with that belief. But if our general beliefs about perception are not of that sort (i.e., if they are consistent with a possible world where there is perception, but where there is also a feature making the truth ratio of perception an even .50), then the envisaged possibility is genuine.

It seems that our actual general beliefs about perception *are* consistent with the sort of possible world in question. For it is highly doubtful that humans uniformly share beliefs about the nature of perception in all possible worlds or even in all possible worlds where perception exists. Perhaps many humans are *disposed to have* such beliefs, yet since few humans have even thought about such matters, only a few have actual beliefs about those matters.[20] But Goldman's

---

20 Here I assume that Goldman's view must preserve the distinction between one's

view requires actual general beliefs as the basis of normal worlds. So it seems that Goldman would be hard put to rule out the possibility of the normal world in question.

Thus although the envisaged situation appears to be a possibility (i.e., a part of a normal world relative to our general beliefs), we must ask whether it is sufficient to preclude justification for the beliefs resulting from the process in question. Goldman's position implies that it is; yet this implication leaves us with an excessive requirement. For, after all, virtually all the normal worlds, including the actual world, preserve the needed reliability, and the single slightly wayward normal world in question decreases the truth ratio only to .50. More to the point, it could be the case that all our justifying evidence (in the sense of §3.2) indicates that the relevant process is highly reliable in the actual world. So normal-world chauvinism is too demanding.

A less stringent requirement available to normal-world chauvinism is that only *a specified high percentage* of the normal worlds need preserve reliability. But such a weakened view faces problems somewhat analogous to those raised above for actualist reliabilism. To show that the present view is too strong, we can consider a situation where a belief process is reliable in a low percentage of normal worlds, but where our justifying evidence (again in the sense of §3.2) indicates that the process is highly reliable in the actual world. Such a discrepancy between our evidence and the majority of normal worlds could stem from the fact, allowed as possible by Goldman, that our general (normal-world–determining) beliefs about the actual world are themselves largely improbable, and thus largely unjustified, relative to our actual evidence. (With slight modification, this case would show also that Goldman's aforementioned less moderate position is too strong.)

The view under consideration is also too weak. Consider a case where a belief process is reliable in a high percentage of normal worlds, but where our justifying evidence indicates overwhelmingly that the process is highly *un*reliable in the actual world. Such a discrepancy, again, could result from our general beliefs' being largely unjustified relative to our evidence. (This sort of case, with

actually believing a proposition and one's being merely disposed to believe a proposition. On this distinction, see §1.1

199

minor alteration, could be used also against Goldman's own, less moderate position.) Thus the problem of relevant worlds is not adequately handled by normal-world chauvinism either of Goldman's sort or of the more moderate sort.

My conclusion gets further support from the fact that not all humans share the same general beliefs about the actual world. Normal worlds for certain humans are *ab*normal for others. Here we need only mention the animism and idealistic mysticism of various tribal communities. Consider, for instance, the Native American tribe whose members hold that they acquire knowledge of the world by means of mystical intuitions of the essential and controlling spiritual features of various nonhuman objects such as trees, mountains, and clouds. Combining animism and mysticism, the members of such a tribe can be called *animystics*, for short.

Normal-world chauvinism implies that the contemporary animystic will be epistemically justified in holding his animism, so long as his belief process of mystical intuition is sufficiently reliable *in his normal worlds*, which of course are radically different from anything like the actual world as depicted by our best physics and psychology. Clearly the process of mystical intuition reliable in the animystic's normal worlds is *not* reliable in our normal worlds, i.e., the normal worlds of those in basic agreement with the main assumptions of contemporary macro-physics and cognitive psychology. Thus the obvious question is whether the reliability provided by the contemporary animystic's normal worlds is sufficient to make his process of mystical intuition justification-conferring for him, despite the available contravening evidence from physics and psychology.

Goldman's normal-world chauvinism leads to relativistic principles of justification each of which is right owing to varying general beliefs about the actual world. A basic principle for the animystic is: Animystic A is epistemically justified in believing that P at time t if and only if A's believing that P at t is permitted by a system of justification rules that permits belief-forming processes that result in a high truth ratio of beliefs *in the animystic's normal worlds*. In contrast, a basic principle of justification for the pro-science believer is: Pro-science believer S is epistemically justified in believing that P at t if and only if S's believing that P at t is permitted by a system of justification rules that permits belief-forming processes that result in a high truth ratio of beliefs *in the pro-science believer's normal worlds*.

Given these contrasting principles, the system of justification rules that is right for the animystic will differ from the system that is right for the pro-science believer.

The right system of rules for the animystic will permit belief-forming processes that are reliable in the animystic's normal worlds. And the right system for the pro-science believer will permit belief-forming processes that are reliable in the pro-science believer's normal worlds. Given the radical difference between those sets of normal worlds, the right systems in question will conflict in the sense that what is *permitted* by one will, at certain points, be *prohibited* by the other. Thus contrary to its aim, Goldman's reliabilism leads to epistemological standard relativism, the view that one system of justification rules is right for one person or culture, while another system is right for another person or culture. The problem with such relativism is *not* that two people can be justified in believing conflicting things – this is not bothersome at all given the variability of justifying evidence. The problem is rather that relativism allows for cases where two equally intelligent people have relevantly similar evidence and believe the same proposition on the basis of that evidence, but where only one of these people is justified in his belief. Such cases should be disallowed on the ground that they foster epistemic arbitrariness: they commit one to a justificational difference without a corresponding evidential difference.

One might counter on Goldman's behalf that *our* general beliefs, and not the animystic's, determine the justificationally relevant normal worlds *for everyone*. Such a reply skirts relativism, but seems unacceptably *ad hoc*. For the following questions remain unanswered: why is epistemic justification a function of *our* (i.e., pro-science believers') general beliefs? That is, what is epistemically special about our mere general beliefs? Why are they more privileged, from an epistemic point of view, than, say, the animystics' mere general beliefs? Lacking answers to such questions, the normal-world chauvinist might turn latitudinarian, and grant the community relativity of viable *concepts* of epistemic justification: the animystics have theirs, and we have ours. But such a move risks undue splintering of the concept of *human* knowledge, given that knowledge entails justification. Or at least it raises the issue of *whose* concept of epistemic justification is essential to the concept of human knowledge. And it leads to the sort of epistemic arbitrariness characterizing epistemic relativism. Reliabilists of Goldman's persuasion, in any case, have not answered the foregoing problem questions.

The threat of relativism arises from the assumption of normal-world chauvinism that epistemic justification is a function ultimately of *mere* general beliefs. Mere general beliefs vary in a way that epistemic justification does not. Thus in making epistemic justification a function of mere general beliefs, normal-world chauvinism does not provide for the needed constraints on such justification. The constraints set by normal-world chauvinism are inadequate mainly because they allow reliability-defining normal worlds to be determined by mere general beliefs, and such beliefs need not satisfy any epistemically relevant, specifically *evidential*, constraints. A symptom of this inadequacy is that normal-world chauvinism allows for epistemically justified belief that is evidentially tenuous in the actual world. Recall the aforementioned implications of the theory for the contemporary animystic's animism. Such a troublesome symptom will characterize any epistemology that makes justified belief a function of *un*justified belief.

The reliabilist cannot avoid the problem at hand, without conceptual circularity, by requiring that the general beliefs in question must themselves be reliable. For the relevant concept of justification-conferring reliability is defined partially in terms of those general beliefs. Or at least the requirement at issue would simply move the problem of relevant worlds to the level of general beliefs, where it is no less troublesome. Barring that useless move, then, normal-world chauvinism leads either to epistemological relativism or to conceptual circularity.

4.3.3 *Reliabilism rejected*

We now can generalize the problem of relevant worlds to challenge *generic reliabilism*, which includes any epistemology that makes epistemically justified belief a function simply of reliable causal processes. The following consideration shows generic reliabilism to be too weak: for any range of possible worlds relevant to justification-conferring reliability, we can imagine that even though a belief-forming process, P, is reliable in those worlds, our justifying evidence (in the sense of §3.2) makes it highly *im*probable that P is reliable in the actual world. In such a situation, the reliability of P would not make P justification-conferring in the actual world.

Generic reliabilism is also too demanding, as the following consideration shows: although P is not reliable across the range of reliability-defining possible worlds, our justifying evidence (again in the sense of §3.2) makes it highly likely that P is reliable in the actual world. In such a situation, our justifying evidence could make P justification-conferring, despite P's being unreliable in certain reliability-defining possible worlds. So we have good reason to hold that generic reliabilism does not set adequate constraints on epistemically justified belief.

A last-ditch effort for the reliabilist might involve an appeal to the sort of no-underminers requirement found above in Goldman's rule-framework principle. The possible response is that the foregoing cases, used to show that reliabilism is too weak, are defective, because they neglect the reliabilist's view that justification requires the absence of undermining evidence. Those cases, so the response goes, are not really cases of justification by reliabilist standards, given the presence of undermining evidence.

But the anticipated response faces an argument that collapses reliabilism into the traditional evidentialist view that justification is a function, not of actual reliability, but of the evidence one has. (See §3.3 on the relevant notion of having evidence.) First, there is no necessary connection between the *actual* reliability of a belief process and one's *having evidence* for its reliability. Thus there can be reliability without one's having supporting evidence. Second, either one's evidence E justifies (i.e., makes maximally probable) the proposition that a belief-forming process, P, is suitably reliable or it does not. If it does, nothing more is needed for P to be justification-conferring; or at least nothing like actual reliability is needed. So we can safely drop the requirement of actual reliability. On the other hand, if E does not justify that proposition, P will not be highly likely to be truth-conducive relative to E, and so will not be justification-conferring for the person whose evidence consists of E.

The upshot of my argument, then, is that once we acknowledge the epistemic significance of justifying evidence, as does the no-underminers requirement in question, we can drop the various reliabilist criteria without epistemological loss. And we may now say good riddance to such criteria, given that the problem of relevant worlds goes with them. More to the point, epistemic reliabilism is not preferable to the foundationalism of Chapter 3.

4.4 Conclusion

The arguments of this chapter lead to two main conclusions. First, my proposed foundationalism has sound motivation from the epistemic regress problem, and withstands likely objections to its reliance on the perceptual given. Second, prominent versions of coherentism, contextualism, and reliabilism face serious problems that this book's foundationalism avoids. A serious defect of coherentism is that it is open to the isolation objection: it neglects the significance of one's *total* empirical evidence to empirical epistemic justification. Once we acknowledge the significance of one's total empirical evidence, we shall be led to reject coherentism. A serious defect of contextualism is its failure to place adequate evidential constraints on an epistemically relevant social consensus. Once we acknowledge such constraints, we can deny that consensus *by itself* is epistemically significant. A serious defect of reliabilism is that it relies on a notion of reliability that is too objective to accommodate the evidential considerations essential to epistemic justification. Once we acknowledge such evidential considerations, we should not be tempted to accept reliabilism. The evidential considerations in question are accommodated, I believe, by the nonreliabilist foundationalism of Chapters 2 and 3. Overall, then, this chapter lends further credibility to this book's foundationalist theory of justification.

The next chapter emphasizes some merits of my proposed theory in connection with procedural epistemic rationality.

5

Procedural epistemic rationality

What in general is the epistemically rational way to be a truth-seeker? This question is different from the question of when one's current evidence epistemically justifies one's current beliefs. The former question, unlike the latter, is directly concerned with guide-lines for one's *regulating* the acquisition of new beliefs. We thus can distinguish conditions for *procedural*, or regulative, epistemic rationality from conditions for *static* epistemic rationality. Conditions for static epistemic rationality are just conditions for one's current evidence epistemically justifying a proposition or a belief for one. Such was the main topic of Chapters 2–4. Conditions for procedural epistemic rationality are, as we shall see, different. (In this chapter my talk of "rationality," unless otherwise indicated, concerns procedural epistemic rationality.)

Epistemologists generally have neglected the question of the conceptual relation between assessments of epistemic *justification* and assessments of procedural epistemic *rationality*. This question merits scrutiny, however, if only because the set of propositions having epistemic justification for one typically includes members that vary in epistemic importance, and that cannot all be believed by one at the same time. This chapter's notion of procedural epistemic rationality concerning propositions is basically the notion of a proposition that it is epistemically more rational for one to believe than not to believe. Such rationality deserves to be called *procedural epistemic rationality*, since it concerns how one epistemically ought to conduct one's believing.

The notions of minimal, overbalancing, and maximal epistemic justification (or evidential probability) from Chapters 2 and 3 do not entail the notion of procedural epistemic rationality, since they do not have implications for the epistemic rationality of one's not believing a proposition. For example, a proposition, P, can have maximal epistemic justification for one, but fail to have procedural epistemic rationality for one, because of its failure to match the epistemic rationality of certain alternative belief candidates that are not its contraries or probabilistic competitors. (On the latter competitors see §3.1.3.) Such alternative belief candidates can be alternatives to P at least in the sense that, for some reason or other, one cannot believe both P and the alternatives in question. Given such alternatives that are more rational than P, P would not have procedural epistemic rationality for one, even if it has maximal epistemic justification for one. In such a case, procedural epistemic rationality would require that one not believe that P, in order to allow for one's believing one or more of the alternatives.

By way of example, suppose that each member of the following endless regress would acquire maximal epistemic justification for me upon my considering and accepting it:

(1) I exist
(2) I believe that (1).
(3) I believe that (2).

.
.
.

Even if the members of this regress would acquire maximal epistemic justification for me, it would not automatically be epistemically rational for me to fill my belief set with such propositions. On the assumption of §1.1 that believing requires assenting (past or present), which takes time, my pursuing the members of such an endless regress would preclude my pursuing other, alternative belief candidates. There is also a sense in which some of these alternatives are epistemically more important than the members of the regress in question. Procedural epistemic rationality would have one conduct one's believing so as not to exclude such epistemically more important alternatives.

Ideally a notion of procedural epistemic rationality specifies the logically necessary and sufficient conditions for (a) its being permissible, from the standpoint of epistemic rationality, for one to believe a proposition and (b) its being permissible, from the standpoint of epistemic rationality, for one not to believe a proposition. The specification of the conditions for (a) and (b) will provide for the familiar distinction between (c) its being epistemically rationally *permissible* for one to believe, or not to believe, a proposition, and

(d) its being epistemically rationally *required* for one to believe, or not to believe, a proposition. We can say that it is epistemically rationally required for one to believe (or not to believe) a proposition if and only if one's not believing (or believing) it is not epistemically rationally permissible for one. Given this distinction, its being epistemically rationally required for one to believe a proposition entails its being epistemically rationally permissible for one to believe that proposition, but the converse entailment does not hold. One's believing a proposition can be epistemically rationally permissible while one's believing an alternative proposition instead is also thus permissible.

The notion of what is *permissible* from the standpoint of epistemic rationality is simply the notion of what satisfies the necessary and sufficient conditions stated by a correct principle of procedural epistemic rationality. A principle of epistemic rationality concerning belief takes the following form:

A proposition, P, of kind K is epistemically rational for a person, S, to believe if and only if X.

Regarding *kinds* of propositions, at least the following categories are relevant: empirical, nonempirical, singular, universal, past tense, and present tense. In the foregoing schema, 'X' stands for a statement of the necessary and sufficient conditions for the epistemic rationality of a certain kind of proposition. Thus given a true epistemic principle, we can say that whatever proposition satisfies the conditions stated by 'X' is epistemically rational.

The necessary and sufficient conditions for epistemic rationality will be represented by one or more declarative sentences that have a truth value. Thus 'X' in the schema above does not itself stand for a prescription, since it stands for something having a truth value. But we can easily derive a prescription from 'X'; and thus we can understand the notion of an epistemically rationally permissible proposition as the notion of what is consistent with what is *prescribed* by a correct principle of epistemic rationality.

Suppose, for example, that we are concerned with empirical propositions, and that 'X' stands for 'S understands P, and P explains the contents of one of S's perceptual experiences decisively better than any other proposition S understands'. The corresponding prescription for S regarding empirical propositions would be: Believe P if and only if you understand P, and P explains the contents of one of your perceptual experiences decisively better than any other proposition you understand. Thus let us take the notion of an epistemically rationally permissible proposition to be equivalent to both (a) the notion of a proposition that is consistent with what is prescribed by a correct principle of epistemic rationality and (b) the notion of a proposition that satisfies the necessary and sufficient conditions stated by a correct principle of epistemic rationality.

Conceivably, more than one proposition about a particular matter satisfies the necessary and sufficient conditions stated by a correct principle of epistemic rationality. In such a case, more than one proposition will be epistemically rationally permissible for one to believe with regard to a particular matter. These propositions taken individually will also be *merely* epistemically rationally permissible for one to believe. None of these propositions will then be epistemically rationally required for one to believe, even if one is epistemically rationally required to believe *some one or other* of these propositions (because one is not rationally permitted to refrain from believing all of them).

Thus far, then, correct principles for the procedural epistemic rationality of propositions indicate not only what is, from an epistemic standpoint, rationally permissible for one to believe, but also what is, from an epistemic standpoint, rationally permissible for one *not* to believe.

However, we can assess at least the following things with regard to their procedural epistemic rationality or irrationality: (a) a proposition construed as a possible object of one's believing or assenting, (b) a state of believing or assenting with regard to the way it has been formed, sustained, or terminated, (c) a state of not believing, or not assenting to, a proposition, and (d) an action with regard to its contributing to the formation, the continuation, or the termination of a belief state or an assent state. Apparently the familiar talk of a *person's* being epistemically rational or irrational is elliptical for talk of the epistemic rationality or irrationality of that person's beliefs, assent states, or actions. Similarly the talk of the epistemic rationality or irrationality of a proposition for a person is often shorthand for talk of its being epistemically rational or irrational for that person *to believe, disbelieve, or withhold* that proposition. But of course a proposition can be epistemically rational for one even when one fails actually to believe it or to assent to it.

Likewise, it can be epistemically rational for one to perform a certain action even when one fails actually to perform it. For example, it can be epistemically rational for me to read certain literature on a particular topic of importance to me even if I now fail to read it because of certain distractions. (Conceivably, I epistemically should read a new book on rationality, but I fail to consider it because of summertime distractions from Lake Michigan.) Philosophers have rarely examined the conditions for epistemically rational action, but this does not mean that these conditions are inherently less important than conditions for epistemically rational belief. This might mean just that conditions for epistemically rational action are highly evasive.

One might propose that the notion of epistemically rational action presupposes the notion of epistemically rational belief. On this proposal, roughly put, the notion of an epistemically rational action is the notion of an action that contributes to epistemically rational believing in a certain way. And on this proposal, we should give the notion of epistemically rational believing relative priority in the order of analysis. In §5.3, however, I shall suggest that this matter may not be quite so straightforward. Yet it does seem clear that the notion of epistemically rational believing presupposes the notion of an epistemically rational proposition. Roughly put, the notion of epistemically rational believing is the notion of one's believing an epistemically rational proposition *on the basis of what makes that proposition epistemically rational for one.*

Chapters 2 and 3, I suggested, were not directly concerned with questions of procedural rationality. But this chapter shows how we can extend the theory of those chapters to answer some basic questions about such rationality. My general strategy now is to examine several notions of truth-seeking relevant to procedural epistemic rationality concerning belief, and to argue for the superiority of a notion that relies on the notion of a maximal probability-maker from §3.2. My proposed notion will have the virtue of specifying the exact relation, regarding relative epistemic importance, between acquiring truth and avoiding error.

In §5.1 I raise doubts about the Cartesian truth-seeking objective according to which one must refuse to believe, and even reject as false, any uncertain proposition. In §5.2 I distinguish and evaluate several noteworthy conceptions of truth-seeking suggested in the epistemological literature. Ultimately I find these conceptions deficient, largely for a single reason. In §5.3 I formulate an alternative conception designed to avoid the defect common to its predecessors: their neglect of the significance of the concept of maximal probability-makers.

5.1 Cartesian truth-seekers

Descartes's characterization of truth-seeking is summarized in Part IV of the *Discourse on Method*:

Because in this case I wished to give myself entirely to the search after truth, I thought that it was necessary for me . . . to reject as absolutely false everything about which I could imagine the least ground of doubt, in order to see if afterwards there remained anything in my belief that was entirely certain.

On Descartes's view the epistemically rational search for truth requires a search for *certainty*, which Descartes understands as a search for indubitable propositions. Specifically Descartes's requirement is that to search after truth, we must refuse to believe and even reject as false every uncertain proposition.

Descartes's requirement is not even initially compelling. It seems that one could rationally search for truth while settling for truth open to some doubt. For instance, the physicist's pursuit of truths about physical objects is not typically accompanied by a quest only for indubitable truths; and yet that pursuit is not obviously irrational. In fact, we should allow for the possibility that such a pursuit is epistemically rational.

Before considering some alleged reasons for endorsing the Cartesian requirement, we should forestall a likely objection to the very notion of an epistemically rational truth-*seeker*. The objection is that this notion is ill formed since it presupposes that believing is under direct voluntary control. I find this objection unconvincing. The notion of an epistemically rational truth-seeker does allow that believing is habit-like and dispositional, and so is not under one's *direct* voluntary control. That is, this notion is compatible with the account of believing in §1.1

Yet it is plausible to hold that believing is typically *indirectly* voluntary.[1] For instance, a person ordinarily can *take measures to*

---

1 Arguments for the indirectly voluntary character of believing have been set forth by Price (1954, pp. 208–13), Chisholm (1968, pp. 223–7), and Naylor (1985). I

cultivate believing of a certain kind, such as believing in accord with a specific sort of evidence. This should not be surprising, given that a person typically can cultivate nonbelief habit-like states. Ordinarily one can indirectly control one's believing either by gathering and focusing on evidence strongly favorable to certain belief candidates, or by ignoring evidence counting against certain beliefs. And one typically can subject oneself to hypnosis to control believing. Thus even if believing is not directly voluntary, we can make sense of the notion of an epistemically rational truth-seeker by acknowledging that believing typically is *indirectly* voluntary. (Or more extremely we could talk simply of rational *assenting* instead of rational believing.)

One useful way to characterize an epistemically rational truth-seeker, and thereby to elucidate the notion of procedural epistemic rationality, is to specify the state of believing in which he, *qua* rational truth-seeker, desires to be. (Hereafter, let us use 'truth-seeker' as short for 'procedurally epistemically rational truth-seeker'.) Thus in attempting to show how the search after truth logically entails a search for certainty, Bernard Williams (1978, pp. 39–40) has proposed that a Cartesian truth-seeker – call him 'S' – would want to achieve this state:

(i) If P, S believes that P, and S's belief has feature E, which is the property of a belief's having been appropriately produced in such a way that beliefs produced in that way are generally true.

Williams finds state (i) preferable to state:

(ii) If P, S believes that P,

on the ground that (i), unlike (ii), accounts for the fact that a truth-seeker needs a *method* of belief acquisition that makes it likely that the acquired beliefs are true. And Williams claims that state (i) will be sufficient for knowledge so long as the relevant feature E excludes accidentally true belief. On this basis Williams concludes that truth-seeking requires a search for *knowledge*.

But of course we need a further step to conclude that truth-

should mention that my notion of a truth-seeker does not conflict with the common view that there are degrees of believing. We might distinguish, for instance, between merely confident believing and believing with absolute certainty as two possibilities for a truth-seeker. For simplicity, however, the subsequent discussion overlooks complications involving degrees of belief. It assumes the notion of believing from §1.1.

seeking requires a search for *certainty*. For knowledge, as standardly conceived and as characterized by (i), does not require any certainty-making feature such as indubitability, incorrigibility, or irrefutability. Williams claims that since a Cartesian truth-seeker's sole aim is to acquire true belief, such a truth-seeker must look for a method of belief acquisition that *guarantees* true belief. The requirement that the method in question guarantee true belief is equivalent, as Williams sees it, to the requirement that the beliefs acquired by the method be certain. On this basis Williams concludes that the search for truth logically requires a search for certainty, or in other words, that the search for certainty is the "only possible road for the pure search for truth" (1978, p. 49).

However, Williams's defense falls far short of supporting the Cartesian requirement. Williams's defense shows *at most* that a Cartesian truth-seeker is required to *try to find* a method of belief acquisition that guarantees the truth of the beliefs thereby acquired. This latter requirement is obviously weaker than the Cartesian requirement that one refuse to believe, and even reject as false, any uncertain proposition. Williams's requirement is *not* violated by a person who looks for, but fails to find, a truth-guaranteeing method, and so settles for believing propositions that are highly likely to be true but less than certain. Yet the Cartesian requirement is violated by such a person. Thus nothing in Williams's defense shows that we must understand the search after truth as requiring one's believing only what is certain. So the Cartesian requirement is, at least as far as Williams's argument goes, unsubstantiated.

It is unclear how one can even begin to substantiate the Cartesian requirement, since a truth-guaranteeing method of belief-acquisition is not necessarily available to all truth-seekers. And it is doubtful that the mere unavailability of such a method precludes one's being an epistemically rational truth-seeker. Another problem with the aforementioned Cartesian view is that it requires that one *reject as false*, and not simply withhold belief from, every proposition about which one can imagine grounds for doubt. This requirement is excessive by any plausible standard of epistemic rationality. Let us turn, then, to some notions of a truth-seeker that are relevant to the notion of procedural epistemic rationality, but that do not rely on the questionable Cartesian approach.

5.2 A plethora of epistemic objectives

Alternatives to the Cartesian notion of a truth-seeker appear in various twentieth-century accounts of a truth-seeker's epistemic objectives and epistemic obligations. The various formulations of such objectives and obligations provide notions of a truth-seeker that are directly relevant to the notion of procedural epistemic rationality. But let us not make much here of the distinction between an epistemic *objective* and an epistemic *obligation*. Instead let us assume (a) that the epistemic objectives essential to a truth-seeker are the objectives a truth-seeker epistemically *should* pursue, and (b) that the epistemic objectives that a truth-seeker epistemically should pursue are objectives essential to a truth-seeker. In due course, I shall clarify further the relevant notion of epistemic obligation. Let us turn now to some purely quantitative approaches to truth-seeking.

5.2.1 Purely quantitative approaches

William James (1896, p. 17) was one of the first to try to clarify the notion of *epistemic obligation*. He explains the notion as follows:

> There are two ways of looking at our duty in the matter of opinion – ways entirely different, and yet ways about whose difference the theory of knowledge seems hitherto to have shown very little concern. *We must know the truth; and we must avoid error* – these are our first and great commandments as would-be knowers; but they are not two ways of stating an identical commandment, they are two separable laws.

James rightly takes the commands 'Acquire truth!' and 'Avoid error!' to be separable epistemic laws, presumably because one can satisfy either without satisfying the other.

One will satisfy the unqualified command to achieve truth simply by believing *every* proposition that comes to mind. In fact, if one believed every available proposition *and* its denial, one thereby would guarantee the acquisition of the largest amount of truth available to one. On the other hand, the unqualified command to avoid error is just as easy to satisfy: it will be satisfied simply by one's refraining from believing anything. Clearly if one believes nothing, one will be free of erroneous belief. But given the *evidentially* undiscriminating ways in which each of these two commands can be satisfied, it is implausible to hold that one's general epistemic

213

obligation is either simply to acquire truth or simply to avoid false belief.[2] For the same reason, it is implausible to suppose that either of these commands specifies the epistemically rational way to be a truth-seeker. One basic problem here is that it is not clear how the command to acquire truth is to be related, *in terms of relative epistemic importance*, to the command to avoid false belief. Unfortunately James does not develop an epistemically relevant solution to this problem.

A directly analogous problem faces an account of a truth-seeker's *epistemic objectives*. Regarding the latter problem, Keith Lehrer has proposed that a truth-seeker's epistemic objective "is to be understood as the twofold objective of seeking to accept as much correct information as one can while at the same time attempting to avoid accepting misinformation."[3] On one interpretation – apparently its intended interpretation – Lehrer's proposal is that a truth-seeker's epistemic objective is perfectionist inasmuch as a truth-seeker aims to acquire truth while avoiding false belief *at any cost*. Given such a perfectionist objective, a truth-seeker would not acquire true belief in a situation where the acquisition of false belief is guaranteed. It is epistemically better on this objective to sacrifice the acquisition of true belief than to sacrifice one's epistemic perfection., i.e., one's being free of guaranteed false belief.

We can clarify the perfectionist objective by contrasting it with some nonperfectionist objectives. Proponents of nonperfectionist objectives typically oppose a perfectionist objective on the ground that it would have one refrain in certain cases from believing propositions that are strongly supported, even justified, by one's evidence. Lottery-style cases are sometimes cited to illustrate this point. But as I suggested in §3.2.3, it is doubtful that the sort of

2 This claim should not be very controversial. But apparently conflicting claims occur in the relevant literature. Price (1969a, p. 128) has stated unqualifiedly that "the end we seek to achieve is to acquire as many correct beliefs as possible on as many subjects as possible." This claim tells at most half the story, as it fails to mention the equally important corresponding aim to avoid error. At the other extreme, Michalos (1978, pp. 206–7) has suggested that commitment to the unqualified obligation to avoid error underlay W. K. Clifford's famous dictum that "one ought to avoid believing anything on insufficient evidence."

3 Lehrer (1975, p. 58). Cf. Lehrer (1980a, p. 42). For a similar view, see Goldman (1980, p. 45) and Keim (1975, p. 75). Keim (p. 77) maintains that "every epistemic viewpoint values getting the truth, avoiding error, and achieving knowledge." The subsequent considerations of this chapter indicate that such a claim hides a multitude of important distinctions.

statistical probabilistic support in lottery cases is sufficient for evidential probability or for epistemic justification. Thus the opponent of a perfectionist objective needs to look elsewhere for examples to illustrate his point. In light of §3.2.3, it is doubtful that clear examples of that sort are forthcoming, if they aim to illustrate one's having a set of justified contingent propositions that is logically inconsistent in the sense that all its members cannot be true. But instead of digressing on that matter, let us consider some nonperfectionist objectives.

Bernard Williams has suggested a noteworthy alternative to a perfectionist objective. He claims that an objective of a truth-seeker is to "maximize true belief," or more accurately, to "raise the truth-ratio [among one's beliefs] to the absolute maximum."[4] This objective is not perfectionist, since it does not require that false belief be avoided at any cost. We might loosely characterize this objective as that of maximizing true belief and minimizing, but not necessarily avoiding altogether, false belief. Williams's talk of maximizing *the ratio* of true to false beliefs is somewhat more precise. But the idea still needs refinement to bear on cases where no false beliefs are acquired. For it is not obvious how we are to compute the ratio in such cases. One natural proposal is that we construe the ratio regarding such cases as the *arithmetical difference* between true and false beliefs. Let us now accept this proposal, if only for the sake of simplicity, and thus construe the first nonperfectionist objective as that of maximizing the arithmetical difference between true and false beliefs.

We should distinguish the present objective from this nonperfectionist objective: that of acquiring as many true beliefs as possible while minimizing, but not necessarily avoiding, false belief. The latter objective does not require that one maximize the arithmetical difference between true and false beliefs. Instead it places a value on one's acquiring *as many true beliefs as possible* while keeping the number of false beliefs to a minimum that may be greater than zero. Thus the latter objective is compatible with the acquisition of guaranteed false beliefs, so long as the largest number of available true beliefs is acquired also. Hence this epistemic objective is conceptually distinct from the aforementioned objectives.

4 See Williams (1978, pp. 49, 200; cf. pp. 46–7, 55, 69). A similar view has been proposed by Alston (1985, p. 25). See also Campbell (1981).

Yet the epistemic objectives under consideration have two features in common. First, they all take a general stand on the relative epistemic importance of the following four possibilities for a truth-seeker:

(a) Believe that P when P is true.
(b) Believe that P when P is false.
(c) Do not believe that P when P is true.
(d) Do not believe that P when P is false.

The unqualified objective to acquire as many true beliefs as possible implies that option (a) is all-important, and thus that option (c) is always to be avoided. Inasmuch as this objective prohibits (c) and does not prohibit (b), we may assume that on this objective (c) is epistemically worse than (b). (Note also that it is this objective alone that is appropriate to a truth-seeker *simpliciter*, taken literally.)

In contrast, the unqualified objective to avoid as many false beliefs as possible implies that option (d) is all-important, and thus that option (b) is always to be avoided. Given this objective, one probably would rank option (d) above (a), and take (b) to be epistemically worse than (c). (Thus this objective is not appropriate to a *truth*-seeker construed literally; at most, it is the aim of a falsehood-avoider.) The aforementioned perfectionist objective suggested by Lehrer implies that it is epistemically worse to believe what is false than to pass up true belief; it thus implies that we should rank option (d) above option (a). But this objective does condone (a) in cases where false belief is not guaranteed.

The two nonperfectionist objectives mentioned above rank (a) above (d), but with distinctive qualifications. The difference objective, suggested by Williams's ratio-oriented goal, values (a) on the condition that the arithmetical difference between true and false beliefs be maximized; whereas the other nonperfectionist objective values (a) on the condition that false beliefs be kept to a minimum that may be greater than zero. Thus the objectives in question take distinctive stands on the relative epistemic importance of the doxastic options above.

The second feature common to the objectives in question is that they are specifically *quantitative* in emphasis: they emphasize the maximizing and/or the minimizing of the *number* of true and/or false beliefs in nonequivalent ways. Such a quantitative emphasis will undoubtedly be taken as misguided by those who find that truths can differ in epistemic importance. If we neglect the relative epistemic importance of truths, we apparently shall have no epistemic ground for faulting a truth-seeker who aims to satisfy his epistemic objective simply by acquiring the member-beliefs of this earlier-mentioned potentially endless regress:

(1) I exist.
(2) I believe that (1).
(3) I believe that (2).
.
.
.

Many of us would fault such a truth-seeker on the ground that he is pursuing only truths that are relatively unimportant from an epistemic point of view. Given the initial plausibility of such a criticism, we should consider some epistemic objectives that are not explicitly quantitative in emphasis. In doing so, we can clarify the relevant notion of epistemic importance.

5.2.2 Nonquantitative approaches

Roderick Chisholm (1977, p. 14) has endorsed this characterization of our general epistemic obligation:

We may assume that every person is subject to a purely intellectual requirement – that of trying his best to bring it about that, for every proposition h that he considers, he accepts h if and only if h is true. One might say that this is the person's responsibility or duty *qua* intellectual being.

Chisholm adds that this purely intellectual requirement is a *prima facie* duty, and so can be overridden by other, perhaps nonintellectual requirements. And Chisholm follows James's view that one's general epistemic obligation consists of two distinct requirements: one should try one's best to bring it about, for any proposition one considers, that one believe that proposition if it is true, *and* one should try one's best to bring it about, for any proposition one considers, that one not believe that proposition if it is false.

Given Chisholm's characterization of epistemic obligation, a truth-seeker should have this objective:

If you consider a proposition, P, try your best to believe that P if and only if P is true.

217

This objective is not a maximization objective: it does not require that one should (try to) acquire *as many true beliefs as possible*. This objective prescribes something only for those propositions that one *actually considers*. But this is a serious defect, if this objective is to characterize the goal of a truth-seeker. For one can satisfy this objective simply by refraining from considering *any* propositions. In failing to satisfy the antecedent of Chisholm's conditional principle, one will never violate that principle. But surely one will not satisfy an appropriate objective of a truth-seeker just in virtue of one's refraining from considering any propositions. Thus Chisholm's objective fails to require that a truth-seeker aim to acquire true beliefs, and so is not a viable alternative to the objectives considered above.[5]

Another problem with Chisholm's objective is that it can be satisfied by one who believes propositions altogether unsupported by one's evidence. One's *trying one's best* to believe that *P* if and only if *P* is true does not require one's believing only propositions supported by one's evidence. This suggests that Chisholm's objective is insufficiently demanding to characterize adequately the state in which an epistemically rational truth-seeker desires to be.

Some other alternatives to the purely quantitative objectives above specify the *kind* of true belief to be acquired. Such alternatives are suggested by the characterizations of scientific inquiry due to Karl Popper, Carl Hempel, and Isaac Levi. As Popper sees scientific inquiry,

Truth is not the only aim of science.... What we look for is interesting truth.... And in the natural sciences (as distinct from mathematics) what we look for is truth which has a high degree of explanatory power. (1965, p. 229; cf. 1972, p. 55)

Under Popper's general influence, Levi writes in a similar vein:

Truth, therefore, cannot be the only desideratum in scientific inquiry. Risking error becomes reasonable because of the demand for [new] information. (1969, p. 59; cf. 1967, Chap. 4; 1980, Chap. 2)

5 One might propose, by way of reply, that Chisholm's epistemic objective be revised as follows: Acquire as large a set of beliefs as possible, each of whose members is such that you hold it if and only if it is true. But this objective does not take a stand on the above-mentioned issue of epistemic perfection. If this objective is construed so as to prohibit the acquisition of a set of contingent beliefs one of whose members must be false, then this objective will be equivalent to the perfectionist objective suggested by Lehrer. But if this objective is not so construed, we need to be told how it differs from the nonperfectionist objectives mentioned earlier.

218

On Levi's view, the objective of our effort to expand our corpus of beliefs should thus involve two desiderata: "the concern to avoid error and the concern to obtain new information, or 'relieve agnosticism' " (1979, p. 96). Here Levi is evidently agreeing with Hempel's view (1962, p. 153) that the "epistemic utility" (i.e., epistemic value) of adding a proposition, h, to a body of scientific knowledge, K, "depends not only on whether h is true or false, but also on how much what h asserts is new, i.e., goes beyond the information already contained in K."

A truth-seeking objective suggested by the remarks of Levi and Hempel is: acquire as many true beliefs with maximal new information as possible while avoiding false belief. We can construe 'maximal new information' in various ways. One way comes from this principle: a contingent proposition (or set of propositions), P, has maximal new information relative to a set of other contingent propositions, and to a belief set, B, if and only if (i) P is not logically entailed by the members of B, and (ii) P is true in fewer, or at most in no more, possible worlds than is each of the members of the set of other propositions in question. On this construal, a proposition such as 'Smith's logic teacher is pedantic' is less informative than a proposition such as 'Smith's logic teacher is pedantic and poor', since the former is true in more possible worlds than the latter.[6] And on this construal a nonredundant disjunction will be less informative than its disjuncts taken individually. But on any such construal, the epistemic objective suggested by Levi and Hempel will not be equivalent to the objective suggested by the quotation from Popper. For maximal new information for one is not necessarily *explanatory* information for one.[7]

6 A minor technical problem confronts this approach to maximal new information if we assume that the propositions 'Smith's logic teacher is pedantic' and 'Smith's logic teacher is pedantic and poor' are each true in an *infinite* number of possible worlds. A straightforward way around this problem comes from the principle stating that the second of the two propositions in question is true in fewer possible worlds than the first inasmuch as the first is true in every possible world where the second is *but not vice versa*. Alternatively we could use the notion of entailment to make the same point.

7 Levi's most recent writings, however, do state that explanatory information is an ingredient of relevant new information. Thus he claims: "By information or informational value I mean whatever features of potential answers such as simplicity, explanatory power, predictive power and the like are deemed useful in gratifying the demands for information which occasion the inquiry" (1982, p. 197; cf. 1980, pp. 34, 45–8).

The objective at hand, however, faces the very same problem I raised above against purely quantitative objectives: it fails to account for the apparent fact that some truths are comparatively *unimportant* from an epistemic point of view. Thus the objective in question could be satisfied by a person who restricts his believing to the members of the endless regress of beliefs about one's existence noted in §5.2.1. Or to take another example, this objective could be satisfied by a person who constructs his belief set solely out of the following series: I call this first blade of grass 'G1'; I call this second blade of grass 'G2'; and so on *ad indefinitum*. At least, it is not clear how this objective would be violated by such believing. But it seems implausible to hold that a truth-seeker would be procedurally epistemically rational, at least in the actual world, just in virtue of the acquisition of such simplistic belief sets. What accounts for this apparent implausibility is the assumption that, other things being equal, to the extent one belief set is lacking in *explanatory power* relative to another, the one belief set is lacking in *epistemic importance* relative to the other.

Somewhat more plausibly, then, Popper's comments on scientific inquiry suggest the following explanation-oriented objective: acquire as many true beliefs with maximal explanatory value as possible while avoiding false belief. There are at least three noteworthy notions of maximal explanatory value in circulation. First, one proposition (or set of propositions), P, has maximal explanatory value relative to a set of other propositions if and only if P explains *more* than does each member of the latter set. Second, P, has maximal explanatory value relative to a set of other propositions if and only if P explains *the same* as each member of the latter set, *and still more*. Third, P, has maximal explanatory value relative to a set of other propositions if and only if P explains *at least as much* as each member of the latter set. This third notion is less strenuous than the preceding notions, but one might use either of the three notions to characterize maximal explanatory value.

Yet whichever notion of maximal explanatory value one prefers, it is doubtful that the objective suggested by Popper will guarantee the acquisition of epistemically important truth. On the plausible assumption that any answer to an explanation-seeking why-question is an explanation,[8] Popper's objective demands that a

8 This is not, of course, to assume that *all* explanations are answers to why-ques-

truth-seeker should acquire either those true beliefs that answer more why-questions than (or at least as many as) their competitors, or those true beliefs that answer the same why-questions as their competitors and still more. But it is quite conceivable in either case that the relevant why-questions are epistemically *un*important. It is doubtful that a belief system is epistemically important simply in virtue of its answering the greatest *number* of why-questions; for such a belief system might nonetheless leave the epistemically important questions unanswered.

By way of example, consider a belief system that (a) explains the truth of a great many propositions having no evidence whatsoever in their favor (not even a minimal probability-maker) and considerable evidence against them, but (b) fails altogether to explain the truth of any of the propositions justified by our total evidence, including all our perceptual evidence. The main problem with such a belief system is of course that it does not explain the truth of those propositions whose truth epistemically *should* be explained (i.e., those propositions justified by our total evidence), and it explains instead the truth of those propositions whose truth should not be explained (i.e., those propositions unjustified relative to our total evidence). Such a belief system, being negligent of justifying evidence, would be defective from an epistemic point of view, even if it were to consist of truths having maximal explanatory value. (We can understand the relevant notion of justifying evidence via the notion of a maximal probability-maker characterized in §3.2.) So we cannot plausibly construe a truth-seeker's epistemic objective as simply the acquisition of truths having maximal explanatory value in any of the three senses noted.

We are thus led to ask about the conditions under which an explanation is epistemically important. Given such conditions, we could recommend generally the sort of true beliefs that one epistemically should pursue. However, some philosophers of a relativist persuasion would propose that what is epistemically important is completely relative to individual truth-seekers. These philosophers would propose that what is epistemically important for an individual truth-seeker is determined by, and so is relative to, the epistemic objectives he actually espouses or prefers. On this proposal,

tions. As I suggested in §2.3.2b, some explanations are answers to *how*-questions, for instances.

what is epistemically important to an adherent of one epistemic objective can be epistemically *un*important to an adherent of another objective, owing simply to the difference between their respective objectives.

A basic assumption of the relativist proposal is that different epistemic objectives can be epistemically appropriate for different people. Such a relativist assumption is suggested by Keith Lehrer's view (1975, p. 71) that the choice between conflicting ultimate epistemic objectives brings one to the "absolutely bottom rock of fundamental epistemic preferences," and that reasonable persons "may have different preferences in this instance." Given this claim, and the further assumption that a truth-seeker is epistemically irrational whenever he believes contrary to an appropriate epistemic objective, we are left with the relativist view that a policy of believing that is epistemically irrational for one truth-seeker might not be thus irrational for another.

We can challenge such relativism by questioning the assumption that the appropriateness of an epistemic objective for one is determined by one's actual epistemic preferences. This assumption leads to an implausible "anything goes" attitude toward what is epistemically appropriate. For instance, on this view it would be epistemically appropriate for one to aim to acquire as many true beliefs as possible without aiming to avoid false beliefs at all, *so long as one preferred to do so*. But such relativism is no more plausible than an "anything goes" attitude in normative ethics,[9] or in normative assessment generally. We can plausibly reject such epistemic relativism on the ground that it would condone one's following a policy of believing in conflict with one's total evidence, so long as one preferred to do so. The condoning of such a belief policy would undercut, in effect, the essential connection between epistemically rational belief and belief supported by one's total evidence.

The following section formulates and defends an epistemic objective that preserves the essential connection between procedurally rational belief and belief supported by one's total justifying evidence. This objective will enable us to resolve the dispute between proponents of perfectionist and nonperfectionist epistemic objectives. And it will give us the basis for an adequate conception of

9 For a challenge to such relativism in ethics, see Moser (1988b) and Carson (1985).

epistemic obligation. In doing so, it will also lead to clarification of the aforementioned notion of epistemic importance.

One significant motivation for the objective to be formulated is a common shortcoming in the aforementioned epistemic objectives: their failure to include the requirement that there be an appropriate *evidence basis* for the beliefs we acquire as epistemically rational truth-seekers.[10] Lacking such a requirement, we shall be unable to fault the acquisition of true beliefs supported only by groundless suspicion, unbridled speculation, lucky guesswork, or wishful thinking. But of course we need to fault the acquisition of such accidentally true belief from an epistemic viewpoint, since there is no relevant epistemic difference between such belief and beliefs that are obviously epistemically irrational due to evidential considerations. Even if lucky guesswork, for instance, is a reliable belief-forming mechanism because of its producing more true than false beliefs, true beliefs based solely on lucky guesswork are epistemically defective, for they are not supported by adequate evidence for their likely truth. Thus they are not relevantly different from epistemically irrational beliefs. Another shortcoming of the objectives above is that they fail to suggest any discriminate way to resolve disagreements concerning perfectionist and nonperfectionist epistemic objectives.

5.3 An evidential epistemic objective

A natural alternative to the foregoing epistemic objectives derives from the account of justifying probability-makers in §3.2. This alternative gives a central role to justifying evidence, specifically maximal probability-makers, and thus it may be called an *evidential* epistemic objective. It is:

10 One might think that Bernard Williams's defense of the Cartesian objective in §5.1 provides an exception here, since Williams introduced the feature *E* that requires that any belief acquired by a truth-seeker be reliably produced, i.e., produced in such a way that beliefs so produced are generally true. However, such reliable belief production does not require that the believer *have justifying evidence* for his belief's being true or reliably produced. One's belief that *P* can be reliably produced, in the sense specified, while the belief that *P* is at best accidentally true from the standpoint of one's total evidence. A similar problem faces various versions of epistemic reliabilism in circulation, as I suggested in §4.3.

EO. Acquire as many true beliefs as possible and avoid the acquisition of as many false beliefs as possible while believing a proposition, P, if and only if P plays an essential role in an ultimately uncontravened decisively best explanation for one of one's unextended justifying evidence.

EO states an *objective* definitive of procedural epistemic rationality concerning belief, and so should not be confused with a statement of the *means* for achieving that objective. EO leaves open the task of characterizing such means. Of course EO is compatible with the view that one's believing all and only propositions adequately supported by one's total justifying evidence (in the sense of §3.2) is an epistemically likely and nonarbitrary means to the maximization of true belief and the minimization of false belief. But EO assumes that we cannot adequately state an objective definitive of procedural epistemic rationality simply by talking about the maximization of true belief and the minimization of false belief.

Thus, in accord with EO, we need to state an evidential requirement as an integral part of an epistemic objective definitive of procedural rationality. Lacking such a requirement, we shall risk allowing that a procedurally rational truth-seeker can achieve an appropriate epistemic objective in any number of evidentially arbitrary ways; and we shall be faced with difficult complications from the question of when it is epistemically rational to acquire false belief and when it is not. (I shall return to the latter point below.) Also in accord with EO, we need to prohibit one's believing only propositions that are relatively epistemically unimportant relative to one's justifying evidence.

The notion of ultimately uncontravened decisively best explanation in EO draws on §3.2. I shall not rehearse the relevant discussion of contravening of an explanation. Let us say that an explanation, P, is *decisively best* for one relative to one's evidence E if and only if P explains E for one and does so decisively better than does *every other explanation of E that one understands*, including every understood contrary and probabilistic competitor for one. Given the notion of a decisively better explanation from §3.2, a decisively best explanation, P, will be informationally more specific than any alternative explanation for one that is as good as P regarding the answering of why-questions and the positing of gratuitous entities. The relevant notion of specificity is this: P is informationally more specific than Q if and only if P logically entails

Q but is not logically entailed by Q. This notion enables EO to prohibit one's expanding one's belief set with ever-increasing disjunctions that fail to add explanatory benefits.

EO uses a notion of *unextended* justifying evidence that is also understandable via §3.2. Unextended justifying evidence is either (a) an unconditional justifier due to one's subjective nonconceptual contents, or (b) a basic propositional justifier that decisively best explains certain of one's nonconceptual contents for one in the absence of uncontravened contravening, or (c) a nonbasic propositional justifier, P, that in the absence of uncontravened contravening either (i) decisively best explains for one a proposition, Q, satisfying (b), or (ii) is decisively best explained for one by Q in such a way that if P is disjunctive, each of P's disjuncts is essential to Q's being a decisively best explanation of any of P's other disjuncts for one.

EO needs its restriction concerning unextended justifying evidence to avoid a problem from justifiable disjunctions. Suppose that P is justifiable for me because P decisively best explains for me certain of my nonconceptual contents in the absence of contravening. Assume also that P decisively best explains Q for me in the absence of contravening, and thus that P also decisively best explains $(Q \lor R)$ for me in the absence of contravening. Further, suppose that H decisively best explains $(Q \lor R)$ for me in the absence of contravening simply because H best explains R for me. In such a case it would not necessarily be epistemically rational for me to believe that H. For H's explanatory value in such a case is inadequately related to my unextended evidence; it has that value, we might say, in a wayward manner. Such a case calls for the restriction of EO to unextended justifying evidence.

The motivation for the requirement of decisively best explanation should be clear in light of §5.2. Briefly, we want to prohibit one's satisfying an epistemic objective definitive of procedural rationality in either of two ways: (a) by maximizing true belief in a series of highly indefinite, relatively uninformative propositions (e.g., a series of disjunctions constructed by the addition of a single new disjunct at each step) or (b) by maximizing true belief in a series of propositions that are informationally specific but relatively epistemically unimportant insofar as they are comparatively lacking in explanatory value (e.g., a series, like that mentioned in §5.2.1, of beliefs of increasing doxastic order about one's existence).

225

Thus EO allows that there can be justifiable propositions for one that are not procedurally epistemically rational for one to believe. And this is how things should be. Yet EO does *not* automatically prohibit one's believing the implications of propositions justifiable for one. It prohibits such believing *only* when such believing does not play an essential role in a decisively best explanation relative to one's unextended justifying evidence. If we reject such a prohibition, we shall risk the epistemic rationality of the just-mentioned options (a) and (b).

We have seen that some demands for maximal explanatory value are not sufficient to promote the acquisition of truths that are comparatively epistemically important. These demands allow that one's belief set has maximal explanatory value but fails to explain the truth of propositions whose truth epistemically *should* be explained, i.e., propositions justifiable on one's total evidence. EO avoids this deficiency by requiring that one's explanatory beliefs be restricted to those propositions that decisively best explain, and are justifiable on, one's unextended justifying evidence. Given this requirement, EO prohibits the acquisition of beliefs that are not evidentially more probable than their understood contraries and probabilistic competitors for one.

We now can see how EO ranks the separable objectives to acquire truth and to avoid error in terms of relative epistemic importance. EO assumes that one's unextended justifying evidence, in conjunction with the requirement of uncontravened decisively best explanation, should determine which of those two objectives has epistemic priority in any case of belief formation. Thus if on one's unextended justifying evidence a false proposition is an uncontravened decisively best explanation for one, one's believing that proposition is *not* epistemically irrational just because it commits one to a falsehood. (Of course in such a case one would not know that the proposition is false.) The procedural constraints on believing and withholding, according to EO, should be set by one's unextended justifying evidence in conjunction with the requirement of uncontravened decisively best explanation. For there is no other epistemically nonarbitrary way to settle the matter of the relative epistemic importance of the objectives in question.

One might object that EO should drop its talk of acquiring truth and avoiding falsehood, on the ground that this talk does not do any real work. Apparently the evidential and explanatory require-

ment of EO does all the real work. But I find this objection misguided. It betrays misunderstanding of the aim of EO: to provide
a suitable objective for an epistemically rational truth-seeker. Such
a truth-seeker, *qua* epistemically rational truth-seeker, does aim to
acquire truth and to avoid error in a certain way, and thus it is
important to represent this twofold aim in EO. The main contri-
bution of EO is that it identifies the evidential and explanatory
component essential to this aim of the epistemically rational truth-
seeker. The significance of this component in no way minimizes
the importance of the aim to acquire truth and to avoid error in a
certain way.

Another likely objection to EO is that its distinctive evidential
requirement is inadequate since it does not require that one *gather*
evidence that may conflict in certain ways with one's current justifying evidence. Suppose that one's justifying evidence indicates
that P, but that with minimal effort one could acquire further justifying evidence indicating that $\sim P$. In such a case, according to
the objection, one would be procedurally epistemically *ir*rational
in believing that P. So EO is defective since it permits one to believe
in accord with one's current justifying evidence without gathering
additional relevant evidence.

I find such an objection inconclusive against EO. Suppose one
has no evidence at all indicating that the gathering of further evidence about P will justify $\sim P$. One would not then be procedurally
epistemically irrational simply because one fails to gather the further
evidence. The mere fact that there *is* such evidence, possessed by
somebody else, does not make one who does not *have* it procedurally epistemically irrational in one's current beliefs. And this is
so even if we suppose that one could *easily* acquire the further
evidence.

Of course if one has justifying evidence indicating that the gathering of further evidence will justify $\sim P$, the situation is significantly different. In such a situation one would not have justifying
evidence for P, since one would have justifying evidence indicating
there is justifying evidence for $\sim P$. One's latter justifying evidence
either would itself justify $\sim P$ or would at least preclude one's having
justifying evidence for P relative to one's overall justifying evidence.

Yet some situations are more complicated. Suppose one does
have considerable, albeit not justifying, evidence indicating that the
gathering of further evidence will justify $\sim P$. And suppose that

one's considerable evidence even indicates specifically how one can easily gather this further evidence. What does procedural epistemic rationality require of one in such a case?

Here the proponent of EO has two fairly straightforward options. The first option assumes that procedural epistemic rationality concerning belief is *evidentially perspectival* inasmuch as it is relative to the justifying evidence, occurrent and nonoccurrent, that one *actually has*. Procedural epistemic rationality, on this option, does not itself require the gathering of new evidence. It is a function just of the evidence one has. So this option raises this question: what does procedural epistemic rationality require of one if one has no evidence, or if one has arrived at a *complete* decisively best explanation of one's current evidence? The answer from the first option is: nothing. Of course one might have *non*epistemic interests, such as prudential and moral interests, that demand that one undergo new perceptual and sensory experiences. But on the first option epistemic rationality does not itself require one to undergo new experiences. One possible motivation for this option is that its denial seems to place excessive, if not unlimited, demands on an epistemically rational truth-seeker. For the gathering of new evidence seems to be a potentially endless task.

The second option grants that EO needs to be supplemented with, and qualified by, principles of epistemically rational *action*. Such principles, according to this option, specify the conditions under which one epistemically should gather new evidence; for gathering evidence is an epistemically relevant sort of action. Presumably, such principles will specify just how easily available additional relevant evidence must be (or at least *evidently* be), if it is to bear on one's epistemically rational beliefs. This second option's answer to our problem question is clear: if the relevant action principles prescribe that one epistemically should gather new evidence regarding P, in the aforementioned case, one should not believe that P (even if P satisfies the conditions of EO with respect to one's current evidence). On this option, EO is overridable at least in certain cases where one has considerable evidence indicating that the gathering of new evidence will undermine some of one's current justifying evidence.

We should refrain now from deciding between the two options at hand. Lacking clear action principles, we cannot determine now whether the second option is ultimately viable, even if this option seems to have an intuitive edge over the first option. Nor need we make this decision now. On either option EO will play a central role in epistemically rational belief. The only pressing question is whether EO is overridable in certain special cases, given certain principles of epistemically rational action. We now must leave this question as unfinished business.

Another likely objection claims that EO is too demanding because of its requirement that one acquire as many decisively best explanations of one's unextended justifying evidence as possible. Apparently this requirement demands by implication that one consider all the propositions one can that are potential decisively best explainers of one's unextended justifying evidence. According to the objection, however, procedural epistemic rationality does not require that one *pursue* truths; it requires only that one conduct one's believing in a certain way relative to the propositions *one happens to consider*.

But such an objection must handle the possible case where one refrains from considering any propositions. I noted in connection with Chisholm's epistemic objective that one cannot achieve procedural epistemic rationality simply by refraining from considering propositions. Thus the objection at hand must require that one consider *some* propositions, although not all the potential decisively best explainers one can. But this is a troublesome requirement, at least because of its vagueness. It fails to specify how many propositions one must consider. (Suppose one considers by intention only a single proposition.) And it fails to specify what *sort* of propositions one must consider. (Suppose one considers only those propositions one desires to be true, or simply likes the components of.) Another problem with the requirement at hand is that it conflicts with the intuition that procedural epistemic rationality requires one to *pursue* explanatorily superior evidence-based truth. Thus the objection at hand is uncompelling.

EO seems to be an epistemic objective essential to a procedurally rational truth-seeker, even if it tells only part of the story about such a truth-seeker. It also seems to state a general *epistemic obligation* for a truth-seeker who aims to be epistemically rational in the procedural sense. If believing in accord with EO is epistemically obligatory for such a truth-seeker, then such believing is of course epistemically permissible too. Epistemically permissible believing, on this view, instantiates the features of adequate evidential support and decisively best explanation relative to one's unextended justifying evidence. A *method* of belief acquisition for achieving the objective stated by EO will specify the exact way such believing should be arrived at and sustained. Construed as a truth-seeker's procedural epistemic obligation, EO is quite compatible with the view that *non*epistemic obligations might come into conflict with, and even override, epistemic obligations. Yet this point raises issues independent of EO that I cannot pursue here.[11]

EO plays a central role in various notions of procedural epistemic rationality. The following simple principle illustrates one role:

A proposition, P, is procedurally epistemically rational for a person, S, to believe if and only if S would believe that P if he were to satisfy EO.

This is an objective notion of procedural epistemic rationality, but it is not the only notion. One less objective notion is this:

A proposition, P, is procedurally epistemically rational for S to believe *from the standpoint of S's evidence* if and only if S's evidence makes justifiable the proposition that S would believe that P if he were to satisfy EO.

There is no reason to think that one of these notions is inherently superior to the other. Each is a viable notion of procedural epistemic rationality that depends on EO.

Thus far my account of EO as providing epistemic objectives and obligations has ignored considerations of epistemic *blame*. Yet we can use EO to provide this sufficient condition for epistemic blamelessness:

S's believing that P is epistemically blameless if S's believing that P is a direct result of S's doing his best to satisfy EO.

Given this notion, one can be epistemically blameless even while violating an epistemic obligation. And normatively this is how things should be. We should also allow that one can satisfy an epistemic obligation while being epistemically blameworthy. But I shall not pursue this matter, since it would take us too far afield. My main point now is simply that there are various important notions of procedural epistemic rationality into which EO fits.

11 For relevant discussion of this point, see Meiland (1980), Moser (1985, Chap. 6), and Foley (1987, Chap. 5).

5.4 Conclusion

In sum, EO improves on the earlier-mentioned epistemic objectives by placing epistemic value on decisively best explanation relative to one's unextended justifying evidence. The earlier objectives neglected one or the other of the basic epistemic values of decisively best explanation and adequate evidential support. They thus failed to specify an epistemic objective appropriate to a procedurally rational truth-seeker. So EO is preferable from a procedural epistemic point of view to those earlier objectives. We now can recommend EO as the belief objective appropriate to an epistemically rational truth-seeker.

And we now can see how this book's account of justification extends to an account of procedural epistemic rationality. Thus this chapter lends further credibility to the account of justification in Chapters 2–4.

Let us turn finally to the Gettier problem and the needed fourth condition for propositional knowledge.

6

Propositional knowledge

Refutation

Propositional knowledge is simply knowledge *that P*, where *P* is some proposition or other. It thus contrasts with knowledge *how* and perhaps with knowledge *who* and knowledge *which*. Since the time of Plato's *Meno*, philosophers have tried to specify what propositional knowledge is. The troubling question is: what are the logically necessary and sufficient conditions for one's having propositional knowledge? Since Plato's time many philosophers have held that propositional knowledge requires justified true belief; Chapter 1 provided some support for this view. Dissenting philosophers there have been, but the topic of serious dissension recently has lain elsewhere: with the needed fourth condition for one's having propositional knowledge.

According to the standard analysis of knowledge suggested by Plato and Kant among others, if one has a justified true belief that *P*, then one knows that *P*. But since Edmund Gettier's famous counterexamples in his (1963), philosophers generally have held that the standard analysis needs modification. Although there is no widespread agreement on exactly what modification we need, there are some prominent proposals. One sort of proposed modification requires that the justification appropriate to knowledge be "undefeated" in the sense that some appropriate subjunctive conditional concerning genuine defeaters of justification be true of that justification.[1] Another noteworthy modification requires that the justification for a true belief qualifying as knowledge not depend on any falsehood.[2] And still another modification proposes that the

---

1 Such a defeasibility approach, with distinctive variations, is represented in Lehrer and Paxson (1969), Swain (1974; 1981, Chap. 5), and Klein (1976; 1981, pp. 137–66). For serious objections to this general approach, see Shope (1983, Chap. 2).
2 Such a view is suggested, even if not explicitly endorsed, in Meyers and Stern

justification appropriate to knowledge must admit of an "epistemic explanation" that does not involve any falsehood.[3]

I shall not review the serious problems facing the first two sorts of modification; they are too well known. In §6.1 I shall consider, but find inadequate, the third sort of modification. Yet shunning the growing despair about successfully analyzing propositional knowledge, I shall argue in §6.2 for an intuitive addition to the justification condition that blocks the various counterexamples inspired by Gettier. The analysis based on this addition might seem initially to be too straightforward to be true, but I shall show that it can withstand various Gettier-inspired counterexamples, including the most difficult. Thus this chapter provides a new fourth condition for knowledge that avoids the defects of its predecessors and solves the Gettier problem.

In §6.3 this chapter challenges a form of strong knowledge skepticism deriving from Descartes's Dreamer Hypothesis: and it proposes a way to solve the famous problem of the criterion and thereby to justify this book's epistemological theory. We shall see that my proposed meta-justification fits nicely with the account of justification in Chapters 2–4.

Some philosophers doubt the importance of providing an analysis of knowledge resistant to Gettier-style counterexamples. I know of only one initially plausible argument for such doubt. In outline it is: one's justified beliefs qualifying as knowledge are *indistinguishable* for oneself from one's merely justified beliefs; so a theory of knowledge should concern itself only with merely justified belief, and not with justification resistant to Gettier-style counterexamples.[4]

To evaluate such an argument, consider any two statements of the following forms:

(J) I justifiedly believe or affirm that *P*.
(K) I know that *P*.

(K) of course entails that *P*, but (J) does not. Given their differing truth conditions, (J) and (K) are not synonymous; they are *semantically* distinguishable.

(1973), Armstrong (1973, p. 152), and Harman (1973, p. 47). This kind of view has been challenged by Feldman (1974). See also Meyers (1988, Chap. 5).
3 This approach has been developed by Shope (1979; 1983, Chap. 7). It derives in part from the analysis of knowledge in Sosa (1974).
4 Such an argument has been suggested by Kaplan (1985). Kaplan finds such an argument suggested by Levi (1980, pp. 28–30).

The suggestion that (J) and (K) are indistinguishable for one might mean that (J) is justifiable for one if and only if (K) is justifiable for one. (If the suggestion does not mean this, it is not clear what it means.) On this construal, the suggestion would imply that (J) and (K) have the same justification conditions for one. The alleged indistinguishability between (J) and (K) would thus be *epistemic*: justifying evidence for (J) would be justifying evidence for (K), and conversely.

Given the argument in §1.3 on the relation between knowledge and justified belief or assent, if the justification conditions for (K) are satisfied for one, then the justification conditions for (J) are also. But let us ask whether we can imagine a case where (J) is justifiable for one, but (K) is not. Clearly if (K) is justifiable for me, then these propositions are also: (a) *P* is true, and (b) I justifiedly believe or affirm that *P*.

Do we get the same entailment from (J)'s being justifiable for me? Of course (b) needs no comment, since it reiterates (J). But regarding (a), it may not be obvious that if (J) is justifiable for me, then so also is the proposition that *P* is true. One might argue that this latter implication does hold on any notion of justification where one's having justification comes from one's having adequate evidence. (Here I have in mind the nondeontological notions mentioned in §1.3.) The assumption would be that any adequate evidence one has for (J) will also serve as adequate evidence for the proposition that *P* is true.[5] Cases where a person's evidence does not serve the latter purpose are, one might argue, cases where (J) is not actually justifiable for that person. Such considerations, one might argue, indicate that when (J) is justifiable for one, so also is the proposition that *P* is true. These considerations are far from decisive, but let us grant the questionable implication at issue if only for the sake of argument.

The decisive complication comes from the fourth condition required for propositional knowledge. Given this condition, for (K) to be justifiable for one, the proposition that the fourth condition for knowledge is satisfied must also be justifiable for one. (We can plausibly take this fourth condition to be a condition for truth-resistant justification of the sort mentioned in §1.3 and to be characterized fur-

---

5 Some philosophers apparently would reject this assumption; see, for example, Alston (1985, p. 48).

ther in §6.2.) But this latter requirement does *not* apply to (J)'s being justifiable for one. (J)'s being justifiable for me does not require that some proposition such as the following be justifiable for me: there is no truth that, when conjoined with my justifying evidence for *P*, ultimately contravenes my justification for *P* (in a sense to be clarified in §6.2). All that is required by (J)'s being justifiable for me is that this proposition be justifiable for me: *relative to my actual total justifying evidence* (in the sense of §3.2), *P* is justifiable for me, and I believe that *P* on the basis of my relevant justifying evidence.

Thus (K)'s being justifiable for one requires one's having justifying evidence concerning *truths in general*, but (J)'s being justifiable for one does not. (J)'s being justifiable for one requires one's having justifying evidence concerning only the justifying evidence one *actually possesses*. Thus (J)'s being justifiable for one does not entail (K)'s being justifiable for one. So one cannot plausibly appeal to the epistemic indistinguishability of (J) and (K) to minimize the significance of an analysis of knowledge that aims to withstand Gettier-style counterexamples.

We can use a simple argument to show that a Gettier-resistant analysis of knowledge is epistemologically important.[6] First, it is epistemologically important for us to understand exactly what propositional knowledge is; after all, one branch of epistemology is the study of the nature of knowledge. Second, our understanding exactly what propositional knowledge is essentially involves our having a Gettier-resistant analysis of propositional knowledge. If our analysis is not Gettier-resistant, it will not provide an exact understanding of what knowledge is. Thus it is epistemologically important for us to have a Gettier-resistant analysis of knowledge. Let us then pursue such an analysis.

6.1 Epistemic explanation and the Gettier problem

Robert Shope's (1983) analysis of propositional knowledge assumes that such knowledge requires a certain kind of *explanation* of the knower's actual justification. I shall discuss this analysis for two

---

6 This argument follows the basic argument of Conee (1988). Conee also provides decisive criticisms of some recent efforts to minimize the philosophical importance of the Gettier problem.

main reasons. It seems very promising in its own right, and it seems to be a natural extension of the explanation-oriented account of justification in Chapters 2–4. Shope suggests that our analysis of knowledge can avoid Gettier-style counterexamples once we recognize that in such examples falsehoods play certain roles in relation to one's actual justification. He suggests that in such examples falsehoods are included in *epistemic explanations* of one's justified beliefs *and* of various epistemically relevant justified propositions that one does not actually believe.

An epistemic explanation, on Shope's account (1983, p. 208), is a set of propositions explaining why some proposition is justified. In a Gettier-style counterexample, Shope claims, there is an inelimimable epistemic explanation that contains a false proposition; and conversely, in a case of propositional knowledge, the relevant belief is justified through its connection with a sequence of epistemic explanations that do not involve falsehoods. Following Shope, let us call a sequence of epistemic explanations a 'justification-explaining chain' (a 'JEC' for short). And let us grant, again following Shope, that the members of a JEC must themselves be justified if there is to be genuine propositional knowledge.

We can clarify Shope's notion of a JEC by characterizing the members of a JEC. The first member, M_1, of a JEC related to a proposition, P, is just a true conjunction of the form: 'F_1 and that makes the proposition that P justified'. In that conjunction the proposition that F_1 describes something sufficient to make the proposition that P justified. If M_1 has a successor, M_2, in the relevant JEC, M_2 will be a true conjunction of the following form: 'F_2 and that makes M_1 justified' (where the proposition that F_2 describes something sufficient to make M_1 justified). A similar point applies to further successors in the relevant JEC. The basic idea of Shope's diagnosis, then, is that by constructing such a JEC for a Gettier-style counterexample, we can expose false propositions, and thereby account for the lack of genuine propositional knowledge.

For purposes of illustration and evaluation, let us consider how Shope's diagnosis would treat the following difficult Gettier-style counterexample:[7]

---

7 This counterexample is inspired in part by Feldman (1974). Cf. Lehrer (1979, p. 75).

236

(I) Suppose a person, *S*, knows the following true proposition, *M*: Mr. Jones, whom *S* has always found to be reliable and whom *S* has no good reason to distrust at present, has told *S*, his office-mate, that *P*: He, Jones, owns a Ford. Suppose also that Jones has told *S* that *P* only because of the state of hypnosis Jones is in, and that *P* is true only because, unknown to himself, Jones has won a Ford in a lottery since entering the state of hypnosis. And suppose further that *S* deduces from *M* its existential generalization, *Q*: There is someone, whom *S* has always found to be reliable and whom *S* has no good reason to distrust at present, who has told *S*, his office-mate, that he owns a Ford. *S*, then, knows that *Q*, since he has correctly deduced *Q* from *M*, which he also knows. But suppose also that on the basis of his knowledge that *Q*, *S* believes that *R*: Someone in the office owns a Ford. Under these conditions, *S* has a justified true belief that *R*, knows his evidence for *R*, but does not know that *R*.

This of course is a variant of the familiar "Lucky Mr. Nogot" counterexample that has proven especially intractable for attempts to analyze the concept of propositional knowledge.[8]

Shope's diagnosis suggests (1983, p. 216) that by constructing a JEC for the present sort of counterexample, we would expose a falsehood when attempting to explain what justifies the proposition that *P*: Jones owns a Ford. On one variant of the familiar Lucky Nogot counterexample, Jones is shamming, and so the relevant falsehood quickly emerges: the false proposition that Jones's giving *S* the relevant evidence stems from an intention to convey true information. But this falsehood clearly is not presupposed by example (I), where it is coherent to suppose that Jones *does* intend to convey true information while in the state of hypnosis. Where then is the relevant falsehood that emerges from a JEC for (I)? This of course is the pressing question for Shope's diagnosis. I shall argue that this question leads to trouble for Shope's account of knowledge.

Suppose we begin to develop the JEC for (I) as follows:

(E1) The proposition that *Q* [= there is someone, whom *S* has always found to be reliable and whom *S* has no good reason to distrust at present, who has told *S*, his office-mate, that he owns a Ford] is justified for *S*; and this fact justifies for *S* the proposition that *R* [= someone in the office owns a Ford].

8 A simple version of the Lucky Nogot counterexample is discussed in Shope (1983, pp. 68–9). The original Nogot counterexample comes from Lehrer (1965).

(E2) The proposition that M [= Jones, whom S has always found to be reliable and whom S has no good reason to distrust at present, has told S, his office-mate, that P: he, Jones, owns a Ford] is justified for S; the proposition that M entails the proposition that Q; S recognizes that this entailment relation holds; and all this makes (E1) justified for S.

(E3) S has found his memory beliefs about what he has heard to be, with very little if any exception, veridical; S has the memory belief that Jones has told him that P; S has no good reason to suppose that the former memory belief is unveridical; S has good reason to hold that justification is transmissible through recognized entailment relations; and all this makes (E2) justified for S.

Consistent with Shope's diagnosis, the talk above of a proposition's (H's) being justified *for* S is not intended to imply that S believes that H; it means rather that relative to all the evidence S possesses, H is justified. (We could also relativize such propositional justification, without any difficulty for the present JEC, to an epistemic *community*.)

If (E1)–(E3) are the initial links of an appropriate JEC for example (I), it is highly doubtful that any falsehoods will emerge from the relevant JEC. Of course one might object that the JEC for (I) must explain what justifies the proposition that Jones owns a Ford, and in doing so would expose a false proposition. But it is not clear why the JEC explaining the justification of R in (I) must explain the justification of *that* proposition, especially since that proposition is not a member of the set of propositions constituting S's justification for R. The JEC beginning with (E1)–(E3) indicates that we can explain the justification of R without explaining the justification of the proposition that Jones owns a Ford. Thus it is doubtful that the JEC for R in (I) will expose a falsehood on which the justification of the latter proposition apparently depends. But if this is so, Shope's diagnosis evidently has the implausible implication that S knows that R in (I). Or at least my objection raises the crucial issue of when a proposition must be included in a JEC that explains the justification of another proposition.

We can anticipate Shope's reply. Consider his view that S's knowledge that H requires S's belief that H to be justified "through its connections with a chain of propositions which themselves are justified in the sense of being ones it would more manifest the rationality of members of the epistemic community to accept in place of competing propositions [and in place of withholding acceptance] when pursuing epistemic goals [e.g., goals like avoiding a false *explanandum* or *explanans*]" (1983, p. 138; cf. p. 217). Shope's notion of a *justified proposition* would lead him to reply to my objection in a specific way. Regarding the variant of the familiar Lucky Nogot counterexample where Jones is shamming (which should not be confused with example [I]), Shope suggests (pp. 216–17, and in correspondence) that the presence or absence of the intention of the speaker to report true information *must* be described in the relevant JEC. The basis for this requirement is the claim that the issue of the presence of such an intention is central to the rationality of an epistemic community considering whether to accept the speaker's report. Shope suggests that the epistemic rationality of a community accepting the report would be undercut by the fact that the report does not stem from an intention to report true information. On this ground Shope proposes (a) that in the familiar Lucky Nogot counterexample where Jones is shamming, the deceptively reported proposition that Jones owns a Ford is *not* justified, and consequently (b) that the inferred proposition that someone in the office owns a Ford is not justified either.

Can we apply a similar strategy, regardless of its ultimate effectiveness, to counterexample (I), where Jones is not shamming? Shope's treatment of the Gettier-style counterexample involving "Tom Grabit's actual twin" (1983, pp. 223–4) indicates that he would apply a similar strategy. In this counterexample, S reports on the basis of his visual experience that his acquaintance, Tom Grabit, stole a book from the library, even though S is unable to detect the difference between Tom's stealing the book and his actual twin's doing so. Shope claims that S's lack of discriminative ability prevents it from being more rational than not for the members of an epistemic community to accept S's report on the basis of S's testimony. Similarly Shope would claim that in counterexample (I) Jones's being in a state of hypnosis would prevent it from being more rational than not for an epistemic community to accept Jones's report that he owns a Ford on the basis of his testimony. And Shope would claim that the proposition that Jones owns a Ford is therefore not a justified proposition in the envisaged circumstances, and that this accounts for the lack of justification and thus knowledge in (I) of the proposition that someone in the office owns a Ford.

Two considerations count against Shope's suggested diagnosis of counterexample (I). First, it is quite implausible to assume that *the mere fact* that Jones is in a state of hypnosis prevents it from being more rational than not for an epistemic community to accept Jones's report on the basis of his testimony. We can easily imagine a case where all the evidence available to the members of an epistemic community either fails to indicate that Jones is in a state of hypnosis or, more strongly, indicates that Jones is a reliable reporter and thus is not in a state of hypnosis. In such a case the mere fact that Jones is in a state of hypnosis would *not* prevent it from being more rational than not for the members to believe Jones's report on the basis of his testimony. (For similar reasons, it is implausible to suppose, with respect to the counterexample where Jones is shamming, that *the mere fact* that Jones does not intend to report true information prevents it from being more rational than not for the members to believe his report.) But if this is so, Shope's diagnosis fails to explain in either case why the proposition reported by Jones is actually unjustified for the members (including the experts) of the relevant epistemic community or for S. Given this failure, the diagnosis also fails to explain why the key inferred proposition that someone in the office owns a Ford is unjustified. Given the envisaged circumstances, there is no reason to think that the propositions in question would be unjustified for the members of the actual epistemic community.

Thus for Shope's diagnosis to succeed, one apparently would have to claim that the justified proposition, Q, in (E1) and (I), does not suffice to justify R, and that some *false* proposition is needed for the justification of R. But it is highly doubtful that the justified Q fails to justify R. And this means that we evidently can construct a genuine JEC like (E1)–(E3) for R in (I) that does not expose a knowledge-precluding falsehood.

The second relevant consideration is that it still is not clear why a JEC for R in (I) *must* explain the justification of the proposition that Jones owns a Ford. The JEC (E1)–(E3) satisfies Shope's aforementioned requirement that propositional knowledge that H must be justified through its connections with a chain of propositions that it would be more rational than not for the members of the epistemic community to accept. Example (I) allows us to assume that each proposition in (E1)–(E3) is justified for the relevant epistemic community. But this means that on Shope's diagnosis we are committed to the implausible view that S knows that R in (I).

The foregoing considerations lead to the conclusion that Shope's diagnosis fails to account for the lack of knowledge in Gettier-style counterexamples like (I). The major problem for the diagnosis is of course that its use of a JEC does not guarantee that a knowledge-precluding falsehood will emerge in such Gettier-style counterexamples. Granted, it would be false to assume with respect to (I) that Jones is not in a state of hypnosis. But this observation does not explain how the presence of falsehood in (I) precludes knowledge; for it does not explain how falsehood figures in the relevant justification. Shope's diagnosis fails to explain why the proposition Q in (I) does not justify R.

What we need from a diagnosis like Shope's is an explanation of the exact roles falsehoods play in Gettier-style examples. Such an explanation will specify why the presence of falsehoods precludes knowledge in certain cases and not in others. But if the considerations above are correct, we cannot rely solely on the notion of a JEC to provide the needed explanation. Thus Shope's diagnosis does not actually solve the Gettier problem.

We cannot salvage Shope's diagnosis with the likely proposal that for one to have propositional knowledge, there must be a relevant JEC that contains no falsehood *and justifies no falsehood.* In the JEC for (I), the justified proposition M in (E2) evidently justifies the false proposition that Jones is not claiming Ford ownership because he is in a state of hypnosis. Given the justified M, one evidently could justifiably believe that Jones is now a reliable reporter about his alleged Ford ownership, and thus that he is not in a state of hypnosis. Yet the proposal at hand is ultimately too demanding. It precludes, for instance, one's knowing the following propositions:

Jones claims he owns a Ford
Jones has always been trustworthy in the past
Jones has often been seen driving a Ford
Jones has a Ford in his garage

whenever the justifying evidence for these propositions justifies the false proposition that Jones owns a Ford. In the latter case, the JEC for these four propositions would justify a false proposition, and so, given the anticipated proposal, would preclude knowledge of these propositions. But this is obviously implausible.

Of course we might revise the anticipated proposal to allow that a certain sort of JEC that justifies a falsehood does not preclude knowledge. Yet it is not clear what sort of JEC qualifies as such an exception.[9] The following section makes a more promising effort to analyze the notion of propositional knowledge. It uses a notion of truth-resistant evidence, but it also allows for the relevance of the notion of epistemic explanation.

6.2 Knowledge and truth-resistant evidence

Let us consider whether we can undercut counterexamples such as (I) with this initially plausible requirement:

> ER. For S to have knowledge that P on evidence E, there must be an epistemic explanation of P that explains, solely by means of true propositions, why S is justified in believing that P on E *even if any other true proposition is conjoined with E.*

ER assumes that the kind of evidence essential to propositional knowledge admits of an epistemic explanation that is not contravened by the addition of any further true propositions. Thus we might say that an epistemic explanation appropriate to knowledge is *resistant* to any truth, including any truth that is not part of the knower's actual evidence. Equivalently, we might say that the kind of evidence knowledge requires is *truth-resistant* in the sense that its justificatory value is not contravened by the addition of *any* true proposition, including true propositions of which the believer is unaware.[10]

In Chapters 2 and 3 I explained the relevant notion of contravening with regard to minimal and justifying, maximal probability-makers. The major difference between *contraveners that are merely knowledge-precluding* (and not actually justification-precluding) for one and *actual contraveners of justification* for one is that the former, unlike the latter, are not part of one's actual evidence, and thus do not actually preclude one's justification. (On the relevant notion of the evidence one has, see §3.3.) The failure to acknowledge the need for something like truth-resistant evidence leaves an analysis of knowledge open to counterexamples like (I). Although ER seems

---

9 For substantiation of this point, see Shope (1983, Chap. 4), where the relevant views of Chisholm and Sosa are critically discussed.

10 Here we could assume that whenever S has truth-resistant justifying evidence for P, there will be a corresponding truth-resistant epistemic explanation of P for S (which consists solely of true propositions), and conversely.

to be sufficiently demanding to explain the lack of knowledge in various Gettier-style counterexamples, our first question should be whether it is too demanding, whether there are cases of actual knowledge that fail to satisfy ER.

One pertinent example resembles the above-described counter-example involving Tom Grabit's actual twin, except it involves Tom's demented mother, Mrs. Grabit:

> (II) S believes on the basis of his visual experience that his acquaintance, Tom Grabit, stole a book from the library. But Tom's twin is simply a fiction of the demented mind of Tom's mother, Mrs. Grabit, who has claimed that F: Tom's twin was at the library at the time of the theft, but Tom was not.[11]

One might claim that once S notes that Mrs. Grabit, being demented, is not a reliable source of information about her son's whereabouts, S may infer that her claim that F is not reliable. Thus one might infer that Mrs Grabit's claim, when added to S's evidence, does *not* make it evidentially improbable for S that Tom stole the book. On this basis, one might deny that Mrs. Grabit's claim that F is a contravener in any relevant sense, with respect to S's justifying evidence. So one might conclude that the proponent of ER need not deny that S has knowledge in the case in question.

Yet, following Klein (1971), we can make the suggested example obviously difficult for ER, if we refrain from adding to S's evidence the true proposition that Mrs. Grabit is demented. Suppose that it still is a fact that Mrs. Grabit is demented, but that we add instead to S's evidence only the true proposition that M: Mrs. Grabit claimed that Tom was nowhere near the library, and mothers are typically highly reliable as a source of information about their sons' general whereabouts. Thus we do not include in S's evidence the proposition that Mrs. Grabit is demented. In this case ER implies that S does not know that Tom stole the book. For S's evidence, when conjoined with the true proposition M, fails to justify for S the proposition that Tom stole the book. But this is an incorrect implication of ER, since Mrs. Grabit is demented. The problem here comes from the assumption of ER that *all* truths that contravene justification (when added to the relevant evidence) preclude knowledge.

Example (II) raises the question of when truths that contravene

11 This example comes from Lehrer and Paxson (1969, p. 228).

justification, when conjoined with it, also preclude knowledge. A simple likely answer to this question, in the spirit of ER, is:

> (A) A truth, T, that contravenes S's justifying evidence E for P, when conjoined with E, precludes S's knowledge that P on E only if there is no further truth, T', that restores the justification of P when conjoined with $(E \& T)$.

We can understand the relevant notion of *restoration* of justification via the notion of uncontravened contravening introduced in Chapters 2 and 3. The basic idea is that T' restores the justification of P on E when (a) T contravenes that justification when conjoined with E, and (b) T' restores the maximal evidential probability for P when conjoined with E and T. (See §3.2 on the relevant notion of maximal probability.) In example (II) involving the demented Mrs. Grabit, there is a further truth that, when conjoined with S's evidence E and the contravener M, restores S's justification for the belief that Tom stole the book. The further truth of course is that Mrs. Grabit is demented. Thus a plausible proposal is that we must supplement ER with the requirement that the contraveners of justification relevant to precluding knowledge must themselves be truth-resistant in the sense specified by (A).

We have then the following emendation of ER:

> ER★. For S to have knowledge that P on justifying evidence E, E must be such that for every true proposition T that, when conjoined with E, contravenes S's justification for P on E, there is a true proposition T' that restores the justification of P for S on $(E \& T)$.

Since it is not obvious that there are cases of knowledge that fail to satisfy the requirement set by ER★, let us postpone the question whether ER★ is too demanding.

Let us ask instead whether the requirement set by ER★ provides a sufficient condition for justifying evidence that satisfies the fourth condition for knowledge. Evidently we can illustrate that ER★ does not provide such a sufficient condition by considering one of Gettier's original counterexamples:

> (III) Smith is justified in believing the false proposition that (i) Jones owns a Ford. On the basis of (i) Smith infers, and thus is justified in believing, that (ii) either Jones owns a Ford or Brown is in Barcelona. As it turns out, Brown happens to be in Barcelona, and so (ii) is true. Thus although Smith is justified in believing the true proposition (ii), Smith does not know (ii).

Here we can suppose that Smith's evidence satisfies ER★. Yet Smith lacks propositional knowledge while having justified true belief. In such an example, S is justified in believing a false proposition, F, on evidence E, and thus, via deductive inference, is justified in believing a disjunction, $(F$ or $B)$, where B is true. When conjoined with S's evidence, the true proposition $\sim F$ contravenes S's justification for $(F$ or $B)$. But there is a true proposition that restores this justification for S, when conjoined with it; this of course is the true proposition B. Thus ER★, when construed as providing a sufficient condition for the fourth condition for knowledge, implies that S knows that $(F$ or $B)$. But this of course is an incorrect implication of ER★ thus construed.

Here is a straightforward notion of truth-resistant evidence that avoids the difficulty of example (III) for ER★:

> TR. S's justifying evidence E for P is truth-resistant if and only if for every true proposition T that, when conjoined with E, contravenes S's justification for P on E, there is a true proposition, T', that, when conjoined with E & T, restores the justification of P for S in a way that S is actually justified in believing that P.

Of course if the relevant true contraveners are themselves uncontravened, they will not be part of S's evidence that actually justifies P; such contraveners would preclude P's being justified for S. We shall see that we need to understand the relevant restorers as truths not justifiable via S's actual justifying evidence for P. So let us take TR's talk of *conjoining* T' to E & T as presupposing that T' is not justifiable via E.

We can clarify the notion of *a way that S is actually justified in believing that P* via the notion of an *alethically variable proposition*. Let us say that a proposition, P, is alethically variable if and only if there is more than one way for P to be true.[12] Nonredundant disjunctions and existential generalizations are paradigm cases, but not the only cases, of alethically variable propositions. A way for a disjunction to be true comes from any set of its disjuncts; and a way for an existential generalization to be true comes from any set of its instantiations. Thus regarding counterexample (III), a way

---

12 Regarding propositions that are not universal generalizations, we can simplify matters by excluding from consideration *conjunctions* that determine "ways" in which a proposition is true. Thus let us not concern ourselves with the fact that both $(P$ & $Q)$ and $(P$ & $\sim Q)$ logically entail P.

for the disjunction that (Jones owns a Ford or Brown is in Barcelona) to be true comes from the true proposition that Brown is in Barcelona; and another way comes from the false proposition that Jones owns a Ford. Given a plurality of propositionally distinct disjuncts and instantiations, alethically variable propositions of this sort qualify as propositions for which there are various ways of being true.

My notion of an alethically variable proposition presupposes a notion of propositional identity. Following Chisholm (1976, pp. 118–24), we can rely on this criterion of propositional identity: a proposition, P, is identical with a proposition, Q, if and only if P and Q are necessarily such that (i) P is true if and only if Q is true, and (ii) one believes that P if and only if one believes that Q. Given this criterion, we can make sense of the notion of a proposition's being true in one way rather than another, since ways of being true are just propositions sufficient for the truth of some proposition.

Returning then to principle TR, we can understand the notion of a way that S is actually justified in believing that P, relative to a disjunction or an existential generalization, as follows:

> For any disjunction, $(P$ or $Q)$, a way that S is actually justified in believing that $(P$ or $Q)$ comes from P if and only if S's justifying evidence for $(P$ or $Q)$ consists, at least in part, of justifying evidence for P.

This explication applies to alethically variable existential generalizations as well as disjunctions, since such generalizations logically behave as disjunctions. And this explication applies to cases where one has justifying evidence for a disjunction, but lacks justifying evidence concerning *which* disjunct is true. In such cases, a way that one is actually justified in believing the disjunction is described by the disjunction itself, and not by any proper subset of its disjuncts. Thus P in the explication above may be disjunctive.

We should not assume that only disjunctions and existential generalizations qualify as alethically variable propositions. A universal proposition such as 'All epistemologists are poor' can be true in various ways. One such way is described by the statement 'Jones is the only epistemologist and Jones is poor', and another such way is described by the statement 'Smith is the only epistemologist and Smith is poor'. Thus Gettier-style cases can arise with universal propositions as well as with disjunctive and existential propositions.

So we should not restrict the notion of a way that S is actually justified in believing that P to disjunctions and existential generalizations. TR allows for cases where there is more than one way that a person is justified in believing a proposition. TR assumes that for there to be knowledge in such cases, a person's justifying evidence must be truth-resistant in *at least one* of the ways that he is justified in believing the relevant proposition.

We now need to consider various Gettier-style counterexamples to test an analysis of knowledge that includes a fourth condition of evidential truth-resistance. For simplicity, let us take the relevant analysis to be this:

> PK. A person, S, has propositional knowledge that P if and only if: P is true; S has justifying evidence E for P that is truth-resistant in the way specified by TR; and S believes or assents to P on the basis of E.

For simplicity, we might take the key thesis of PK to be the requirement that knowledge requires justified true belief or assent *sustained by the collective totality of truths*. I intend this only as shorthand for the actual key thesis, since in light of Grim (1984), it is not obvious that there is a set of all truths.

Considering first the example (III), we should recall that in that example Smith is justified in believing the false proposition:

(i) Jones owns a Ford,

which, according to (III), justifies the following true disjunction for Smith:

(ii) Either Jones owns a Ford or Brown is in Barcelona.

But Smith does not know (ii). Once we expand Smith's justifying evidence to include the true proposition that Jones does not own a Ford, we see that PK explains Smith's lack of knowledge in example (III). For then we see that Smith is no longer justified in believing that (i). The explanation of this contravening of justification is simple: Smith's initial justifying evidence for (i), when supplemented by the true proposition that Jones does not own a Ford, does not make (i) evidentially more probable than not. The epistemic justification of a proposition, P, requires that P be evidentially more probable than its denial. Thus if on the expanded evidence Smith is justified in believing that Jones does not own a Ford, he is not on that evidence justified in believing that Jones owns a Ford.

So a true proposition has contravened Smith's justification for the proposition that Jones owns a Ford.

Given PK, there is not in (III) the appropriate kind of restorer of the contravened justification. One inadequate restoration comes from the true proposition that Brown is in Barcelona. PK explains the inadequacy of that restoration on the ground that it has nothing to do with Smith's actual justification for the disjunction (Jones owns a Ford or Brown is in Barcelona). Smith's actual justification consists solely of justifying evidence for the false disjunct that Jones own a Ford; it does not include justifying evidence for the disjunct that Brown is in Barcelona. Thus a restoration of Smith's contravened justification that supports only the latter disjunct is, given PK, inadequate to sustain knowledge. In such a case, it is not Smith's actual evidence relative to the false disjunct that is truth-resistant. So PK explains Smith's lack of knowledge in example (III).

Considering next the counterexample (I), we should recall that in that example S knows the following proposition:

(i) Mr. Jones, whom S has always found to be reliable and whom S has no good reason to distrust at present, has told S, his office-mate, that he, Jones, owns a Ford.

According to (I), S correctly deduces from (i), and thus is justified in believing, this true existential generalization:

(ii) There is someone, whom S has always found to be reliable and whom S has no good reason to distrust at present, who has told S, his office-mate, that he owns a Ford.

On the basis of (ii), then, S infers and is justified in believing this true proposition:

(iii) Someone in the office owns a Ford.

However, S does not know (iii), because:

(a) Jones has told S that he owns a Ford only because of the hypnotic state he is in.

PK accounts for S's lack of knowledge in this case, because when we add the true proposition (a) to S's justifying evidence, S is not justified in believing (iii) on the basis of that expanded evidence; for that evidence does not make (iii) evidentially more probable than not. The reason it does not make (iii) evidentially more probable than not is simple: that expanded evidence undercuts the presumed reliability of Jones's claim that he owns a Ford.

Example (I) involves no relevant truth that provides an adequate restoration of S's contravened justification. Given PK, the true proposition that Jones owns a Ford is not relevant to such a restoration, since this proposition is justifiable via S's actual justifying evidence. PK's requirement of truth-resistant evidence, in the sense of TR, presupposes that the relevant restorers are truths not justifiable by one's actual justifying evidence. This presupposition fits with the fact that Gettier-style cases involve a sort of contravening that is *independent* of one's actual justifying evidence. Thus S's evidence is not truth-resistant in the sense required by PK; and so PK accounts for S's lack of knowledge in example (I).

PK also explains the lack of knowledge in the aforementioned familiar Lucky Nogot counterexample where Jones is shamming. When we expand S's evidence to include the true proposition that Jones is shamming, the expanded evidence justifies for S neither the proposition that someone who is currently a reliable office-mate has said that he owns a Ford nor the proposition that someone in the office owns a Ford. And that example does not involve the sort of restorer of justification required by PK. The considerations explaining the lack of knowledge in example (I) apply here as well.

PK is equally effective with this example due to Gettier himself:

(IV) Smith and Jones have applied for the same job. Smith is justified in believing that (i) Jones will get the job, and that (ii) Jones has ten coins in his pocket. On the basis of (i) and (ii) Smith infers, and thus is justified in believing, that (iii) the person who will get the job has ten coins in his pocket. As it turns out, Smith himself will get the job, and he also happens to have ten coins in his pocket. Thus although Smith is justified in believing the true proposition (iii), Smith does not know (iii).

In this example Smith is justified in believing the false proposition:

(ii) Jones will get the job,

and the proposition:

(ii) Jones has ten coins in his pocket.

According to (IV), when conjoined these propositions justify for Smith this true proposition:

(iii) The person who will get the job has ten coins in his pocket.

But (IV) includes a true proposition that contravenes Smith's actual justification for (iii) as well as (i) when that proposition supplements his justification. The proposition of course is that Smith will get the job. When this proposition supplements Smith's evidence, it is not evidentially more probable than not for Smith that Jones will get the job. For the true proposition that Smith will get the job implies that Jones will not get the job. And (IV) includes no relevant restorer of Smith's actual justification for (iii); specifically it includes no relevant restorer of Smith's actual justification for the proposition that Jones will get the job. Thus Smith's justifying evidence in (IV) is not truth-resistant in the way required by PK. So PK accounts for the lack of knowledge in (IV).

Let us also consider the bearing of PK on the counterexample involving Tom Grabit's actual twin: S believes on the basis of his visual experience that his acquaintance, Tom Grabit, stole a book from the library; but unknown to S, Tom has an identical twin brother who was in the library during the theft. Given PK, we can deny that S knows that Tom Grabit stole the book. When we add to S's justifying evidence the true proposition that S is unable to detect the difference between Tom's stealing the book and his twin's doing so, that evidence fails to justify for S the proposition that Tom stole the book. Nor does this case include the appropriate sort of restorer of S's justification. Given the intended construal of TR, the proposition that Tom stole the book does not provide such a restorer. So S's justification is not truth-resistant in the manner required by PK. Thus PK handles this example.

Apparently PK can explain the lack of knowledge in every Gettier-style counterexample. The characteristic feature of such a counterexample seems to be that it identifies a case of justified true belief where the justification is not truth-resistant in the manner required by PK. In any such case, one apparently lacks justifying evidence that is truth-resistant in the required manner. Thus PK seems to remove the perplexity from Gettier-style counterexamples.

But we now must ask whether PK is too demanding, whether there are cases of propositional knowledge that fail to satisfy the requirement of truth-resistant justification. This leads us to reconsider the example (II) that raised problems for principle ER. In that example, S believes on the basis of his visual experience that his acquaintance, Tom Grabit, stole a book from the library, but Tom's twin is just a fiction of the imagination of Tom's demented mother,

Mrs. Grabit, who has claimed that F: Tom's twin was at the library at the time of the theft, but Tom was not. PK accounts for S's having knowledge in this example, on the ground that S's justification is truth-resistant in the required way. When we add to S's evidence the truth that Mrs. Grabit's claim that F is mistaken, we preclude her claim's serving as a contravener of S's justifying evidence. And this is true even of the more difficult variation on the Grabit example where we add to S's evidence only the potentially contravening truth that Mrs. Grabit has claimed that F and mothers are typically highly reliable as a source of information about their sons' general whereabouts. Thus PK handles the example that troubled ER.

Another example possibly suggesting that PK is too strong also resembles the counterexample involving Tom Grabit's actual twin, except it includes the following situation: while observing Tom's theft, S momentarily entertains the proposition that Tom has an identical twin who was in the library during the time of the theft; but S also knows that he does not actually believe that proposition.[13] In this example, one might argue, the momentarily entertained proposition – call it 'D' – is, if true, a knowledge-precluding contravener of S's justification for the belief that B: he does not believe D. For if D supplements S's justifying evidence for believing that B (in the sense that S believes that D), then S is not justified in believing that B. Therefore, the argument concludes, PK improperly leads us to deny that S knows that B.

But this argument rests on a confusion: a confusion between the proposition that D and the proposition that S *believes that D*. Although the latter proposition is, if true, a knowledge-precluding contravener of S's justifying evidence for B, the former clearly is not. And when D supplements S's evidence in accord with PK, only the proposition that D is added. The proposition that S believes that D does not thereby supplement S's evidence, even if we thereby *assume* that S believes that D. Of course our *assuming* the proposition that S believes that D (simply for purposes of testing PK) neither makes this proposition true nor makes it part of S's actual evidence. And one's adding the proposition that S believes that D to S's actual evidence for B is definitely *not* condoned by the testing of PK, for

13 This example comes from Shope (1983, p. 71). Shope uses it to oppose Peter Klein's (1980) defeasibility analysis.

that proposition, being the contradictory of the true B, is actually false. So we have no reason to think that the present case threatens PK.

Still another case deserves brief consideration for purposes of testing PK:

> (V) Mr. Relator, a teacher whom S knows to be generally reliable as a source of information about events at school, reports to S the information that led Mr. Relator justifiably to believe that Q: Mr. Nogot owns a Ford. The relevant information is P: Mr. Nogot, one of my students, drove a Ford in front of me, affirmed that he owns it, showed me papers to that effect, and has been generally reliable in past dealings with me. So S knows that P. And Mr. Relator and S are justified in believing that Q; neither of them has any reason to believe that Q is false. But as it turns out, Q is false.[14]

This example prompts the question whether PK improperly denies that S knows that P in the specified situation where S does not believe that $\sim Q$. Specifically, does the addition of the true proposition that $\sim Q$ to S's evidence contravene S's justification for P and thereby preclude S's knowledge that P? The answer clearly is no. For even if S justifiably assumes that Nogot does not own a Ford, it still can be maximally evidentially probable, and thus justifiable, on S's evidence that the report of the generally reliable Mr. Relator is correct: that is, the report that Nogot drove a Ford in front of Relator, claimed to own it, displayed papers to that effect, and has been generally reliable in past dealings with Relator. Indeed, the justification for P still can be truth-resistant in the manner required by PK. For $\sim Q$ neither is incompatible with P nor makes P evidentially improbable. Thus PK does not preclude S's knowledge that P. So example (V) does not threaten PK.

Here is another noteworthy example:

> (VI) S attends a wedding ceremony where two of his friends become married. The local bishop performs the ceremony without error. After witnessing the ceremony, S knows that his friends are married. But unknown to anyone witnessing the ceremony, the local cardinal goes insane at the time of the ceremony, and falsely denounces the bishop as a fraud who is not authorized to perform weddings.[15]

This example is no more challenging to PK than is the aforementioned case of the demented Mrs. Grabit. In fact, a direct analogue

14 This example comes from Shope (1983, p. 62).
15 This example comes from Swain (1974, p. 18). Cf. Swain (1981, pp. 164–5).

of the above explanation of the demented Mrs. Grabit case provided by PK applies with equal effectiveness to example (VI).

Here is a final pair of examples that deserves consideration for purposes of testing PK:

> (VII) *S* has a justified true belief that his two friends were just married by the local bishop, but there is a true proposition, *T*, which contravenes *S*'s justification when conjoined with it (in the way required by PK), and which is such that it is humanly impossible (i.e., impossible given human limitations) for *S* to be justified in believing that *T*.

> (VIII) *S* has a justified true belief that his two friends were just married by the local bishop but there is a true proposition, *T*, which contravenes *S*'s justification when conjoined with it (in the way required by PK), and which is such that it is physically impossible (i.e., impossible given the correct laws of physics) for *S* to be justified in believing that *T*.

One might argue that examples (VII) and (VIII) are cases where *S* has propositional knowledge, and thus that PK is too strong. But I believe the more enlightening moral to these examples is that we should countenance varying strengths of propositional knowledge. Such strengths are determined by accessibility qualifications on the set of relevant true propositions that are contraveners when conjoined to justifying evidence. Given this moral, we should countenance a variety of concepts of propositional knowledge weaker than PK, concepts formulated by means of various accessibility-to-contraveners qualifications added to PK (where the relevant contraveners are of course merely knowledge-precluding in the sense noted earlier).

PK is our most demanding concept of propositional knowledge. It assumes that (at most) it need only be *logically* possible for one to be justified in believing the relevant knowledge-precluding contraveners. Apparently some philosophers would endorse PK as *the* concept of propositional knowledge. But it would be gratuitous to deny that there are concepts of propositional knowledge less strenuous than PK. Example (VIII) suggests one weaker concept. On this concept, it must be physically possible for one to be justified in believing the relevant contraveners. Example (VII) suggests a weaker concept. On this concept, it must be humanly possible for one to be justified in believing the relevant contraveners. (I assume of course that not all physical possibilities are human possibilities.)

Apparently various philosophers have presupposed each of these three viable concepts of propositional knowledge.

The difference between the suggested concepts comes from differing degrees of accessibility-to-contraveners involved with the key notion of truth-resistant justifying evidence. The availability of these differing degrees of accessibility should lead us to countenance various concepts of propositional knowledge stemming from PK. Some of these concepts will appear to be too demanding relative to certain Gettier-style counterexamples, whereas others will appear to be too weak. But so long as these concepts build on the truth-resistance requirement set by PK, and differ only on the accessibility-to-contraveners qualification, they will survive the range of Gettier-style examples where our epistemic intuitions are quite clear. The remaining Gettier-style examples allow for divergent treatments, since they constitute cases where our intuitions waver and thus where we may entertain divergent concepts of propositional knowledge.

Thus although PK does not have a monopoly on the concept of propositional knowledge, it provides the essential core for that concept. In doing so, PK takes the mystery out of the Gettier-style counterexamples that intuitively demand the formulation of evidential constraints on propositional knowledge. I have roughly characterized the evidential constraints provided by PK as justification sustenance by the collective totality of truths.

In summary, we have seen that the analysis of propositional knowledge due to PK explains not only Gettier's two original counterexamples, but also some of the most difficult Gettier-style counterexamples, e.g., example (I) above, the familiar Lucky Mr. Nogot case, and the cases involving Tom Grabit and his demented mother. We have also seen how this analysis improves substantially on the use of epistemic explanation in Shope's initially promising analysis, and how it can meet several likely objections claiming that it is too demanding.

Unlike typical defeasibility analyses, PK does *not* employ a subjunctive conditional in its fourth condition, and so does not fall prey to the objection that it commits the conditional fallacy with that condition.[16] We can easily put PK in standard quantificational form: for every proposition, P, and every instance of justifying

16 For the details of this fallacy, see Shope (1978; 1983, Chap. 2).

evidence, *E*, *S* knows that *P* on *E* if and only if *P* is true; *S* has justifying evidence, *E*, for *P* that is truth-resistant in the sense specified by the (subjunctive-free) principle TR; and *S* believes or assents to *P* on the basis of *E*. Nor does this analysis run afoul of the principle that the probability of a nonredundant conjunction is less than the probability of its individual conjuncts having a probability less than 1. The analysis assumes that any true proposition, *T*, is added to *S*'s evidence, *E*, in the sense that *S* *is* justified in believing that (*E* & *T*). Thus we cannot take the relevant conjunction to be unjustified for *S* because of low probability.

Another virtue of PK is that it allows for *non*deductive justifying evidence as a component of propositional knowledge. PK also enables us to see how to generate less strenuous, but equally plausible, concepts of propositional knowledge, particularly in connection with Gettier-style examples where our intuitions waver. Given these considerations, we may reasonably endorse PK as a most promising explication of the basic concept of propositional knowledge. Or, more boldly, we may conclude that it provides an analysis of propositional knowledge that puts the Gettier problem to rest once and for all.

The Gettier problem has revealed an important lesson. Propositional knowledge requires a fourth condition, in addition to the belief/assent, truth, and justification conditions. And this condition is not simply a function of the evidence a knower possesses. Thus the fourth condition for knowledge is externalist in a way that the justification condition is not.

6.3 Knowledge skepticism and meta-justification

Having clarified the necessary and sufficient conditions for propositional knowledge, we should ask whether humans can possess such knowledge. A strong version of knowledge skepticism states that we *cannot* possess propositional knowledge about the external world. This section opposes two noteworthy arguments for such skepticism, and explains how this book's epistemological theory is itself justified.

6.3.1 Knowledge and a Cartesian Dreamer Hypothesis

The first noteworthy argument for strong knowledge skepticism stems from Descartes's famous "Dreamer Hypothesis": the hypothesis that for one who takes oneself to perceive that something is so, it is possible that one is dreaming that it is so. I shall focus on this argument in its most recent garb, as presented by Stroud (1984).

The Cartesian skeptic often assumes that if one is dreaming that something is so, one does not *thereby* know that it is so. But this assumption does not quite explain how the Dreamer Hypothesis, which concerns the mere possibility of dreaming, is actually a skeptical hypothesis. Thus Stroud relies on the following assumption to infer a skeptical implication from the Dreamer Hypothesis: for any possibility incompatible with our knowing something, we must know that possibility not to obtain if we are to know the thing in question. Given this Cartesian assumption, according to Stroud, we cannot know anything about the external world, since we cannot know at any particular time that we are not dreaming.

Stroud's argument that we cannot know at any time that we are not dreaming runs as follows (1984, pp. 20–2):

1. One knows that one is not dreaming only if one has a test enabling one to determine that one is not dreaming.
2. One has a test enabling one to determine that one is not dreaming only if one knows that the test in question is reliable, and that one is not dreaming that one has such a reliable test.
3. But one cannot know that one has, and is not dreaming that one has, the reliable test in question.
4. Hence one cannot know that one is not dreaming.

Premises 2 and 3 obviously invite questions, and premise 1 is far from compelling without independent argument. Stroud supports premise 3 with this claim: "[A person] would have to have known at some time that he was not dreaming in order to get the information he needs to tell at *any* time that he is not dreaming – and that cannot be done" (p. 21). But one is left wondering just why that cannot be done. Stroud's remarks in support of premise 3 certainly do not show that we cannot tell that we are not dreaming; at most they raise the question of how we can tell this.

As for premise 2, Stroud owes us an explanation why it is inadequate that one's test simply *be* reliable, why one needs to know that it is reliable. Stroud's requirement here is excessive since it generates an endless regress of required known propositions. To illustrate this, let us state the requirement explicitly:

One knows that one is not dreaming that $P1$ only if one knows that $P2$: one has, and is not dreaming one has, a reliable test specifying that one is not dreaming that $P1$.

This requirement is perfectly general, and thus it applies to $P2$ also. So we have this implication:

One knows that $P2$ [= one has, and is not dreaming one has, a reliable test specifying that one is not dreaming that $P1$] only if one knows that $P3$: one has, and is not dreaming one has, a reliable test specifying that one is not dreaming that $P2$.

In addition, the requirement in question applies to $P3$, and to each member of the ensuing endless regress of required known propositions. But surely it is implausible to hold that one's knowing any single proposition requires one's knowing an *infinity* of propositions. Thus premise 2 of Stroud's skeptical argument is unacceptable.

We can illustrate further the implausibility of Stroud's skeptical argument by considering his Cartesian requirement that "there are always certain possibilities which must be known not to obtain if I am to know what I claim to know" (p. 26). The relevant possibilities, according to Stroud, are possibilities incompatible with one's knowing what one claims to know (p. 27). Thus let us state the Cartesian requirement explicitly as follows:

CR. For any possibility, X, necessarily if X is incompatible with S's knowing a physical-object proposition, P, then if S knows that P, then S knows that X does not obtain.

Without this principle, Stroud's case for strong knowledge skepticism is hopeless, and Stroud himself recognizes as much.

Problems face not only CR itself, but also what Stroud takes to satisfy its antecedent. Regarding CR, we should ask why S is required to know that X does not obtain, or why X's simply not obtaining is inadequate for the relevant necessary condition. Given this requirement, CR is excessive: it generates an endless regress of the sort arising from premise 2. To see this, consider the following requirement due to CR:

S knows that $P1$ only if S knows that $P2$: possibility X incompatible with S's knowing that $P1$ does not obtain.

This requirement, being perfectly general, applies to $P2$ also; thus:

S knows that *P2* only if S knows that *P3*: possibility *X* incompatible with *S*'s knowing that *P2* does not obtain.

The requirement at hand also applies to *P3*, and to each member of the resulting endless regress of required propositions. But again it is implausible to hold that one's knowing any single proposition requires one's knowing an infinity of propositions.

Regarding the satisfaction of CR's antecedent, Stroud would have us believe that:

(a) Possibly I now am dreaming that there is a blue book before me

is incompatible with:

(b) I know that there is a blue book before me.

But this seems wrong. What reason do we have to think that my knowing that there is a blue book before me excludes the *mere logical possibility* that I now am dreaming that there is a blue book before me? Clearly, this mere possibility of my dreaming does not entail either (i) that there is no blue book before me, (ii) that I do not believe that there is a blue book before me, (iii) that I am not justified in believing that there is a blue book before me, or (iv) that the fourth condition for knowledge, specified in §6.2, is not satisfied. Why then should we grant that the mere possibility of my dreaming is incompatible with my knowing?

Perhaps Stroud would have us understand his basic skeptical argument as follows (where *P* is any contingent physical-object proposition):

1. Necessarily, if it is logically possible that I am dreaming that *P*, while having evidence *E*, then it is logically possible that (*E* & ~*P*). (Dreamer Hypothesis Assumption)
2. It is logically possible that I am dreaming that *P* while having *E*, for any of my evidence. (Assumption)
3. Necessarily, if *E* justifies *P* for me, then *E* logically entails *P*. (Assumption)
4. Necessarily, if it is logically possible that (*E* &~*P*), then *E* does not justify *P* for me. (From 3 by transposition)
5. Hence *E* does not justify *P* for me. (From 1–4)
6. Hence I do not know that *P*. (From 5 and the assumption that propositional knowledge requires justification)

Of course this argument supports only weak knowledge skepticism, according to which I do not actually know that *P*. It does not support strong knowledge skepticism, according to which I *cannot* know that *P*. But if this is not the sort of argument underlying Stroud's skepticism, it is a mystery what his positive support for skepticism actually is.

In any case, premise 3 of the reconstructed argument is highly implausible. Why should we accept a principle of epistemic justification that rules out the very possibility of *non*deductive justifying evidence? Stroud gives no answer to this basic question. And once the skeptic demands that justification constitute deductive, entailing evidence, his challenge becomes uninteresting. For empirical knowledge of the external world, on virtually every nonskeptical epistemology, is *not* alleged to be based on deductive evidence. Nonskeptical philosophers widely admit that deductive evidence is not available for our justified physical-object beliefs.

What Stroud and other skeptics owe us, then, is a skeptical argument that does not rely on premise 3. The skeptic might argue, for instance, that our being in a dream state now is not merely possible, but is evidentially as *probable* as the physical-object propositions he calls into question. Such an argument would have to rely on specific principles of epistemic justification. But what might these principles be? In light of §3.5, we now can say that the justification skeptic has a lot of explaining to do. For the lesson of that section is that justification skepticism in its standard dress is inferior, from an explanatory point of view, to the familiar nonskeptical realist position about physical-object propositions.

Thus far, then, it is doubtful that we have adequate reasons to accept either strong or weak knowledge skepticism, or strong or weak justification skepticism. At least, nothing in Stroud's arguments provides the needed reasons. Regarding strong knowledge and justification skepticism, it certainly seems logically possible for one to satisfy the conditions for justification and knowledge stated in §§3.2 and 6.2. There seems to be no incoherence in supposing that one satisfies those conditions. Thus in the absence of argument to the contrary, we can reasonably reject strong knowledge and justification skepticism.

As for weak knowledge and justification skepticism, the key question is whether any of us actually has knowledge or justification. This question is largely empirical since it requires an examination of individual humans to see whether they satisfy the conditions specified in §§3.2 and 6.2. Such an examination involves, for instance, the empirical question whether anyone believes or assents to P in such a way that one satisfies the evidential basing relation. Thus weak skepticism is not *logically* false; for even if this book's epistemological principles are analytically true, it is not necessarily true that someone satisfies them. Yet I see no reason to deny that some of us have knowledge in the sense of §6.2, or that some of us have justification in the sense of §3.2. In fact, it seems plausible to suppose that some of us sometimes satisfy the principles of §§3.2 and 6.2. But let us not pursue such empirical matters here. I now am concerned mainly with the issue whether knowledge and justification are possible.

Stroud (1984, p. 118) has suggested that a prerequisite of a viable alternative to strong skepticism about knowledge of the external world is that it provide a general explanation of all such knowledge at once, without appealing to any particular instance of supposed knowledge about the external world. What the nonskeptic needs, according to Stroud, is an explanation of how we can get knowledge of the external world on the basis of something that is not knowledge of the external world, such as sense experience. Of course Stroud doubts that such an explanation is actually forthcoming. However, this book has tried to provide the needed explanation in considerable detail. I shall lend further credibility to this proposed explanation by turning to the second noteworthy argument for knowledge skepticism: the argument from the famous problem of the criterion. My consideration of this argument will lead to a justification of this book's epistemological theory.

6.3.2 Explanatory particularism and the problem of the criterion

In Book II of his *Outlines of Pyrrhonism*, Sextus Empiricus presents the problem of the criterion by raising two general questions: (a) what do we know and (b) how do we know anything? Question (a) asks about the extent of our knowledge, whereas question (b) asks about the criteria for our knowledge. These simple questions generate the problem that without an answer to (a) we apparently cannot answer (b), and without an answer to (b) we apparently cannot answer (a). Some skeptics think this problem of the criterion shows that propositional knowledge is impossible.

I suspect that the important lesson here is simply that we should not try to justify our criteria for knowledge or justification, i.e.,

260

our epistemic principles, solely by what those principles count-enance as knowledge or justification. Apparently such an effort will always confront circularity. But what other means of meta- Q justification, or justification of epistemic principles, is there? The answer to this question will lead to a resolution of the problem of the criterion. R

Moral theorists sometimes appeal to a strategy of "reflective equi-librium" to justify an ethical theory. It seems that we can use an analogue of this strategy in epistemology. The analogue in epis-temology begins with one's having certain tentative, revisable ep-istemic intuitions about particular instances of justification and knowledge. It then involves one's asking what explanatory epi-stemic principles, if any, entail those putative instances of justifi-cation and knowledge. The desired epistemic principles must also entail that one does not have knowledge or justification in those cases that one's tentative intuitions exclude from knowledge and justification.

One's tentative epistemic intuitions are simply one's *considered, but revisable, judgments* that in certain specified cases one has knowl-edge or justification, and that in certain other specified cases one does not have knowledge or justification. On the basis of such considered judgments, the epistemologist aims to formulate a set of explanatory epistemic principles that entail those judgments and explain why they are true. The epistemologist often works back and forth between epistemic principles and considered judgments. One sometimes revises considered judgments about particular cases in light of effective explanatory principles; and one sometimes re-vises epistemic principles in light of new considered judgments about particular cases. Such a policy of reciprocating benefits cases where one's epistemic intuitions are inconsistent, and where one's epistemic principles conflict with certain considered judgments about cases of knowledge and justification. Such a policy should lead to maximal explanatory coherence between one's epistemic principles and one's considered epistemic judgments. Such maximal explanatory coherence can justify an epistemological theory for one.

Such meta-justification resembles the sort of justification for physical-object propositions characterized in §3.2. In both cases justification derives from propositions' having a sort of maximal explanatory power for one relative to a data base and to a set of competing propositions. Such an analogy between justification of physical-object propositions and meta-justification for epistemic principles is highly desirable; for both are, after all, species of epistemic justification. Chapters 2 and 3 gave an account of the data base and the competing propositions relevant to the justification of physical-object propositions. The relevant ultimate data base for such justification consists of one's subjective nonconceptual contents.

Regarding meta-justification for epistemic principles, the ultimate data base consists of one's epistemic intuitions, i.e., one's considered epistemic judgments. And the competing propositions consist of the alternative epistemic principles one understands. When one set of epistemic principles explains certain epistemological intuitions (i.e., why they are correct) better than does each of its alternatives, then the set in question has maximal explanatory power relative to those intuitions and alternatives. And when a set of epistemic principles has such maximal explanatory power for one, that set of principles is justifiable for one. Such is the strategy of meta-justification that can apply to this book's epistemic principles.

Several points deserve emphasis. First, the proposed strategy does not require that justified epistemic principles actually be truth-conducive in the sense that believing in accord with them will actually produce more true than false beliefs. We saw reason to reject a reliabilist criterion for justification in §4.3; and there seems to be no reason to revive such a criterion for meta-justification. Epistemic principles can be justified even in a world where, owing to the deceptions of a Cartesian evil demon, they are not truth-conducive.

Second, the justification for physical-object propositions, as characterized in Chapters 2 and 3, does not itself require meta-justification. The denial of this leads to an epistemic level confusion: a confusion between the claim that (a) P is justified for one and the claim that (b) 'P is justified for one' is justified for one. In addition, such a denial threatens to generate an endless regress of required justifications of ever-increasing orders. If justification requires meta-justification, then meta-justification requires meta-meta-justification, and so on *ad infinitum*. Obviously we should not go down that road of no return.

Third, my proposed meta-justification allows that meta-

262

justification, like any justification, is perspectival, i.e., relative to one's data base and alternative explainers. Thus the epistemic principles justified for one epistemologist need not be justified for another. Epistemologists can have differing considered epistemic judgments and differing alternative explainers. Such variability of justification is common regarding physical-object beliefs, and it is no less common at the level of meta-justification. The perspectival feature of meta-justification also allows that what has meta-justification for one can change upon one's acquiring new explainers of one's epistemic data base.

The fourth important point is that my proposed strategy for meta-justification is not question-begging against knowledge skepticism or justification skepticism. This strategy leaves open the possibility that skeptical epistemic principles best explain one's epistemic intuitions. On this strategy, one's relevant epistemic intuitions are tentative and revisable; and thus one may withdraw one's judgment that one has knowledge or justification in a certain case if a set of skeptical epistemic principles turned out to have maximal explanatory power for one relative to other epistemic intuitions one has. So my proposed strategy for meta-justification leaves open the possibility that the various *non*skeptical epistemological theories are all inferior, from an explanatory view, to their skeptical competitors. Such a strategy improves on certain recent treatments of the problem of the criterion that are question-begging against skepticism inasmuch as they rule out skepticism *from the start.*[17] The nonskeptic need not preempt the skeptic, since powerful antiskeptical arguments are available. (See §3.5 on this point.)

Fifth, and finally, my strategy for meta-justification gives us a solution to the problem of the criterion. Recall that according to this problem we evidently cannot answer the question of what we know without first answering the question of how we know, and we evidently cannot answer the question of how we know without first answering the question of what we know. The traditional *particularist* response to this problem begins with an answer to the question of what we know, and thus typically begs the main question against the skeptic. The traditional *methodist* response to the problem begins with an answer to the question of how we know, and thus typically risks divorcing knowledge and justification from

17 See, for example, Chisholm (1982).

263

our considered judgments about what qualifies as knowledge and justification. On my strategy for meta-justification, we avoid the undesirable implications of these two approaches by adopting a policy of reciprocating between considered epistemic judgments and explanatory epistemic principles.

The goal of the policy of reciprocating is, I suggested, maximal explanatory coherence relative to one's epistemic data base consisting of one's considered epistemic judgments. We may call this policy *explanatory particularism*, as it recognizes the role in meta-justification of both epistemic intuitions *and* explanatory epistemic principles. But this is not traditional particularism, since I take the relevant epistemic intuitions to be revisable in cases where explanatory power increases relative to other epistemic intuitions one has. Explanatory particularism also differs from the traditional methodist response, as it relies on a data base consisting of epistemic intuitions about individual cases of knowledge and justification. So explanatory particularism avoids the undesirable extremes of traditional particularism and methodism.

Explanatory particularism also avoids the problem of circularity by denying that we can justify our epistemic principles solely by what those principles countenance as knowledge or justification. On this method, the role of epistemic intuitions in meta-justification frees us from such circularity. Thus explanatory particularism gives us a noncircular solution to the problem of the criterion.

Explanatory particularism also provides for a straightforward meta-justification of this book's epistemological theory. The desired meta-justification requires that this book's epistemological theory exceed its available competitors in explanatory power relative to our considered epistemic judgments. We have seen how the various alternative theories face serious problems, relative to our epistemic intuitions, that the theory of Chapters 2–4 avoids. For instance, §2.2 identified the explanatory defects in the various epistemic principles committed solely to propositional evidential probability-makers. It showed the flaws, relative to our epistemic intuitions, in Probability Coherentism, Probability Infinitism, the Thesis of Self-Probability, and the thesis of Circular Probability. And §2.3 identified the explanatory defects in the alternative epistemic principles committed to nonpropositional evidential probability-makers. It showed the flaws, again relative to our epistemic intuitions, in Radical Externalism, Moderate Externalism,

264

and Radical Internalism. We thus were left with Moderate Internalism, a version of which I developed in Chapters 2 and 3. Perhaps we could develop other versions of Moderate Internalism, but until we do so, we can recommend the theory of Chapters 2 and 3 over its nonskeptical competitors.

Thus the remaining competitor for my Moderate Internalism is justification skepticism. In §3.5 we saw that the prominent variations on such skepticism are seriously defective from an explanatory point of view. So given the strategy for meta-justification described above, we now have a general meta-justification of this book's Moderate Internalism.

We can employ a similar meta-justification for the fourth condition for knowledge proposed in §6.2, but I cannot pursue the details here. Alternative fourth conditions form a labyrinth, if not an inescapable maze. All the prominent variations evidently suffer grave defects relative to our epistemic intuitions.[18] Thus §6.1 focused on a new fourth condition that initially promised to succeed where the earlier variations failed. However, that condition also was ultimately unpromising. The fourth condition of §6.2 apparently succeeded where the former condition failed. Thus we have at least a rough sketch of a meta-justification for my proposed fourth condition for knowledge.

So this book's epistemological theory can itself be justified, and thus recommended, on explanatory grounds.

6.4 Conclusion

Given the analysis of knowledge culminating in §6.2, we can *naturalize* an important part of epistemology. We can analyze the concept of propositional knowledge solely in terms of concepts that are *non*epistemic and *non*-normative. My analysis relies on the nonnormative concepts of belief, truth, explanation, entailment, causation, subjective contents of experience, contravening, and truth-resistant evidence. In freeing the concepts of epistemic justification and propositional knowledge from normative concepts, this book's analysis removes a considerable amount of epistemological mystery. This, I believe, is one of the major benefits of this book's theory of knowledge.

18 The relevant arguments against the prominent variations can be found in Shope (1983, Chaps. 2–5).

I have sidestepped the question whether this book's epistemic principles are analytic as opposed to synthetic, and *a priori* as opposed to *a posteriori*. An easy answer might be simply that this book's epistemic principles have whatever status a philosophical theory is supposed to have. But like most easy answers, this one would not be very helpful. Clearly my epistemic principles are not *a posteriori* in the sense of being justified as generalizations from perceptual experience. Rather, as §6.3 suggested, they are explanatory generalizations from epistemic intuitions. And inasmuch as epistemic intuitions are nonempirical, we must regard my proposed epistemic principles as having *a priori* justification.

Thus if my epistemic principles are synthetic, they provide a species of the controversial synthetic *a priori*. But are they really synthetic, in the sense that their being true is not due solely to the meanings of their constituent terms? I think not. There seems to be no reason to deny their being analytic; and they certainly seem to be definitional in status. Like Hume, I fail to see how synthetic truths could be justified *a priori*. But I cannot pursue that vexing topic here, mainly because it calls for a separate book.

Thus in the absence of argument to the contrary, I recommend this book's epistemic principles as analytic truths justified *a priori* via my strategy of meta-justification called 'explanatory particularism'. This recommendation does not imply that, given the theory of this book, dissenting theorists do not understand at all what terms such as 'justification' and 'knowledge' mean. We can understand the meaning of such terms at various levels of generality; and there surely is common understanding at some general level. However, this book's theory aims to provide epistemological understanding at a very specific level of conceptual analysis.

Only time and good reasoning will tell how this book's theory fares in the hectic explanatory competition of contemporary epistemology. And this of course is how things should be, epistemically. This book's explanation-oriented foundationalism would not have it any other way.

References

Achinstein, Peter. 1983. *The Nature of Explanation*. New York: Oxford University Press.

Alston, William. 1976. "Self-Warrant: A Neglected Form of Privileged Access." *American Philosophical Quarterly* 13, 257–72.

1980. "Level-Confusions in Epistemology." In P. A. French, T. E. Uehling, and H. K. Wettstein, eds., *Midwest Studies in Philosophy*, vol. 5: *Studies in Epistemology*, pp. 135–50. Minneapolis: University of Minnesota Press.

1983. "What's Wrong with Immediate Knowledge?" *Synthese* 55, 73–95.

1985. "Concepts of Epistemic Justification." *The Monist* 68, 57–89. Reprinted in Moser (1986, pp. 23–54). Page references are to this reprint.

1986a. "Epistemic Circularity." *Philosophy and Phenomenological Research* 47, 1–30.

1986b. "Internalism and Externalism in Epistemology." *Philosophical Topics* 14, 179–221.

1988. "An Internalist Externalism." *Synthese* 74, 265–83.

Annis, David. 1978. "A Contextualist Theory of Epistemic Justification." *American Philosophical Quarterly* 15, 213–19. Reprinted in Moser (1986, pp. 203–13).

Appiah, Anthony. 1986. *For Truth in Semantics*. Oxford: Blackwell Publisher.

Armstrong, David. 1961. *Perception and the Physical World*. London: Routledge and Kegan Paul.

1973. *Belief, Truth, and Knowledge*. Cambridge: Cambridge University Press.

1978. *Nominalism and Realism*. Cambridge: Cambridge University Press.

Audi, Robert. 1982. "Believing and Affirming." *Mind* 91, 115–20.

1986. "Belief, Reason, and Inference." *Philosophical Topics* 14, 27–65.

Ayer, A. J. 1973. *The Central Questions of Philosophy*. London: Weidenfeld and Nicolson.

Bach, Kent. 1987. *Thought and Reference*. Oxford: Clarendon Press.

Bauer, Russell, and Alen Rubens, 1985. "Agnosia." In K. M. Heilman and Edward Valenstein, eds., *Clinical Neuropsychology*, pp. 187–241. New York: Oxford University Press.

Belnap, Nuel, and Thomas Steel. 1976. *The Logic of Questions and Answers.* New Haven, Conn.: Yale University Press.

Black, Ira, J. E. Adler et al. 1987. "Biochemistry of Information Storage in the Nervous System." *Science* 236, 1263–8.

BonJour, Laurence. 1976. "The Coherence Theory of Empirical Knowledge." *Philosophical Studies* 30, 281–312. Reprinted in Moser (1986, pp. 116–44).

   1985. *The Structure of Empirical Knowledge.* Cambridge, Mass.: Harvard University Press.

   1988. "Reply to Moser." *Analysis* 48, 164–5.

Brentano, Franz. 1924. *Psychology from an Empirical Standpoint*, 2d ed. English trans. by A. C. Rancurello, D. B. Terrell, and L. L. McAlister. London: Routledge and Kegan Paul, 1973.

   1929. *Sensory and Noetic Consciousness.* English trans. by Margarete Schaettle and L. L. McAlister. London: Routledge and Kegan Paul, 1981.

Bromberger, Sylvain. 1966. "Why-Questions." In R. G. Colodny, ed., *Mind and Cosmos*, pp. 86–111. Pittsburgh: University of Pittsburgh Press.

Brown, Harold. 1977. *Perception, Theory, and Commitment.* Chicago: University of Chicago Press.

Brown, Jason. 1972. *Aphasia, Apraxia, and Agnosia.* Springfield, Ill.: Thomas.

Burge, Tyler, 1977. "Belief *De Re.*" *The Journal of Philosophy* 74, 338–62.

Butchvarov, Panayot. 1966. *Resemblance and Identity.* Bloomington: Indiana University Press.

   1970. *The Concept of Knowledge.* Evanston, Ill.: Northwestern University Press.

   1979. *Being qua Being: A Theory of Identity, Existence, and Predication.* Bloomington: Indiana University Press.

Campbell, Richmond. 1981. "Can Inconsistency Be Reasonable?" *The Canadian Journal of Philosophy* 11, 245–70.

Carson, Thomas. 1985. "Relativism and Nihilism." *Philosophia* 15, 1–23.

Changeux, J.-P. 1986. *Neuronal Man: The Biology of Mind.* New York: Oxford University Press.

Chisholm, Roderick. 1956a. "Epistemic Statements and the Ethics of Belief." *Philosophy and Phenomenological Research* 16, 447–60.

   1956b. " 'Appear', 'Take', and 'Evident'." *The Journal of Philosophy* 53, 722–31. Reprinted in R. J. Swartz, ed., *Perceiving, Sensing, and Knowing*, pp. 473–85. Garden City, N.Y.: Doubleday, 1965.

   1957. *Perceiving: A Philosophical Study.* Ithaca, N.Y.: Cornell University Press.

   1964. "Theory of Knowledge in America." In Chisholm et al., *Philosophy*, pp. 261–86. Englewood Cliffs, N.J.: Prentice-Hall. Reprinted in Chisholm, *The Foundations of Knowing*, pp. 109–93. Minneapolis: University of Minnesota Press.

   1966. *Theory of Knowledge.* Englewood Cliffs, N.J.: Prentice-Hall.

1968. "Lewis's Ethics of Belief." In P. A. Schilpp, ed., *The Philosophy of C. I. Lewis*, pp. 223–42. LaSalle, Ill.: Open Court.

1974. "On the Nature of Acquaintance: A Discussion of Russell's Theory of Knowledge." In George Nakhnikian, ed., *Bertrand Russell's Philosophy*, pp. 47–56. New York: Barnes and Noble.

1976. *Person and Object*. LaSalle, Ill.: Open Court.

1977. *Theory of Knowledge*, 2d ed. Englewood Cliffs, N.J.: Prentice-Hall.

1980. "A Version of Foundationalism." In P. A. French, T. E. Uehling, and H. K. Wettstein, eds., *Midwest Studies in Philosophy*, vol. 5: *Studies in Epistemology*, pp. 543–64. Minneapolis: University of Minnesota Press. Reprinted in Moser and vander Nat (1987, pp. 293–308).

1982. "The Problem of the Criterion." In Chisholm, *The Foundations of Knowing*, pp. 61–75. Minneapolis: University of Minnesota Press.

1988. "The Indispensability of Internal Justification." *Synthese* 74, 285–96.

1989. *Theory of Knowledge*, 3d ed. Englewood Cliffs, N.J.: Prentice-Hall.

Church, Alonzo. 1956. "Propositions and Sentences." In Church et al., *The Problem of Universals*, pp. 3–11. Notre Dame, Ind.: University of Notre Dame Press. Reprinted in J. F. Rosenberg and Charles Travis, eds., *Readings in the Philosophy of Language*, pp. 276–82. Englewood Cliffs, N.J.: Prentice-Hall.

Clark, Romane. 1979. "Sensing, Perceiving, Thinking." In Ernest Sosa, ed., *Essays on the Philosophy of Roderick Chisholm*, pp. 273–95. Amsterdam: Rodopi.

1987. "Objects of Consciousness: The Non-Relational Theory of Sensing." In James Tomberlin, ed., *Philosophical Perspectives*, vol. 1: *Metaphysics*, pp. 481–500. Atascadero, Calif.: Ridgeview.

Cohen, Stewart. 1984. "Justification and Truth." *Philosophical Studies* 46, 279–95.

Conee, Earl. 1988. "Why Solve the Gettier Problem?" In David Austin, ed., *Philosophical Analysis*, pp. 55–8. Dordrecht: Kluwer.

Cornman, James. 1972. "Materialism and Some Myths about Some Givens." *The Monist* 56, 215–33.

1975a. "Chisholm on Sensing and Perceiving." In Keith Lehrer, ed., *Analysis and Metaphysics*, pp. 11–33. Dordrecht: Reidel.

1975b. *Perception, Common Sense, and Science*. New Haven, Conn.: Yale University Press.

1980. *Skepticism, Justification, and Explanation*. Dordrecht: Reidel.

Craig, E. J. 1976. "Sensory Experience and the Foundations of Knowledge." *Synthese* 33, 1–24.

Davidson, Donald. 1969. "True to the Facts." *The Journal of Philosophy* 66, 748–64. Reprinted in Davidson (1984, pp. 37–54).

1973. "In Defence of Convention T." In Hugues Leblanc, ed., *Truth, Syntax, and Modality*, pp. 76–85. New York: North Holland. Reprinted in Davidson (1984, pp. 65–75).

1983. "A Coherence Theory of Truth and Knowledge." In Dieter Henrich, ed., *Kant oder Hegel*, pp. 423–38. Stuttgart: Klett-Cotta. Reprinted in Ernest Le Pore, ed., *Truth and Interpretation*, pp. 307–19. Oxford: Blackwell Publisher.

    1984. *Inquiries into Truth and Interpretation*. Oxford: Clarendon Press.

Davis, Wayne. 1988. "Knowledge, Acceptance, and Belief." *The Southern Journal of Philosophy* 26, 169–78.

Devitt, Michael. 1984. *Realism and Truth*. Princeton, N.J.: Princeton University Press.

Dretske, Fred. 1979. "Simple Seeing." In D. F. Gustafson and B. L. Tapscott, eds., *Body, Mind, and Method*, pp. 1–15. Dordrecht: Reidel.

    1981. *Knowledge and the Flow of Information*. Cambridge, Mass.: MIT Press.

Ducasse, C. J. 1944. "Propositions, Truth, and the Ultimate Criterion of Truth." *Philosophy and Phenomenological Research* 4, 317–40. Reprinted in Ducasse, *Truth, Knowledge, and Causation*, pp. 150–78. London: Routledge and Kegan Paul, 1968.

    1951. *Nature, Mind, and Death*. LaSalle, Ill.: Open Court.

Evans, Gareth. 1982. *The Varieties of Reference*. Oxford: Clarendon Press.

Feldman, Richard. 1974. "An Alleged Defect in Gettier Counter-Examples." *The Australasian Journal of Philosophy* 52, 68–9. Reprinted in Moser (1986, pp. 252–3).

    1985. "Reliability and Justification." *The Monist* 68, 159–74.

    1988. "Having Evidence." In David Austin, ed., *Philosophical Analysis*, pp. 83–104. Dordrecht: Kluwer.

Feldman, Richard, and Earl Conee. 1985. "Evidentialism." *Philosophical Studies* 48, 15–34. Reprinted in Moser and vander Nat (1987, pp. 334–45).

Field, Hartry. 1972. "Tarski's Theory of Truth." *The Journal of Philosophy* 69, 347–75.

    1986. "The Deflationary Conception of Truth." In Graham Macdonald and Crispin Wright, eds., *Fact, Science, and Morality*, pp. 55–117. Oxford: Blackwell Publisher.

Firth, Roderick. 1949. "Sense-Data and the Percept Theory." *Mind* 58. Reprinted in R. J. Swartz, ed., *Perceiving, Sensing, and Knowing*, pp. 219–42. Garden City, N.Y.: Doubleday, 1965.

    1969. "Lewis on the Given." In P. A. Schilpp, ed., *The Philosophy of C. I. Lewis*, pp. 329–50. LaSalle, Ill.: Open Court.

    1978. "Are Epistemic Concepts Reducible to Ethical Concepts?" In Alvin Goldman and Jaegwon Kim, eds., *Values and Morals*, pp. 215–29. Dordrecht: Reidel.

Fodor, Jerry. 1984. "Observation Reconsidered." *Philosophy of Science* 51, 23–43.

Fogelin, Robert. 1985. *Hume's Skepticism in the Treatise of Human Nature*. London: Routledge and Kegan Paul.

Foley, Richard. 1979. "Justified Inconsistent Beliefs." *American Philosophical Quarterly* 16, 247–57.

    1986. "Is It Possible To Have Contradictory Beliefs?" In P. A. French, T. E. Uehling, and H. K. Wettstein, eds., *Midwest Studies in Philos-*

ophy, vol. 10: *Studies in the Philosophy of Mind*, pp. 327–55. Minneapolis: University of Minnesota Press.

1987. *The Theory of Epistemic Rationality*. Cambridge, Mass.: Harvard University Press.

Forbes, Graeme. 1986. "Truth, Correspondence, and Redundancy." In Graham Macdonald and Crispin Wright, eds., *Fact, Science, and Morality*, pp. 27–54. Oxford: Blackwell Publisher.

Gettier, Edmund. 1963. "Is Justified True Belief Knowledge?" *Analysis* 23, 121–3. Reprinted in Moser (1986, pp. 231–3).

Ginet, Carl. 1975. *Knowledge, Perception, and Memory*. Dordrecht: Reidel.

1983. "Justification of Belief." In Carl Ginet and Sydney Shoemaker, eds., *Knowledge and Mind*, pp. 26–49. New York: Oxford University Press.

Goldman, Alan. 1988. *Empirical Knowledge*. Berkeley and Los Angeles: University of California Press.

Goldman, Alvin. 1976. "Discrimination and Perceptual Knowledge." *The Journal of Philosophy* 73, 771–91. Reprinted in Moser and vander Nat (1987, pp. 269–82).

1979. "What Is Justified Belief?" In George Pappas, ed., *Justification and Knowledge*, pp. 1–23. Dordrecht: Reidel. Reprinted in Moser (1986, pp. 171–92).

1980. "The Internalist Conception of Justification." In P. A. French, T. E. Uehling, and H. K. Wettstein, eds., *Midwest Studies in Philosophy*, vol. 5: *Studies in Epistemology*, pp. 27–52. Minneapolis: University of Minnesota Press.

1986. *Epistemology and Cognition*. Cambridge, Mass.: Harvard University Press.

1988. "Strong and Weak Justification." In James Tomberlin, ed., *Philosophical Perspectives*, vol. 2: *Epistemology*. Atascadero, Calif.: Ridgeview.

Goldstein, Kurt, and Martin Scheerer. 1941. "Abstract and Concrete Behavior." *Psychological Monographs* 53 (whole no. 239), 1–150.

Goodman, Nelson. 1960. "The Way the World Is." *The Review of Metaphysics* 14, 48–56. Reprinted in Goodman, *Problems and Projects*, pp. 24–32. Indianapolis: Bobbs-Merrill, 1972.

1978. *Ways of Worldmaking*. Indianapolis: Hackett.

Grim, Patrick. 1984. "There Is No Set of All Truths." *Analysis* 44, 206–8.

Hallett, Garth. 1988. *Language and Truth*. New Haven, Conn.: Yale University Press.

Hamlyn, David. 1970. *The Theory of Knowledge*. London: Macmillan.

Hardin, C. L. 1988. *Color for Philosophers*. Indianapolis: Hackett.

Harman, Gilbert. 1965. "The Inference to the Best Explanation." *The Philosophical Review* 74, 88–95.

1970. "Induction." In Marshall Swain, ed., *Induction, Acceptance, and Rational Belief*, pp. 83–99. Dordrecht: Reidel.

1973. *Thought*. Princeton, N.J.: Princeton University Press.

271

1980. "Reasoning and Explanatory Coherence." *American Philosophical Quarterly* 17, 151–7.

1986. *Change in View*. Cambridge, Mass.: MIT Press.

Harnad, Stevan. 1987. "Category Induction and Representation." In Harnad, ed., *Categorical Perception*, pp. 535–65. Cambridge: Cambridge University Press.

Harrah, David. 1963. *Communication: A Logical Model*. Cambridge, Mass.: MIT Press.

Hecaen, Henri, and M. L. Albert. 1978. *Human Neuropsychology*. New York: Wiley.

Heidelberger, Herbert. 1979. "The Self-Presenting." In Ernest Sosa, ed., *Essays on the Philosophy of Roderick Chisholm*, pp. 59–76. Amsterdam: Rodopi.

Hempel, Carl. 1962. "Deductive-Nomological vs. Statistical Explanation." In Herbert Feigl and Grover Maxwell, eds., *Minnesota Studies in the Philosophy of Science*, vol. 3: *Scientific Explanation, Space, and Time*, pp. 98–169. Minneapolis: University of Minnesota Press.

Hirst, William. 1986. "The Psychology of Attention." In J. E. LeDoux and William Hirst, eds., *Mind and Brain*, pp. 105–41. Cambridge: Cambridge University Press.

Hiz, Henry. 1962. "Questions and Answers." *The Journal of Philosophy* 59, 253–65.

1978. "Difficult Questions." In Hiz, ed., *Questions*, pp. 211–26. Dordrecht: Reidel.

Jackson, Frank. 1977. *Perception: A Representative Theory*. Cambridge: Cambridge University Press.

James, William. 1896. "The Will To Believe." *New World*. Reprinted in James, *The Will To Believe and Other Essays*. New York: Mackay, 1911. Page references are to this reprint.

Johnsen, Bredo. 1986. "The Given." *Philosophy and Phenomenological Research* 46, 597–613.

1987. "Relevant Alternatives and Demon Skepticism." *The Journal of Philosophy* 84, 643–53.

Johnston, William, and Veronica Dark. 1986. "Selective Attention." *Annual Review of Psychology* 37, 43–75.

Kaplan, Mark. 1985. "It's Not What You Know That Counts." *The Journal of Philosophy* 82, 350–63.

Keim, Robert. 1975. "Epistemic Values and Epistemic Viewpoints." In Keith Lehrer, ed., *Analysis and Metaphysics*, pp. 75–91. Dordrecht: Reidel.

Kiefer, Ferenc, ed., 1983. *Questions and Answers*. Dordrecht: Reidel.

Klein, Peter. 1971. "A Proposed Definition of Propositional Knowledge." *The Journal of Philosophy* 68, 471–82.

1976. "Knowledge, Causality, and Defeasibility." *The Journal of Philosophy* 73, 792–812.

1980. "Misleading Evidence and the Restoration of Justification." *Philosophical Studies* 37, 81–9.

1981. *Certainty: A Refutation of Scepticism.* Minneapolis: University of Minnesota Press.

1985. "The Virtues of Inconsistency." *The Monist* 68, 105–35.

Kneale, William, and Martha Kneale. 1962. *The Development of Logic.* Oxford: Clarendon Press.

Kosslyn, Stephen. 1980. *Image and Mind.* Cambridge, Mass.: Harvard University Press.

Kuhn, Thomas. 1970. *The Structure of Scientific Revolutions,* 2d ed. Chicago: University of Chicago Press.

Kyburg, Henry. 1970a. *Probability and Inductive Logic.* New York: Macmillan.

1970b. "Conjunctivitis." In Marshall Swain, ed., *Induction, Acceptance, and Rational Belief,* pp. 55–82. Dordrecht: Reidel. Reprinted in Kyburg (1983b, pp. 232–54).

1971. "Epistemological Probability." *Synthese* 23, 309–26. Reprinted in Kyburg (1983b, pp. 204–18).

1983a. "The Nature of Epistemological Probability." In Kyburg (1983b, pp. 153–7).

1983b. *Epistemology and Inference.* Minneapolis: University of Minnesota Press.

Lehrer, Keith. 1965. "Knowledge, Truth, and Evidence." *Analysis* 25, 168–75.

1974. *Knowledge.* Oxford: Clarendon Press.

1975. "Reason and Consistency." In Lehrer, ed., *Analysis and Metaphysics,* pp. 57–74. Dordrecht: Reidel.

1979. "The Gettier Problem and the Analysis of Knowledge." In George Pappas, ed., *Justification and Knowledge,* pp. 65–78. Dordrecht: Reidel.

1980a. "Self-Profile." In R. J. Bogdan, ed., *Keith Lehrer,* pp. 3–104. Dordrecht: Reidel.

1980b. "Reply to Pastin." In R. J. Bogdan, ed., *Keith Lehrer,* pp. 233–41. Dordrecht: Reidel.

1983. "Belief, Acceptance, and Cognition." In Herman Parret, ed., *On Believing,* pp. 172–83. Berlin: Walter de Gruyter.

1986. "The Coherence Theory of Knowledge." *Philosophical Topics* 14, 5–25.

1988. "Metaknowledge: Undefeated Justification." *Synthese* 74, 329–47.

Lehrer, Keith, and Thomas Paxson. 1969. "Knowledge: Undefeated Justified True Belief." *The Journal of Philosophy* 66, 225–37. Reprinted in Pappas and Swain (1978, pp. 146–54).

Levi, Isaac. 1967. *Gambling with Truth.* Cambridge, Mass.: MIT Press.

1969. "Information and Inference." *Synthese* 17, 369–91. Reprinted in Levi (1984, pp. 51–69). Page references are to this reprint.

1979. "Abduction and Demands for Information." In Ilkka Niiniluoto and Raimo Tuomela, eds., *The Logic and Epistemology of Scientific Change,* pp. 405–29. New York: North Holland. Reprinted in Levi (1984, pp. 87–106). Page references are to this reprint.

1980. *The Enterprise of Knowledge.* Cambridge, Mass.: MIT Press.

1982. "Self-Profile." In R. J. Bogdan, ed., *Henry E. Kyburg, Jr., and Isaac Levi*, pp. 181–216. Dordrecht: Reidel.

1984. *Decisions and Revisions*. Cambridge: Cambridge University Press.

Lewis, C. I. 1926. "The Pragmatic Element in Knowledge." *University of California Publications in Philosophy* 6, 205–27. Reprinted in Moser and vander Nat (1987, pp. 201–11). Page references are to this reprint.

1929. *Mind and the World Order*, New York: Scribner.

1946. *An Analysis of Knowledge and Valuation*. LaSalle, Ill.: Open Court.

1952. "The Given Element in Empirical Knowledge." *The Philosophical Review* 61, 168–75. Reprinted in J. D. Goheen and J. L. Mothershead, eds., *The Collected Papers of Clarence Irving Lewis*, pp. 324–30. Stanford, Calif.: Stanford University Press.

Lewis, David. 1984. "Putnam's Paradox." *The Australasian Journal of Philosophy* 62, 221–36.

Lycan, William. 1988. *Judgement and Justification*. Cambridge: Cambridge University Press.

Lynch, Gary. 1986. *Synapses, Circuits, and the Beginnings of Memory*. Cambridge, Mass.: MIT Press.

Mackie, J. L. 1970. "Simple Truth." *The Philosophical Quarterly* 20, 321–33.

1973. *Truth, Probability, and Paradox*. Oxford: Clarendon Press.

1976. *Problems from Locke*. Oxford: Clarendon Press.

Meiland, J. W. 1980. "What Ought We To Believe?" *American Philosophical Quarterly* 17, 15–24.

Meyers, Robert. 1988. *The Likelihood of Knowledge*. Dordrecht: Kluwer.

Meyers, Robert, and Kenneth Stern. 1973. "Knowledge without Paradox." *The Journal of Philosophy* 70, 147–60.

Michalos, Alex. 1978. *The Foundations of Decision-Making*. Ottawa: Canadian Library of Philosophy.

Moore, G. E. 1903. "The Refutation of Idealism." *Mind* 12, 433–53. Reprinted in Moore, *Philosophical Studies*. London: Kegan Paul, Trench, Trubner, 1922.

Morawetz, Thomas. 1978. *Wittgenstein and Knowledge*. Amherst: University of Massachusetts Press.

Moser, Paul. 1984. "Types, Tokens, and Propositions." *Philosophy and Phenomenological Research* 44, 361–75.

1985. *Empirical Justification*. Dordrecht: Reidel.

1987. "Harman's *Change in View*." *Grazer Philosophische Studien* 30, 179–87.

1988a. "Meaning, Justification, and Skepticism." *Philosophical Papers* 17, 88–101.

1988b. "A Dilemma for Normative Moral Relativism." *The Southern Journal of Philosophy* 26, 207–16.

1988c. "Foundationalism, the Given, and C. I. Lewis." *History of Philosophy Quarterly* 5, 189–204.

1989a. Critical notice of Foley's *The Theory of Epistemic Rationality*. *Noûs* 23. Forthcoming.

1989b. "Inferential Justification and Foley's Foundations." *Analysis* 49, 89–93.

1989c. "Lehrer's Coherentism and the Isolation Objection." In John Bender, ed., *The Current State of the Coherence Theory*. Dordrecht: Kluwer. Forthcoming.

Moser, Paul, ed. 1986. *Empirical Knowledge*. Totowa, N.J.: Rowman and Littlefield.

Moser, Paul, and Arnold vander Nat, eds. 1987. *Human Knowledge: Classical and Contemporary Approaches*. New York: Oxford University Press.

Naylor, M. B. 1985. "Voluntary Belief." *Philosophy and Phenomenological Research* 45, 427–36.

Neisser, Ulric, ed. 1987a. *Concepts and Conceptual Development*. Cambridge: Cambridge University Press.

1987b. "From Direct Perception to Conceptual Structure." In Neisser (1987a, pp. 11–24).

O'Connor, D. J. 1975. *The Correspondence Theory of Truth*. London: Hutchinson.

Pappas, George. 1982. "Non-Inferential Knowledge." *Philosophia* 12, 81–98.

Pappas, George, and Marshall Swain, eds. 1978. *Essays on Knowledge and Justification*. Ithaca, N.Y.: Cornell University Press.

Parasuraman, Raja, and D. R. Davies, eds. 1984. *Varieties of Attention*. New York: Academic Press.

Peacocke, Christopher. 1979. *Holistic Explanation*. Oxford: Clarendon Press.

1983. *Sense and Content*. Oxford: Clarendon Press.

1986. "Analogue Content." *Proceedings of the Aristotelian Society*, suppl. vol. 60, 1–17.

1988. "Perceptual Content." In Joseph Almog, John Perry, and H. K. Wettstein, eds., *Themes from Kaplan*. New York: Oxford University Press.

Pinker, Steven, ed. 1985. *Visual Cognition*. Cambridge, Mass.: MIT Press.

Pollock, John. 1974. *Knowledge and Justification*. Princeton, N.J.: Princeton University Press.

1979. "A Plethora of Epistemological Theories." In George Pappas, ed., *Justification and Knowledge*, pp. 93–113. Dordrecht: Reidel.

1982. *Language and Thought*. Princeton, N.J.: Princeton University Press.

1983. "Epistemology and Probability." *Synthese* 55, 231–52.

1984. "Reliability and Justified Belief." *The Canadian Journal of Philosophy* 14, 103–14. Reprinted in Moser (1986, pp. 193–202).

1986. *Contemporary Theories of Knowledge*. Totowa, N.J.: Rowman and Littlefield.

1987. "Defeasible Reasoning." *Cognitive Science* 11, 481–518.

Popper, Karl. 1965. *Conjectures and Refutations*, 2d ed. New York: Harper and Row.

1972. *Objective Knowledge*. Oxford: Clarendon Press.

Post, John. 1980. "Infinite Regresses of Justification and of Explanation." *Philosophical Studies* 38, 31–52.

1987. *The Faces of Existence*. Ithaca, N.Y.: Cornell University Press.

Price, H. H. 1950. *Perception*, 2d ed. London: Methuen.

1954. "Belief and Will." *Proceedings of the Aristotelian Society*, suppl. vol. 28. Reprinted in R. F. Dearden, P. H. Hirst, and R. S. Peters, eds., *Reason*, pp. 198–217. London: Routledge and Kegan Paul, 1972.

1969a. *Belief.* London: Allen and Unwin.

1969b. *Thinking and Experience.* 2d ed. London: Hutchinson.

Prior, A. N. 1967. "Correspondence Theory of Truth." In Paul Edwards, ed., *The Encyclopedia of Philosophy*, vol. 2, pp. 223–32. New York: Macmillan.

Putnam, Hilary. 1960. "Do True Assertions Correspond to Reality?" In Putnam, *Mind, Language, and Reality: Philosophical Papers*, vol. 2, pp. 70–84. Cambridge: Cambridge University Press, 1975.

1981. *Reason, Truth, and History.* Cambridge: Cambridge University Press.

1983a. *Realism and Reason: Philosophical Papers*, vol. 3. Cambridge: Cambridge University Press.

1983b. "On Truth." In Leigh Cauman, Isaac Levi, Charles Parsons, and Robert Schwartz, eds., *How Many Questions?* pp. 35–56. Indianapolis: Hackett.

1983c. "Beyond Historicism." In Putnam (1983a, pp. 287–303).

Quine, W. V. 1955. "The Scope and Language of Science." In Lewis Leary, ed., *The Unity of Knowledge.* Garden City, N.Y.: Doubleday. Reprinted in Quine, *The Ways of Paradox*, pp. 215–32. New York: Random House, 1966. Page references are to this reprint.

1960. *Word and Object.* Cambridge, Mass.: MIT Press.

1969. "Epistemology Naturalized." In Quine, *Ontological Relativity and Other Essays*, pp. 68–90. New York: Columbia University Press. Reprinted in Moser (1986, pp. 214–28). Page references are to this reprint.

1970. *Philosophy of Logic.* Englewood Cliffs, N.J.: Prentice-Hall.

1974. *The Roots of Reference.* LaSalle, Ill.: Open Court.

Rescher, Nicholas. 1973. *Conceptual Idealism.* Oxford: Blackwell Publisher.

1982. *Empirical Inquiry.* Totowa, N.J.: Rowman and Littlefield.

Robinson, D. L., and S. E. Petersen. 1986. "The Neurobiology of Attention." In J. E. LeDoux and William Hirst, eds., *Mind and Brain*, pp. 142–71. Cambridge: Cambridge University Press.

Rorty, Richard. 1972. "The World Well Lost." *The Journal of Philosophy* 69, 649–65. Reprinted in Rorty (1982, pp. 3–18).

1979. *Philosophy and the Mirror of Nature.* Princeton, N.J.: Princeton University Press.

1982. *Consequences of Pragmatism.* Minneapolis: University of Minnesota Press.

Runzo, Joseph. 1982. "The Radical Conceptualization of Perceptual Experience." *American Philosophical Quarterly* 19, 205–17.

Russell, Bertrand. 1911. "Knowledge by Acquaintance and Knowledge by Description." *Proceedings of the Aristotelian Society* 11, 108–28. Reprinted in Russell, *Mysticism and Logic*, pp. 202–24. Garden City, N.Y.: Doubleday, 1957. Page references are to this reprint.

1912. *The Problems of Philosophy.* New York: Oxford University Press.

1914a. "On the Nature of Acquaintance." *The Monist* 24. Reprinted in Russell, *Logic and Knowledge*, ed. R. C. Marsh, pp. 125–74. New York: Putnam, 1956. Page references are to this reprint.

1914b. *Our Knowledge of the External World*. LaSalle, Ill.: Open Court.

1927. *The Analysis of Matter*. London: Allen and Unwin.

Salmon, Wesley, 1984. *Scientific Explanation and the Causal Structure of the World*. Princeton, N.J.: Princeton University Press.

Scheffler, Israel. 1982. *Science and Subjectivity*, 2d ed. Indianapolis: Hackett.

Schiffer, Stephen. 1987. *Remnants of Meaning*. Cambridge, Mass.: MIT Press.

Scholnick, E. K., ed. 1983. *New Trends in Conceptual Representation*. Hillsdale, N.J.: Erlbaum.

Searle, John. 1983. *Intentionality*. Cambridge: Cambridge University Press.

Sellars, Wilfrid. 1963. *Science, Perception, and Reality*. London: Routledge and Kegan Paul.

1967. *Philosophical Perspectives*. Springfield, Ill.: Thomas.

1973. "Givenness and Explanatory Coherence." *The Journal of Philosophy* 70, 612–24.

1979. "More on Givenness and Explanatory Coherence." In George Pappas, ed., *Justification and Knowledge*, pp. 169–82. Dordrecht: Reidel.

Shepard, R. N., and L. A. Cooper. 1982. *Mental Images and Their Transformations*. Cambridge, Mass.: MIT Press.

Shiner, Roger. 1977. "Wittgenstein and the Foundations of Knowledge." *Proceedings of the Aristotelian Society* 78, 102–24.

Shope, Robert. 1978. "The Conditional Fallacy in Contemporary Philosophy." *The Journal of Philosophy* 75, 397–413.

1979. "Knowledge and Falsity." *Philosophical Studies* 36, 389–405. Reprinted in Moser (1986, pp. 254–69).

1983. *The Analysis of Knowing*. Princeton, N.J.: Princeton University Press.

Smith, E. E., and D. L. Medin. 1981. *Categories and Concepts*. Cambridge, Mass.: Harvard University Press.

1984. "Concepts and Concept Formation." *Annual Review of Psychology* 35, 113–38.

Soames, Scott. 1984. "What Is a Theory of Truth?" *The Journal of Philosophy* 81, 411–29.

Sosa, Ernest. 1974. "How Do You Know?" *American Philosophical Quarterly* 11, 113–22. Reprinted in Pappas and Swain (1978, pp. 184–205).

1980a. "The Raft and the Pyramid: Coherence versus Foundations in the Theory of Knowledge." In P. A. French, T. E. Uehling, and H. K. Wettstein, eds., *Midwest Studies in Philosophy*, vol. 5: *Studies in Epistemology*, pp. 3–25. Minneapolis: University of Minnesota Press. Reprinted in Moser (1986, pp. 145–70).

1980b. "The Foundations of Foundationalism." *Noûs* 14, 547–64.

1985. "Knowledge and Intellectual Virtue." *The Monist* 68, 226–45.

1988. "Beyond Scepticism, to the Best of Our Knowledge." *Mind* 97, 153–88.

Squire, Larry. 1987. *Memory and Brain*. New York: Oxford University Press.

Stove, D. C. 1973. *Probability and Hume's Inductive Skepticism*. Oxford: Clarendon Press.

Stroud, Barry. 1984. *The Significance of Philosophical Scepticism*. Oxford: Clarendon Press.

Swain, Marshall. 1974. "Epistemic Defeasibility." *American Philosophical Quarterly* 11, 15–25. Reprinted in Pappas and Swain (1978, pp. 160–83).

　　1979. "Justification and the Basis of Belief." In George Pappas, ed., *Justification and Knowledge*, pp. 25–49. Dordrecht: Reidel.

　　1981. *Reasons and Knowledge*. Ithaca, N.Y.: Cornell University Press.

　　1985. "Justification, Reasons, and Reliability." *Synthese* 64, 69–92.

Tarski, Alfred. 1936. "The Concept of Truth in Formalized Languages." In Tarski, *Logic, Semantics, Metamathematics*, pp. 152–278. Oxford: Clarendon Press, 1956.

　　1944. "The Semantic Conception of Truth and the Foundations of Semantics." *Philosophy and Phenomenological Research* 4, 341–75. Reprinted in A. P. Martinich, ed., *The Philosophy of Language*, pp. 48–71. New York: Oxford University Press, 1985.

　　1967. "Truth and Proof." *Scientific American* 220, 63–77.

Teller, Paul. 1974. "On Why-Questions." *Noûs* 8, 371–80.

Temple, Dennis. 1988. "The Contrast Theory of Why-Questions." *Philosophy of Science* 55, 141–51.

Thagard, Paul. 1988. *Computational Philosophy of Science*. Cambridge, Mass.: MIT Press.

Tye, Michael, 1984. "The Adverbial Approach to Visual Experience." *The Philosophical Review* 93, 195–225.

Unger, Peter. 1975. *Ignorance: A Case for Scepticism*. Oxford: Clarendon Press.

Van Cleve, James. 1985. "Epistemic Supervenience and the Circle of Belief." *The Monist* 68, 90–104.

van Fraassen, Bas. 1980. *The Scientific Image*. Oxford: Clarendon Press.

Vision, Gerald. 1988. *Modern Anti-Realism and Manufactured Truth*. London: Routledge.

Watkins, John. 1984. *Science and Scepticism*. Princeton, N.J.: Princeton University Press.

Weitz, Morris. 1988. *Theories of Concepts*. London: Routledge.

White, A. R. 1981. "Knowledge, Acquaintance, and Awareness." In P. A. French, T. E. Uehling, and H. K. Wettstein, eds., *Midwest Studies in Philosophy*, vol. 6: *The Foundations of Analytic Philosophy*, pp. 159–72. Minneapolis: University of Minnesota Press.

Williams, Bernard. 1970. "Deciding To Believe." In Milton Munitz and H. E. Kiefer, eds., *Language, Belief, and Metaphysics*, pp. 95–111. Albany: State University of New York Press. Reprinted in Williams, *Problems of the Self*, pp. 136–51. Cambridge: Cambridge University Press, 1973. Page references are to this reprint.

1978. *Descartes: The Project of Pure Enquiry*. Atlantic Highlands, N.J.: Humanities.

Williams, Michael. 1977. *Groundless Belief*. Oxford: Blackwell Publisher.

Wittgenstein, Ludwig. 1953. *Philosophical Investigations*. English trans. by G. E. M. Anscombe. Oxford: Blackwell Publisher.

1969. *On Certainty*. English trans. by Denis Paul and G. E. M. Anscombe. Oxford: Blackwell Publisher.

Wright, Crispin. 1985. "Facts and Certainty." *Proceedings of the British Academy* 71, 429–72.

Wurtz, Robert, Michael Goldberg, and Daniel Robinson. 1982. "Brain Mechanisms of Visual Attention." *Scientific American* 246, 124–35.

Yolton, John. 1984. *Perceptual Acquaintance from Descartes to Reid*. Oxford: Blackwell Publisher.

Index

282